D0302253

REVOLUTIONARY
CONNECTIONS

REVOLUTIONARY CONNECTIONS

PSYCHOTHERAPY AND NEUROSCIENCE

Edited on behalf of the
United Kingdom Council for Psychotherapy
by

Jenny Corrigall

and

Heward Wilkinson

KARNAC
LONDON   NEW YORK

Published in 2003 by
H. Karnac (Books) Ltd.
6 Pembroke Buildings, London NW10 6RE

Copyright © 2003 Arrangement and Introduction copyright UKCP,
Chapters copyright 2003 to individual contributors

Reprinted 2004

The contributors assert the moral right to be identified as the authors
of this work.

All rights reserved. No part of this publication may be reproduced, stored in
a retrieval system, or transmitted, in any form or by any means, electronic,
mechanical, photocopying, recording, or otherwise, without the prior written
permission of the publisher.

British Library Cataloguing in Publication Data

A C.I.P. for this book is available from the British Library

ISBN 1 85575 941 1

Edited, designed, and produced by The Studio Publishing Services Ltd,
Exeter EX4 8JN

Printed and bound in Great Britain by Biddles Ltd, *www.biddles.co.uk*

10 9 8 7 6 5 4 3 2

www.karnacbooks.com

UKCP conference planning committee 2001:
Roz Carroll, Cairns Clery, Jenny Corrigall, Del Loewenthal,
Elizabeth Model, Amy Turner and Heward Wilkinson.

CONTENTS

ACKNOWLEDGEMENTS   ix

FOREWORD   xi

CONTRIBUTORS   xiii

Introduction
   Roz Carroll, Jenny Corrigall and Heward Wilkinson   1

CHAPTER ONE
The seventh annual John Bowlby Memorial Lecture
   Allan N. Schore   7

CHAPTER TWO
Neuroscience and intrinsic psychodynamics:
   current knowledge and potential for therapy
   Colwyn Trevarthen   53

CHAPTER THREE
Psychotherapy in an age of neuroscience:
   bridges to affective neuroscience
   Douglas F. Watt   79

CHAPTER FOUR
Early experience, attachment and the brain
　　Danya Glaser   117

CHAPTER FIVE
Emotion, false beliefs, and the neurobiology of intuition
　　Oliver Turnbull   135

CHAPTER SIX
Psychotherapy and neuroscience:
　　how close can they get?
　　Chris Mace   163

CHAPTER SEVEN
Constructing a psychobiological context—
　　science, neuroscience, and therapeutic collaboration
　　Cairns Clery   175

CHAPTER EIGHT
"At the border between chaos and order":
　　what psychotherapy and neuroscience have in common
　　Roz Carroll   191

INDEX   213

ACKNOWLEDGEMENTS

Chapter One (pp. 7–51), Schore, A. (2001) *Minds in the Making: Attachment, The Self-Organising Brain, and Developmentally-Oriented Psychoanalytic Psychotherapy*. First delivered as the 7th of the annual Bowlby Memorial Lectures organised by the Centre for Attachment-Based Psychoanalytic Psychotherapy. First published in the *British Journal of Psychotherapy*, Vol. 17: 299. Reprinted with permission.

Chapter Three, Figure 2 (p. 97), Mesulam, M. (2000) *Principles of Behavioural and Cognitive Neurology*, first published by Oxford University Press. Reprinted with permission.

Chapter Three, Figure 3 (p. 98), Kandel, E. R., Schwarz, J. H. and Jessel, T. M. (2000) *The Principles of Neural Science*, first published by McGraw-Hill. Reprinted with permission.

Chapter Four (pp. 117–133), "Early experience, attachment and the brain" by Danya Glaser. This chapter has been developed from ideas in an article by Danya Glaser and Robin Balbernie, which was first published in *Fragile, Handle with Care: Protecting Babies From Harm*, edited by Evender Harran and Rosemary Gordon, published by NSPCC, 2001.

Chapter Six, Figure 1 (p. 168), Thase, M. E., Buysee, D. J., Frank, E., Cherry, C. R., Cornes, C. L., Mallinger, A. G. and Kupfer, D. J. (1997) "Which depressed patients will respond to interpersonal psychotherapy? The role of abnormal EEG profiles". First published in *American Journal of Psychiatry*, Vol. 154: 505, 1997, The American Psychiatric Association: http://ajp.psychiatryonline.org. Reprinted by permission.

Chapter Six, Figure 2 (p. 171), Martin, S. D., Martin, E., Rai, S. S., Richardson, M. A., Royall, R. (2001) "Brain blood flow changes in depressed patients treated with interpersonal psychotherapy or venlafaxine hydrochloride". First published in the *Archives of General Psychiatry*, Vol. 58: 645, 2001. Reprinted by permission.

FOREWORD

The formation of the UKCP ten years ago represented a major step forward for psychotherapy. It succeeded in drawing together psychotherapists from across the wide range of schools that developed as the last century unfolded.

Central to the vision that lay behind the UKCP was the acceptance of diversity within the field of psychotherapy and the importance of dialogue between what have come to be known as the different modalities of psychotherapy.

The UKCP set out to build a common framework for that dialogue and to create a structure that could serve the public by maintaining standards of professional conduct and ensuring high standards of training.

At the same time the UKCP has sought to promote professional contact and the exploration of issues of common interest. A similar commitment lies behind the engagement between psychotherapy and neuroscience. It is, therefore, particularly appropriate that the UKCP's first venture into book publishing should focus on this interdisciplinary engagement. The engagement is in its infancy and the connections that can be made are potentially revolutionary.

I warmly welcome this book and am grateful to all those who

have contributed to it and to all those, particularly Jenny Corrigall and Heward Wilkinson, who have contributed so much to the development of the UKCP's Professional Conference.

James Pollard
Chair UKCP

CONTRIBUTORS

Roz Carroll is a body psychotherapist and a member of the Society of Neuro-Psychoanalysis. She has specialized in integrating concepts from neuroscience, psychoanalysis and body psychotherapy. Roz teaches short and long workshops and seminars in a wide range of clinical training contexts. One of these is the seminar series "Emotion and Embodiment: a new relationship between neuroscience and psychotherapy", hosted by Confer, for health professionals. She has a private practice in North West London, and also offers supervision and consultation on issues relating to the body in psychotherapy. Many of her articles and lectures are available on www.thinkbody.co.uk.

Cairns Clery is employed as Principal Psychotherapist (Systemic and Family) in a NHS Child and Adolescent Mental Health Service in England, and can be contacted at cairnsclery@yahoo.co.uk. His particular field of enquiry in recent years has been deliberate self injury in adolescence. He has written widely on the subject.

Jenny Corrigall is a research psychologist, and a psychoanalytic psychotherapist and supervisor, working in Cambridge.

Danya Glaser is Consultant Child and Adolescent Psychiatrist in the Department of Psychological Medicine, Great Ormond Street Hospital for Children, London.

Chris Mace heads the NHS psychodynamic psychotherapy service in South Warwickshire and is Senior Lecturer in Psychotherapy at Warwick University. He has also trained as a neuropsychiatrist, conducting clinical and research studies at the Institute of Neurology into hysteria, epilepsy and the psychiatric impact of neurosurgery.

Allan Schore is Assistant Clinical Professor in the Department of Psychiatry and Biobehavioural Sciences at the University of California at Los Angeles School of Medicine. He is on the teaching faculties of the Institute for Contemporary Psychoanalysis, and the Southern California Psychoanalytic Institute, Los Angeles, California, USA. An overview and compilation of his work is provided in his books *Affect Regulation and Disorders of the Self*, and *Affect Regulation and the Repair of the Self*, published by W. W. Norton, 2003.

Colwyn Trevarthen is Emeritus Professor of Child Psychology and Psychobiology, and Honorary Research Fellow, in the Department of Psychology at the University of Edinburgh. After training in psychobiology and neuropsychology, his research has employed micro-descriptive longitudinal methods to elucidate the expressive behaviour and the intersubjective co-ordination of communicating and co-operative action in young children. Recently, in collaboration with a musical acoustic expert, Stephen Malloch, he has produced a new way of analysing the 'musicality' of vocal interactions between babies and parents, which helps explain the remarkable efficiency of their 'dance' together.

Oliver Turnbull is a neuropsychologist, and Senior Lecturer at the Centre for Cognitive Neuroscience in the School of Psychology, University of Wales in Bangor. He is Associate Editor of the journal Neuro-Psychoanalysis, and the Secretary of the International Neuro-Psychoanalysis Society.

Douglas Watt is the Director of Neuropsychology at Quincy Medical

Centre in Massachusetts and at the Boston University School of Medicine. A member of the Society of Neuro-Psychoanalysis, he has focused on emotion as a central organizing process for consciousness.

Heward Wilkinson is the Senior Editor, International Journal of Psychotherapy (journal of the EAP); Chair of the Humanistic and Integrative Psychotherapy Section of the UKCP; a member of the UKCP Governing Board; External Relations Officer for the Minster Centre, London; and co-founder of Scarborough Psychotherapy Training Institute. In private practice in London, he has a special interest in the philosophy of psychotherapy.

Introduction

Roz Carroll, Jenny Corrigall and Heward Wilkinson

The Professional Conference for the UK Council for Psychotherapy in 2001 aimed to create a forum to explore what is, to many psychotherapists, the very new and rapidly changing field of neuroscience. The relationship between psychotherapy and the branch of neuroscience called "affective neuroscience" is challenging and potentially revolutionary for both sides.

As Roz Carroll has written (*The Psychotherapist*, 2001, *16*: 20–24), from the early years of the twentieth century the two fields of neuroscience and psychotherapy (initially in its form of Freudian psychoanalysis, but now vastly widened) went in very different directions and seemed to have little contact or hold any interest for each other. Gradually, with changes in both fields, the two have more to say to each other as evidenced, for example, by the existence of a new journal, *Neuro-Psychoanalysis*.

Neuroscience has moved away from trying to draw direct causal connections between individual anatomical structures and mental processes, to an understanding that psychological phenomena emerge from the complex interaction between systems in the body and the brain. And psychotherapy, in many forms, has moved away from the pure mentalistic vision of psychoanalysis after the

Interpretation of Dreams, to more interactive and embodied views of experience and intervention (though in the light of recent developments, Freud's seminally prescient *Project for a Scientific Psychology* has turned out to be a veritable Rosetta Stone, as Karl Pribram noted, for neuropsychology).

So, now that affective neuroscience is integrating aspects of human functioning into its conceptual models which include the staples of clinical interest (emotions, relationships, the construction of meaning and of internal working models), psychotherapy has much to gain from the impetus and dynamism of contemporary affective neuroscience, and even *vice versa*, as the psychotherapeutically fluent pioneers are beginning to show.

The UKCP conference planning committee, therefore, organized a conference to which we were lucky enough to bring speakers who have made significant contributions and connections in this area by their ability to integrate material and theories from more than one field.

The conference, though held in September 2001, actually started in July of that year with an introductory lecture on the conference theme by the distinguished neuropsychoanalyst, Dr Allan Schore. His talk entitled "Clinical Implications of a Psycho-neurobiological Model of Projective Identification" is to appear as a chapter in *Primitive Mental States, Volume II*, edited by S. Alhanati, for Karnac Books. For copyright reasons, we cannot reproduce his talk in this volume, but are delighted to have been able to include instead his Bowlby Memorial Lecture, with its detailed and comprehensive introduction to the intricate interrelationship between the vicissitudes of attachment and its effects on the developing brain and the individual's ego function. This is an excellent introduction to the themes of the conference and we are grateful to Allan Schore, and to the editor of the *British Journal of Psychotherapy*, for their permission to include it here.

Our first speaker of the weekend conference, Professor Colwyn Trevarthen, Emeritus Professor of Child Psychology and Psychobiology in the University of Edinburgh, has made rich use of micro-descriptions of mothers and infants in "proto-conversation", to explore the dynamics of the infant's first companionship. It was very fitting that Professor Trevarthen was our first plenary speaker, because his study of communicative and cooperative exchanges between infants and adults was an early indicator of revolutionary change. He sees the mother's availability to engage in emotional transactions with her infant as a crucial factor in the healthy development of the child's brain. This will not surprise psychotherapists, but it should not leave us complacent that we "already know it" either. The specificity of the tracking of development through neuroscientific means offers us substantive and precise information with which to refine our models and interventions.

Professor Trevarthen's work on infant intersubjectivity is a challenge to both the reductive cognitive perspective and the classical psychoanalytical view of primary narcissism. Since the late 1970s he has used his own and others' research to reorient, reform, and reformulate the picture of young babies' emotional, communicative, and relational capacities. The idea of babies as primitive and unskilled is turned on its head by his account of their incipient narrative awareness, musical intelligence, and social sophistication. He contends that babies are born with intrinsic regulatory capacities, by which they are motivated to engage in a relationship. Along with other pioneers in this science, and with an emphasis that psychotherapists would wholeheartedly share, Colwyn Trevarthen vigorously insists on the fundamental role of emotion and relationships in the infant's development.

One of the thinkers leading and articulating the change in neuroscience's orientation towards its human subject is Douglas Watt, Director of Neuropsychology in the Quincy Medical Centre, Boston University, who argues that emotion has for too long been "relegated to the back of the bus" in cognitive science. He has both the specialized knowledge of the intricate—and still controversial theories about—workings of the brain, and a wide-ranging reference in related fields, including psychoanalytic metapsychology. In a series of articles on emotion and consciousness, he has made a strong case, in parallel with Damasio's recent thinking (*The Feeling of What Happens*, Heinemann, 2000), for emotion binding together "virtually every type of information that the brain can encode". Indeed, he suggests that emotion is "the glue that holds the whole system together", reflecting "fundamental adaptive integrations". His work throws new light on the distinctions made in psychotherapy between neurotic and psychotic processes. The keynote address he gave at the conference provided a vastly detailed, fascinating, and cogently argued case for both the importance of integrating affective neuroscience with psychotherapy, and some of the difficulties that still remain for both sides.

The next two plenary speakers, Danya Glaser, a child psychiatrist, and Oliver Turnbull, a neuropsychologist, show how neuroscience may also be able to help facilitate more understanding between branches of psychotherapy, psychoanalysis, psychology, and psychiatry. Its capacity to measure, now with much more sophistication, the effects of experience on brain–body systems means that it can offer independent verification of theories, and particularly diagnostic categories. Within the framework provided by complexity, there is not such a need to adjudicate between the respective claims of object relational, genetic, environmental, and social influences on the aetiology of disorders. Each factor and its interrelation with other factors can be given its due. Danya Glaser's work at Great Ormond Street Hospital with abused and neglected children underpinned by neurodevelopmental theory, also draws on social and biological psychology, psychiatry, and attachment theory. She has drawn attention to the fact that emotional *neglect* and its developmental ramifications have been overlooked in neuroscience until recently, although the effects of emotional deprivation have long been central to psychotherapeutic models. Oliver Turnbull, working at the University of Bangor, a neuro-psychologist with a particular interest in the neurology of analytic concepts, provided us with a fascinating study of the neurobiology of false beliefs, expanding neuroscience for us away from its earlier and purely cognitive trends to grappling with the part of the mental apparatus which includes emotion. He described affects as the "internal sense organs" and stressed, in a way that echoes the earlier presentations, the growing importance of affect in neuroscience. Such studies highlight the best points of contact for cooperation between medicine, neuroscience research, psychology, and psychotherapy.

David Boadella gave the fifth plenary talk (not included here for copyright reasons) in which he emphasized the systems in the body (hormonal, immune, autonomic) which are part of the process we call mind. He offered some general pointers to ways therapists can implement these ideas in their clinical practice by attuning to body rhythms, pacing, and keeping the balance between flooding and freezing.

In the final plenary of the conference, three speakers spoke in ways that integrated the weekends' events and which asked us all to think how neuroscience research impacts on our work as psychotherapists. Chris Mace, senior lecturer in psychotherapy at Warwick University, both investigated the potential of neuroscience research for psychotherapeutic practice, and sounded a note of caution at adopting an instrumental view of therapy, based on the current models from neuroscience. Cairns Clery, a family therapist working in an inpatient setting, gave us a moving and powerful case study, describing how the work of affective neuroscience, especially in the field of responses to early trauma, helped him in his work. Roz Carroll, a body psychotherapist, described the impact of neuroscience research and thinking on psychotherapy in a more general way, emphasizing the importance of "critical reorganization" as essential to therapeutic change, and expanding, most interestingly, on how the therapist maximizes opportunities for this change through the therapeutic relationship.

The conference did indeed engender lively interest and debate, both in the plenary discussions, and in workshops and discussion groups, formal and informal, throughout the weekend. In order to continue that debate, and to bring it to those unable to attend the conference itself, we are delighted to have these contributions from Dr Schore and all but one of the plenary speakers.

CHAPTER ONE

The seventh annual John Bowlby Memorial Lecture

Minds in the making: attachment,
the self-organizing brain, and developmentally-
oriented psychoanalytic psychotherapy

Allan N. Schore

I t is an honour to be invited to present the Seventh Annual John Bowlby Memorial Lecture. Indeed, this has been a double privilege, in that it follows another (in 2000) in which I was asked to write the Foreword to the reissue of Bowlby's ground-breaking volume, *Attachment*. In that work I surveyed, from a perspective at the close of what has been called "the decade of the brain", his far-sighted proposals about the biological and neuro-logical nature of attachment. Indeed, in a number of contributions I am describing how a spectrum of psychological and biological disciplines have adopted his ideas as the dominant model of human development available to science.

Each of these fields of scientific inquiry, when documenting the origins of the theory, points to Bowlby's integration of ethology (the study of behavioural biology) and psychoanalysis. In a contemporary description of the volume, Ainsworth wrote, "In effect what Bowlby has attempted is to update psychoanalytic theory in the light of recent advances in biology" (1969, p. 998). I suggest that in the three decades since the publication of *Attachment*, although the connections between attachment theory and science have deepened, those between itself and psychoanalysis, especially clinical psychoanalysis, have not. This situation is currently improving, however, due to the contributions of developmental psychoanalytic and psychological attachment research that demonstrate the clinical relevance of the concepts of mental representations of internal working models and reflective functions. Experimental and clinical attachment researchers are now describing, in detail, these two fundamental characteristics of "minds in the making", the theme of this meeting.

It has sometimes been forgotten that attachment theory is a direct outgrowth of Freud's developmental perspective, not just a repudiation of some of his early speculations. Indeed, in the very first paragraph of *Attachment* Bowlby (1969) begins his ground-breaking work with specific reference to Freud's fundamental goal of understanding early development. In his opening passage, he contrasts Freud's methodology for generating developmental hypotheses—analysing the dreams and symptoms of adult neurotic patients and the behaviour of primitive peoples—to his own, and so he states, "although in his search for explanation [Freud] was in each case led to events of early childhood, he himself only rarely drew for his basic data on direct observation of children" (p. 3). Expanding this latter theme is the focus of the book, yet in the final chapter he returns to a summary of developmental psychoanalytic concepts with a chapter, "The child's tie to his mother: a review of the psychoanalytic literature".

In this paper I want to present some recent interdisciplinary advances that are forging tighter links between the common goals of classical psychoanalysis and attachment theory. It may appear surprising that the new developments that are re-coupling Freud and Bowlby come from neuroscience. Yet this information bears upon a shared interest of the two most important contributors to a theory of the development of the early mind, specifically, an interest in internal psychic structure, and how it is influenced by early relational interactions.

At the very outset of his first chapter Bowlby (1969) quotes Freud's (1915a) final paragraph of *Repression*: "We must select first one and then another point of view, and follow it up through the material as long as the application of it seems to yield results". In ongoing writings, I am presenting, from a psychoneurobiological point of view, a specification of the structural systems of the developing unconscious in terms of recent brain research. This work on "the origin of the self" (a phrase I deliberately used to evoke an echo of Darwin's phylogenetic speculations on "the origin of species") attempts to document the ontogenetic evolution of the neurobiology of subjectivity and intersubjectivity, which I equate with specifically the experience-dependent self-organization of the early developing right hemisphere. In a 1997 article in the *Journal of the American Psychoanalytic Association* and another in 1999 in *Neuro-Psychoanalysis*, I suggested that the structural development of the right hemisphere mediates the functional development of the unconscious mind. And this year, in *Attachment and Human Development*, I offer further evidence to demonstrate that the right hemisphere is the repository of Bowlby's unconscious internal working models of the attachment relationship (Henry, 1993; Schore, 1994, 2000b; Siegel, 1999).

Taking this even further, in the following I want to suggest that an integration of current findings in the neurobiological and developmental sciences can offer a deeper understanding of the origins and dynamic mechanisms of the system that represents the core of psychoanalysis, the system unconscious. Psychoanalysis has been called the scientific study of the unconscious mind (Brenner, 1980), clearly implying both that the unconscious is its definitional realm of study, and that this realm is accessible to scientific analysis. This has been so from its very inception. Although Freud was well aware of Darwin's groundbreaking biological concepts, the major science that influenced his thinking was neurology (Schore, 1997a). Despite the fact that he failed to produce "a psychology which shall be a natural science" in the *Project for a Scientific Psychology* (1895), Freud transplanted its germinal hypotheses concerning the regulatory structures and dynamics of the system unconscious in the seventh chapter of his masterwork, *The Interpretation of Dreams* (1900).

As you remember, Freud predicted that there would someday be a rapprochement between psychoanalysis and neurobiology. A number of current rapidly expanding trends indicate that this convergence with the other sciences is now under way. Indeed, in this last year we have seen the appearance of a new journal, *Neuro-Psychoanalysis*, with a dual editorial board composed of both psychoanalysts and neuroscientists. The first issue centres on Freud's theory of affect, and in that journal I (1999a) present evidence from both domains of science, the study of the brain, and the study of the mind, to argue that the early developing right brain, or as the neuroscientist Robert Ornstein (1997) calls it, "the right mind", is the neurobiological substrate of Freud's system unconscious. Freud, of course, deduced that the unconscious system appears very early in life, well before verbal conscious functions. A body of research now indicates that the right hemisphere is dominant in human infancy, and indeed for the first three years of life (Chiron *et al.*, 1997).

Freud (1920) described the unconscious as "a special realm, with its own desires and modes of expression and peculiar mental mechanisms not elsewhere operative". Due to its central role in unconscious functions and primary process activities, psychoanalysis has been intrigued with the unique operations of the early developing right brain for the last quarter of a century. In the 1970s Galin (1974), Hoppe (1977), Stone (1977), and McLaughlin (1978), stimulated by the split brain studies of the time, began to link up psychoanalysis and neurobiology by positing that the right hemisphere is dominant for unconscious and the left for conscious processes.

The relevance of hemispheric specialization to psychoanalysis continued in the work of Miller (1991), Levin (1991), and particularly Watt (1990), who offered data to show that the right hemisphere contains an affective–configurational representational system, one that encodes self-and-object images, while the left utilizes a lexical–semantic mode. In fact, current neurobiological studies are revealing greater right than left hemispheric involvement in the *unconscious* processing of affect-evoking stimuli (Wexler *et al.*, 1992). Most intriguingly, a neuroimaging study of Morris, Ohman, and Dolan (1998) demonstrates that unconscious processing of emotional stimuli is specifically associated with activation of the right and not left hemisphere, and the reporter in the journal *Science* described this finding as indicating that "the left side is involved with conscious response and the right with the unconscious mind" (Mlot, 1998, p. 1006).

In an updated description of the unconscious, Winson concludes:

> Rather than being a cauldron of untamed passions and destructive wishes, I propose that the unconscious is a cohesive, continually active mental structure that takes note of life's experiences and reacts according to its scheme of interpretation. [1990, p. 96]

Notice his use of the term, structure. Although psychoanalysis has used this term to describe internal cognitive *processes*, such as representations and defences, and content, such as conflicts and fantasies, I suggest that *structure* refers to those specific brain systems, particularly right brain systems, that underlie these various mental functions. In other words the internal psychic systems involved in processing information at levels beneath awareness, described by Freud in his topographic (1900) and structural (1923) models, can now be identified by neuroscience.

A common ground of psychoanalysis, neurobiology, and psychology is an emphasis on the centrality of early development. In 1913 Freud proclaimed, "from the very first, psychoanalysis was directed towards tracing developmental processes. It ... was led ... to construct a genetic psychology" (1913b, pp. 182–183). Continuing this tradition, I would argue that the most significant psychoanalytic contributor to our understanding of developmental processes was, indeed, John Bowlby (Schore, 2000a,b). As mentioned earlier, in *Attachment* he applied then current biology to a psychoanalytic understanding of infant–mother bonding, and in so doing offered his "Project", an attempt to produce *a natural science of developmental psychology*. This volume focused upon one of the major questions of science, specifically, how and why do certain early ontogenetic events have such an inordinate effect on everything that follows? Bowlby's scientifically-informed curiosity about this question envisioned the centre stage of human infancy, on which is played the first chapter of the human drama, to be a context in which a mother and her infant experience connections and disconnections of their vital emotional communications.

Because these communications are occurring in the period of the brain growth spurt that continues through the second year of life (Dobbing & Sands, 1973), attachment transactions mediate "the social construction of the human brain" (Eisenberg, 1995), specifically the social emotional brain that supports the unique operations of "the right mind". Attachment is thus inextricably linked to developmental neuroscience. Stern has recently written, "Today it seems incredible that until Bowlby no one placed attachment at the centre of human development" (2000, p. xiii). I suggest that the great advances in our knowledge of early development have been the engine which has transformed contemporary psychoanalysis, which according to Cooper is "anchored in its scientific base in developmental psychology and in the biology of attachment and affects" (1987, p. 83).

In 1920 Freud proclaimed that *"the unconscious is the infantile mental life"*. This fundamental tenet is directly relevant to the topic of today's Bowlby Memorial Conference, *Minds in the Making*, and suggests that what particularly interests us here are *unconscious minds in the making*. We now know that an infant functions in a fundamentally unconscious way, and unconscious processes in an older child or adult can be traced back to the primitive functioning of the infant. Knowledge of how the maturation of the right brain, "the right mind", is directly influenced by the attachment relationship offers us a chance to more deeply understand not just the contents of the unconscious, but its origin, structure, and dynamics.

In *Affect Regulation and the Origin of the Self* (1994), I described a number of psychoneurobiological mechanisms by which attachment experiences specifically impact the experience-dependent maturation of the right hemisphere. In a continuation of this work (Schore, 2000b), I offer an overview of Bowlby's classic volume and argue that attachment theory is fundamentally a regulatory theory. In the following talk I want to offer some ideas about the *psychobiological* regulatory events that mediate the attachment process, and the *psychoneurobiological* regulatory mechanisms by which "the right mind" organizes in infancy.

In the latter part of this lecture I will suggest that regulation theory describes the mechanisms by which the patient forms an attachment, that is a working alliance with the therapist. This construct—created to define the subtle, interactive dynamic relationship between patient and therapist—is the most important conceptualization of the common elements of the different therapy modalities (Horvath & Greenberg, 1994). Bradley (2000) points out that all psychotherapies, psychodynamic, cognitive–behavioural, experiential, and interactional, show a similarity in promoting affect regulation.

In other words, this information about attachment, regulation, and the emotion-processing right brain is describing the "non-specific factors" that are common to all forms of clinical treatment, factors particularly accessed in developmentally-oriented psycho-analytic psychotherapy (Schore, 2000e). The major contribution of attachment theory to clinical models is thus its elucidation of the nonconscious dyadic affect transacting mechanisms that mediate a positive therapeutic working alliance between the patient and the empathic therapist. Complementing this, the neurobiological aspects of attachment theory allow for a deeper understanding of how an affect-focused developmentally oriented treatment can alter internal structure within the patient's brain/mind/body systems.

The neurobiology and psychobiology of a secure attachment

The essential task of the first year of human life is the creation of a secure attachment bond between the infant and primary caregiver. Indeed, as soon as the child is born it uses its maturing sensory capacities, especially smell, taste, and touch, to interact with the social environment. But at two months, a developmental milestone occurs in the infant brain, specifically the onset of a critical period in the maturation of the occipital cortex (Yamada *et al.*, 2000). This allows for a dramatic progression of its social and emotional capacities. In particular, the mother's emotionally expressive face is, by far, the most potent visual stimulus in the infant's environment, and the child's intense interest in her face, especially in her eyes, leads him to track it in space, and to engage in periods of intense mutual gaze. The infant's gaze, in turn, reliably evokes the mother's gaze, thereby acting as a potent interpersonal channel for the transmission of "reciprocal mutual influences". It has been observed that the pupil of the eye acts as a nonverbal communication device (Hess, 1975) and that large pupils in the infant release caregiver behaviour (*Figure 1*).

As described by Feldman, Greenbaum, and Yirmiya:

> Face-to-face interactions, emerging at approximately two months of age, are highly arousing, affect-laden, short interpersonal events that expose infants to high levels of cognitive and social information. To regulate the high positive arousal, mothers and infants ... *synchronize* the intensity of their affective behaviour within lags of split seconds. [1999, p. 223, my italics]

In this process of "affect synchrony" the intuitive (Papousek & Papousek, 1995) mother initially attunes to and resonates with the

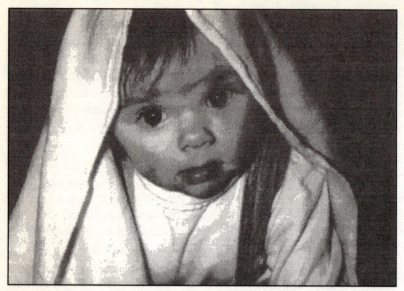

Figure 1. Notice the size of the pupils of this 9 month-old-infant, and the strong positive valence of the facial expression.

infant's resting state, but as this state is dynamically activated (or deactivated or hyperactivated) she fine tunes and corrects the intensity and duration of her affective stimulation in order to maintain the child's positive affect state. As a result of this moment-by-moment state-matching both partners increase together their degree of engagement. The fact that the coordination of responses is so rapid suggests the existence of a bond of unconscious communication.

In this interpersonal context of "contingent responsivity" the more the mother tunes her activity level to the infant during periods of social engagement, the more she allows him to recover quietly in periods of disengagement, and the more she contingently responds to his signals for re-engagement, the more synchronized their interaction (see *Figure 2*). Lester, Hoffman, and Brazelton (1985, p. 24) state that "*synchrony* develops as a consequence of each partner's learning the rhythmic structure of the other and modifying his or her behaviour to fit that structure". The primary caregiver thus facilitates the infant's information processing by adjusting the mode, amount, variability, and timing of stimulation to its actual temperamental–physiological abilities. These mutually attuned

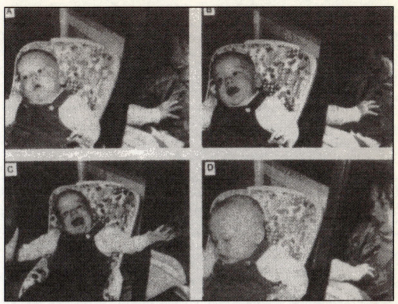

Figure 2. A typical sequence observed during "attuned" interactions of normal infants and their mothers: (a) the infant looks at the mother and the mother shows an exaggerated facial expression (mock surprise); (b) the infant and mother smile; (c) the infant laughs, the mother "relaxes" her smile; and (d) the infant looks away, the mother ceases smiling and watches her infant. Note the synchronization during both the engagement and disengagement. From Field and Fogel, 1982.

synchronized interactions are fundamental to the ongoing affective development of the infant.

Reciprocal facial signalling thus represents an open channel of social communication, and this interactive matrix promotes the outward expression of internal affects in infants. In order to enter into this communication, the mother must be psychobiologically attuned, not so much to the child's overt behaviour as to the reflections of his internal state. In light of the fact that misattunements are a common developmental phenomena, she also must modulate nonoptimal high levels of stimulation which would trigger hyperarousal, or low levels which engender hypoarousal in the infant.

Most importantly, the arousal-regulating primary caregiver must participate in interactive repair to regulate interactively induced stress states in the infant. If attachment is interactive synchrony, stress is defined as an *asynchrony* in an interactional sequence, and, following this, a period of re-established *synchrony* allows for stress recovery. In this reattunement pattern of "disruption and repair" the "good-enough" caregiver, who induces a stress response in her infant through a misattunement, self-corrects and in a timely fashion, reinvokes her psychobiologically attuned regulation of the infant's negative affect state that she has triggered. The key to this is the caregiver's capacity to monitor and regulate her own affect, especially negative affect.

These regulatory processes are precursors of psychological attachment and its associated emotions. An essential attachment function is "to promote the synchrony or regulation of biological and behavioural systems on an organismic level" (Reite & Capitanio, 1985, p. 235). Indeed, psychobiological attunement, interactive resonance, and the mutual synchronization and entrainment of physiological rhythms are fundamental processes that mediate attachment bond formation, and attachment can be defined as the interactive regulation of biological synchronicity between organisms (Schore, 1994, 2000a,b, 2001b,c).

To put this another way, in forming an attachment bond of somatically expressed emotional communications, the mother is synchronizing and resonating with the rhythms of the infant's dynamic internal states and then regulating the arousal level of these negative and positive states. Attachment is thus the dyadic (interactive) regulation of emotion (Sroufe, 1996). The baby becomes attached to the psychobiologically attuned regulating primary caregiver, who not only minimizes negative affect but also maximizes opportunities for positive affect. Attachment is not just the re-establishment of security after a dysregulating experience and a stressful negative state, it is also the interactive amplification of positive affects, as in play states. Regulated interactions with a familiar, predictable primary caregiver create not only a sense of safety, but also a positively charged curiosity that fuels the burgeoning self's exploration of novel socio-emotional and physical environments.

Furthermore, attachment is more than overt behaviour, it is internal, "being built into the nervous system, in the course and as a result of the infant's experience of his transactions with the mother" (Ainsworth, 1967, p. 429). Next question—in this "transfer of affect between mother and infant", what do we know of "the processes whereby the primary object relations become internalized and transformed into psychic structure?" The work of Trevarthen on maternal–infant proto-conversations bears directly on this problem (*Figure 3*). He notes, "the intrinsic regulators of human brain growth in a child are specifically adapted to be coupled, by emotional communication, to the regulators of adult brains" (1990, p. 357). In these transactions, the *resonance* of the dyad ultimately permits the intercoordination of positive affective brain states. His work underscores the fundamental principle that the baby's brain is not only affected by these transactions, its growth requires brain–brain interaction and occurs in the context of an intimate positive affective relationship. These findings support Emde's assertion that "It is the emotional availability of the caregiver in intimacy which seems to be the most central growth-promoting feature of the early rearing experience" (1988, p. 32).

There is now consensus that interactions with the environment during sensitive periods are necessary for the brain as a whole to

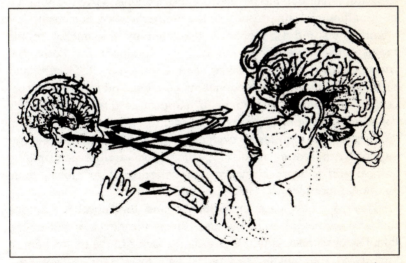

Figure 3. Channels of face-to-face communication in proto-conversation. Proto-conversation is mediated by eye-to-eye orientations, vocalizations, hand gestures, and movements of the arms and head, all acting in coordination to express interpersonal awareness and emotions. Adapted from Trevarthen, 1993.

mature. But we know that different regions of the brain mature at different times. Can we tell what specific parts of the growing brain are affected by these emotion transacting events? It has been observed that:

> The emotional experience of the infant develops through the sounds, images, and pictures that constitute much of an infant's early learning experience, and are disproportionately stored or processed in the right hemisphere during the formative stages of brain ontogeny. [Semrud-Clikeman & Hynd, 1990, p. 198]

A body of evidence shows that the right hemisphere matures before the left, a finding in line with Freud's assertion that primary process ontogenetically precedes secondary process functions.

The learning mechanism of attachment, imprinting, is defined as *synchrony* between sequential infant maternal stimuli and behaviour (Petrovich & Gewirtz, 1985). I suggest that in these affectively *synchronized*, psychobiologically attuned face-to-face interactions, the infant's right hemisphere, which is dominant for the infant's recognition of the maternal face, and for the perception of arousal-inducing maternal facial affective expressions, visual emotional information, and the prosody of the mother's voice, is focusing her attention on and is, therefore, regulated by the output of the mother's right hemisphere, which is dominant for nonverbal communication, the processing and expression of facially and prosodically expressed emotional information, and for the maternal capacity to comfort the infant. In support of this, Ryan and his colleagues, using EEG and neuroimaging data, now report that, "The positive emotional exchange resulting from autonomy-supportive parenting involves participation of right hemispheric cortical and subcortical systems that participate in global, tonic emotional modulation" (1997, p. 719).

There are now clear experimental and theoretical indications that this emotional exchange also affects the development of the infant's consciousness (another primary factor to the theme here of "minds in the making"). Tronick and his colleagues are now describing how microregulatory social–emotional processes of communication generate intersubjective states of consciousness in the infant–mother dyad. In such there is "a mutual mapping of (some of) the elements of each interactant's state of consciousness into each of their brains" (Tronick & Weinberg, 1997, p. 75). Tronick *et al.* (1998) argue that the infant's self-organizing system, when coupled with the mother's, allows for a brain organization which can be expanded into more coherent and complex states of consciousness. I suggest that Tronick is describing an expansion of what the neuroscientist Edelman (1989) calls primary consciousness, which relates visceral and emotional information pertaining to the biological self, to stored information processing pertaining to outside reality. Edelman lateralizes primary consciousness to the right brain.

Thus, regulation theory suggests that *attachment is, in essence, the right brain regulation of biological synchronicity between organisms.* Feldman *et al.* (1999) have recently published a study entitled, "Mother–infant affect synchrony as an antecedent of the emergence of self-*control*". At the same time Garavan, Ross, and Stein (1999) reported, in a functional magnetic resonance imaging (fMRI) study, "Right hemispheric dominance of inhibitory *control*". These data bear upon Bowlby's (1969) assertion, thirty years ago, that attachment behaviour is organized and regulated by means of a "*control system*" within the central nervous system.

Maturation of an orbitofrontal regulatory system

Bowlby hypothesized that the maturation of the attachment control system is open to influence by the particular environment in which development occurs. Current neurobiological studies show that the mature orbitofrontal cortex acts in "the highest level of *control* of behaviour, especially in relation to emotion" (Price *et al.*, 1996, p. 523) and plays "a particularly prominent role in the emotional modulation of experience" (Mesulam, 1998, p. 1035). The orbito-frontal regions are not functional at birth. Over the course of the first year limbic circuitries emerge in a sequential progression, from amygdala to anterior cingulate to insula and finally to orbitofrontal (Schore, 1997b, 2000c, 2001b). And so, as a result of attachment experiences, this system enters a critical period of maturation in the last quarter of the first year, the same time that working models of attachment are first measured.

The orbital prefrontal cortex is positioned as a convergence zone where the cortex and subcortex meet. It is the only cortical structure with direct connections to the hypothalamus, the amygdala, and the reticular formation in the brainstem that regulates arousal (*Figure 4*), and through these connections it can modulate instinctual behaviour and internal drives. But because it contains neurons that process face and voice information, this system is also capable of appraising changes in the external environment, especially the social, object-related environment. Due to its unique connections, at the orbitofrontal level cortically processed information concerning the *external* environment (such as visual and auditory stimuli emanating from the emotional face of the *object*) is integrated with subcortically processed information regarding the *internal* visceral environment (such as concurrent changes in the emotional or bodily *self* state). In this manner, the (right) orbitofrontal cortex and its connections function in the "integration of adaptive bodily responses with ongoing emotional and attentional states of the organism" (Critchley *et al.*, 2000a, p. 3033).

The orbitofrontal system is now described as "a nodal cortical

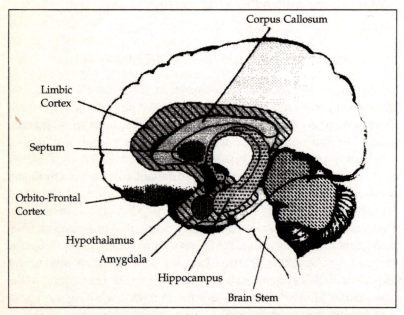

Figure 4. Limbic structures of the right hemisphere, lateral view. Cingulate is labelled limbic cortex. From Trevarthen, Aitken, Papoudi, and Roberts, 1998.

region that is important in assembling and monitoring relevant past and current experiences, including their affective and social values" (Cavada *et al.*, 2000, p. 238). In a recent entire issue of the journal *Cerebral Cortex* on "The mysterious orbitofrontal cortex", the editors conclude, that "the orbitofrontal cortex is involved in critical human functions, such as social adjustment and the control of mood, drive and responsibility, traits that are crucial in defining the 'personality' of an individual" (Cavada & Schultz, 2000, p. 205).

This frontolimbic cortex is situated at the hierarchical apex of an "anterior limbic prefrontal network" interconnecting the orbital and medial prefrontal cortex with the temporal pole, cingulate, and amygdala. This cortical–subcortical limbic network is involved in "affective responses to events and in the mnemonic processing and storage of these responses" (Carmichael & Price, 1995, p. 639). The limbic system is now thought to be centrally implicated in the implicit processing of facial expressions without conscious awareness (Critchley *et al.*, 2000b), in the capacity "to adapt to a rapidly changing environment", and in "the organization of new learning" (Mesulam, 1998, p. 1028). Current findings thus support Bowlby's (1969) and Anders and Zeanah's (1984) speculation that the limbic system is the site of developmental changes associated with the rise of attachment behaviours. Indeed, it is now held that "The integrity of the orbitofrontal cortex", the highest level of the limbic system, "is necessary for acquiring very specific forms of knowledge for regulating interpersonal and social behaviour" (Dolan, 1999, p. 928).

The orbitofrontal system, the "Senior Executive" of the social–emotional brain, is especially expanded in the right cortex (Falk *et al.*, 1990), and in its role as an executive of limbic arousal it comes to act in the capacity of an executive control function for the entire right brain (*Figure 5*). This hemisphere, which is dominant for unconscious processes, performs, on a moment-to-moment basis, a "valence tagging" function, in which perceptions receive a positive or negative affective charge, in accord, as Freud speculated, with a calibration of degrees of pleasure–unpleasure. Very recent studies show that the right hemisphere is faster than the left in performing valence-dependent, automatic, pre-attentive appraisals of emotional facial expressions (Pizzagalli *et al.*, 1999). It also contains a "nonverbal affect lexicon", a vocabulary for nonverbal affective signals such as facial expressions, gestures, and vocal tone or

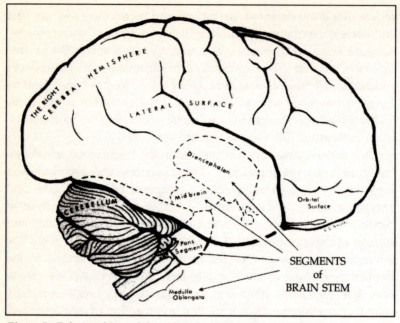

Figure 5. Relationships of the orbitofrontal cortex to subcortical structures of the right hemisphere From Smith, 1981.

prosody (Bowers *et al.*, 1993; Snow, 2000), a finding directly relevant to Bowlby's (1969, p. 120) speculation that, in intimate settings, human feelings are detected through "facial expressions, posture, tone of voice, physiological changes, tempo of movement, and incipient action".

The right hemisphere is, more so than the left, deeply connected into not only the limbic system but also both the sympathetic and parasympathetic branches of the autonomic nervous system (ANS). For this reason the representation of visceral and somatic states and the processing of "self-related material" (Keenan *et al.*, 1999) is under primary control of the "non-dominant" hemisphere. The ANS has been called the "physiological bottom of the mind" (Jackson, 1931). The connections of the highest centres of the limbic system into the hypothalamus, the head ganglion of the ANS and anatomical locus of drive centres, supports Freud's idea about the central role of drive in the system unconscious. The fact that the right hemisphere contains "the most comprehensive and integrated map of the body state available to the brain" (Damasio, 1994, p. 66) indicates that Freud's (1915b) definition of "drive" as "the psychical representative of the stimuli originating from the organism and reaching the mind" may be more properly characterized as reaching the "right mind" (Ornstein, 1997). It may also elucidate Freud's remark to Groddeck: "the unconscious is the proper mediator between the somatic and the mental, perhaps the long-sought 'missing link'" (Groddeck, 1977, p. 38).

For the rest of the lifespan the right brain plays a superior role in the regulation of fundamental physiological and endocrinological functions whose primary control centres are located in subcortical regions of the brain. Since the hypothalamo–pituitary–adrenocortical axis and the sympathetic–adrenomedullary axis are both under the main control of the right cerebral cortex, this hemisphere contains "a unique response system preparing the organism to deal efficiently with external challenges", and so its adaptive functions mediate the human stress response (Wittling, 1997, p. 55). It, therefore, is centrally involved in the vital functions that support survival and enable the organism to cope actively and passively with stress (Sullivan & Gratton, 1999; Schore, 2001b). In support of Bowlby's speculation that the infant's "capacity to cope with stress" is correlated with certain maternal behaviours (1969, p. 344), the attachment relationship directly shapes the maturation of the infant's right brain stress-coping systems that act at levels beneath awareness.

The right hemisphere contributes to the development of reciprocal interactions within the mother–infant regulatory system and mediates the capacity for biological synchronicity, the regulatory mechanism of attachment. In further support of its role in organismic synchronicity, the activity of this hemisphere is instrumental to the empathic perception of the emotional states of other human beings (Schore, 1994, 1996, 1997c, 1998a,b,c,d, 2002a). According to Adolphs et al., "recognizing emotions from visually presented facial expressions requires right somatosensory cortices", and in this manner "we recognize another individual's emotional state by internally generating somatosensory representations that stimulate how the individual would feel when displaying a certain facial expression" (2000, p. 2683). The interactive regulation of right brain attachment biology is thus the substrate of empathy.

The right brain stores an internal working model of the attachment relationship which encodes strategies of affect regulation that maintain basic regulation and positive affect even in the face of environmental challenge (Schore, 1994). Since the right hemisphere is centrally involved in unconscious processes and in "implicit learning" (Hugdahl, 1995), this unconscious model is stored in right cerebral implicit–procedural memory. Neuropsychological studies now also reveal that the right hemisphere, "the right mind", and not the later forming verbal–linguistic left, is the substrate of affectively-laden autobiographical memory (Fink *et al.*, 1996).

Current psychobiological models refer to representations of the infant's affective dialogue with the mother which can be accessed to regulate its affective state (Polan & Hofer, 1999). The orbitofrontal area "is particularly involved in situations in which internally generated affective representations play a critical role" (Zald & Kim, 1996). Because this system is responsible for "cognitive–emotional interactions" (Barbas, 1995), it generates internal working models. These mental representations, according to Main, Kaplan, and Cassidy (1985), contain cognitive as well as affective components and act to guide appraisals of experience. Recent findings that the orbitofrontal cortex generates nonconscious biases that guide behaviour before conscious knowledge does (Bechara *et al.*, 1997), codes the likely significance of future behavioural options (Dolan, 1999), and represents an important site of contact between emotional information and mechanisms of action selection (Rolls, 1996), are consonant with Bowlby's (1981) assertion that unconscious internal working models are used as guides for future action.

According to Fonagy and Target (1997) an important outcome of a secure attachment is a reflective function, a mental operation that enables the perception of another's state. Brothers (1995, 1997) describes a limbic circuit of orbitofrontal cortex, anterior cingulate gyrus, amygdala, and temporal pole which functions as a social "editor" that is "specialized for processing others' social intentions" by appraising "significant gestures and expressions" (Brothers, 1997, p. 27) and "encourages the rest of the brain to report on features of the social environment" (p. 15). The editor acts as a unitary system "specialized for responding to social signals of all kinds, a system that would ultimately construct representations of the mind" (p. 27). A recent neuropsychological study indicates that the orbitofrontal cortex is "particularly involved in theory of mind tasks with an affective component" (Stone *et al.*, 1998, p. 651).

As previously mentioned, the orbitofrontal control system plays an essential role in the regulation of emotion. This frontolimbic system provides a high level coding that flexibly coordinates exteroceptive and interoceptive domains and functions to correct responses as social conditions change, processes feedback information, and thereby monitors, adjusts, and corrects emotional responses and modulates the motivational control of goal-directed behaviour. It thus acts as a recovery mechanism that efficiently monitors and regulates the duration, frequency, and intensity of not only positive but negative affect states. Damasio's recent publication emphasizes that developmental neurological damage of this system in the first two years leads to abnormal development of social and moral behaviours (Anderson *et al.*, 1999).

The orbital cortex matures in the middle of the second year, a time when the average child has a productive vocabulary of less than 70 words. The core of the self is thus nonverbal and unconscious, and it lies in patterns of affect regulation. This structural development allows for an internal sense of security and resilience that comes from the intuitive knowledge that one can regulate the flows and shifts of one's bodily-based emotional states either by one's own coping capacities or within a relationship with caring others. In developmental neurobiological studies, Ryan and colleagues (1997) conclude that the operation of the right prefrontal cortex is integral to autonomous regulation, and that the activation of this system facilitates increases in positive affect in response to optimally challenging or personally meaningful situations, or decreases in negative affect in response to stressful events. Confirming earlier proposals for a central role of the right orbitofrontal areas in essential self functions (Schore, 1994, 1996), current neuroimaging studies now demonstrate that the processing of self occurs within the right prefrontal cortices (Keenan *et al.*, 2000), and that the self concept is represented in right frontal areas (Craik *et al.*, 1999).

The functioning of the "self-correcting" orbitofrontal system is central to self-regulation, the ability to flexibly regulate emotional states through interactions with other humans (interactive regulation in interconnected contexts via a two-person psychology), and without other humans (autoregulation in autonomous contexts via a one-person psychology). The adaptive capacity to shift between these dual regulatory modes, depending upon the social context, emerges out of a history of secure attachment interactions of a maturing biological organism and an early attuned social environment. The essential aspect of this function is highlighted by Westen (1997, p. 542) who asserts that "The attempt to regulate affect—to minimize unpleasant feelings and to maximize pleasant ones—is the driving force in human motivation".

The right hemisphere, attachment theory, and the empathic reception of unconscious emotional communications

Earlier I described an optimal developmental scenario, one that facilitates the experience-dependent growth of an efficient regulatory system in the right hemisphere that supports functions associated with a secure attachment. On the other hand, growth-inhibiting environments negatively impact the ontogeny of self-regulatory prefrontal systems and generate attachment disorders, and such early disturbances of personality formation are mechanisms for the transmission of psychopathology. Recall Bowlby's (1978) prediction that:

> In the fields of aetiology and psychopathology [attachment theory] can be used to frame specific hypotheses which relate different family experiences to different forms of psychiatric disorder and also, possibly, to the neurophysiological changes that accompany them. [1978]

Very recent neuropsychiatric research demonstrates that reduced volume of prefrontal areas serves as an "endophenotypic marker of disposition to psychopathology" (Matsui *et al.*, 2000, p. 155).

In a number of works I have provided clinical and neurobiological evidence to show that various forms of attachment pathologies specifically represent inefficient patterns of organization of the right brain, especially the right orbitofrontal areas (Schore, 1994, 1996, 1997b; see 2000d for a theory of trauma). Yet all share a common deficit—due to the impaired development of the right cortical preconscious system that decodes emotional stimuli by actual felt emotional responses to stimuli, individuals with poor attachment histories display empathy disorders, the limited capacity to perceive the emotional states of others. An inability to read facial expressions leads to a misattribution of emotional states and a misinterpretation of the intentions of others. Thus, there are deficits in the processing of socioemotional information and in affect regulation.

In addition to this deficit in social cognition, the deficit in self-regulation is manifest in a limited capacity to modulate the intensity and duration of affects, especially biologically primitive affects like shame, rage, excitement, elation, disgust, panic-terror, and hopeless-despair. Under stress such individuals experience not discrete and differentiated affects, but diffuse, undifferentiated, chaotic states accompanied by overwhelming somatic and visceral sensations. The poor capacity for what Fonagy and Target (1997) call mentalization leads to a restricted ability to reflect upon their emotional states. And Solms has also described a mechanism by which disorganization of a damaged or developmentally deficient right hemisphere is associated with a "collapse of internalized representations of the external world" in which "the patient regresses from whole to part object relationships" (1996, p. 347), a hallmark of early forming personality disorders.

There is now consensus that the psychotherapy of these "developmental arrests" is directed toward the mobilization of fundamental modes of development (Emde, 1990) and the completion of interrupted developmental processes (Gedo, 1979). This development is specifically emotional development. Recall Winnicott's dictum that the therapist must understand, at an intuitive level, specifically the emotional history of the patient:

> In order to use the mutual experience one must have *in one's bones* a theory of the emotional development of the child and the relationship of the child to the environmental factors. [1971, p. 3, my italics]

With patients, especially those manifesting early forming attachment pathologies and therefore developmental disorders of self-regulation, the psychotherapeutic interaction functions as an attachment relationship. Very recent models suggest that affect dysregulation is a fundamental mechanism of all psychiatric disorders (Taylor *et al.*, 1997), that all psychotherapies show a similarity in promoting affect regulation (Bradley, 2000), and that the goal of attachment-focused psychotherapy is the mutual regulation of affective homeostasis and the restructuring of interactive representations encoded in implicit-procedural memory (Amini *et al.*, 1996).

In 1913 Freud proclaimed, "It remains the first aim of treatment to *attach* him [the patient] to it [the process of analysis] and to the person of the doctor" (Freud, 1913a, p. 139). What can current ideas about attachment as the dyadic regulation of emotion and research on the right brain tell us about this process? The direct relevance of developmental attachment studies to the psychotherapeutic process derives from the commonality of interactive right brain to right brain emotion-transacting mechanisms in the caregiver–infant attachment relationship and in the clinician–patient therapeutic relationship (Schore, 1994, 1997c, 1998c, 1999b, 2001a, 2002a). A number of authors have pointed out the direct parallels between the clinical attributes of an effective therapist and the parental characteristics of the psychobiologically attuned intuitive caregiver of a securely attached child (e.g., Holmes, 1993a; Dozier *et al.*, 1994; Schore, 1994; Sable, 2001).

Embedded in Freud's description of the aim of the treatment is the centrality of the concept of attachment to the operational definition of the therapeutic alliance. For a working alliance to be created, the therapist must be experienced as being in a state of vitalizing attunement to the patient, that is, the crescendos and decrescendos of the therapist's affective state must be in *resonance* with similar states of crescendos and decrescendos of the patient (Schore, 1994, 1997c). Studies of empathic processes between the "intuitive" attuned mother and her infant demonstrate that this affective *synchrony* is entirely nonverbal and that resonance is not so much with his mental (cognitive) states as with his psychobiological (affective-bodily) states. Similarly, the intuitive empathic therapist psychobiologically attunes to and resonates with the patient's shifting affective state, thereby co-creating with the patient a context in which the clinician can act as a regulator of the patient's physiology (Schore, 1994; 1997c; Amini *et al.*, 1996).

The right cortical hemisphere, which is centrally involved in attachment functions, is dominant for the perception of the emotional states of others, by a right posterior cortical mechanism involved in the perception of nonverbal expressions embedded in facial and prosodic stimuli (Schore, 1994, 1999a). It is also dominant for "*subjective* emotional experiences" (Wittling & Roschmann, 1993) and for *the detection of subjective objects* (Atchley & Atchley, 1998). The *interactive* "transfer of affect" between the right brains of the members of the mother–infant and therapeutic dyads is thus best described as *"intersubjectivity"*. So what can current developmental neuropsychoanalysis tell us about psychotherapeutic intersubjectivity?

The right brain is centrally involved in unconscious activities, and just as the left brain communicates its states to other left brains via conscious linguistic behaviours, so the right nonverbally communicates its unconscious states to other right brains *that are tuned to receive these communications*. Freud asserted that, "It is a very remarkable thing that the Ucs. of one human being can react upon that of another, *without passing through the Cs"* (1915c, p. 194, my italics). He also proposed that the therapist should "turn his own unconscious like a receptive organ towards the transmitting unconscious of the patient ... so the doctor's unconscious is able ... to reconstruct [the patient's] unconscious" (1912, p. 115). He called the state of receptive readiness "evenly suspended attention". Bion (1962) referred to "reverie" or "dream state alpha", clearly implying a right-brain state. Indeed, Marcus has recently written "The analyst, by means of reverie and intuition, listens with the right brain directly to the analysand's right brain" (1997, p. 238).

This same right-brain to right-brain system is described in the neuropsychological literature by Buck as "spontaneous emotional communication":

Spontaneous communication employs species-specific expressive displays in the sender that, given attention, activate emotional preattunements and are directly perceived by the receiver ... The "meaning" of the display is known directly by the receiver ... This spontaneous emotional communication constitutes a *conversation between limbic systems* ... It is a biologically-based communication system that involves individual organisms directly with one another: the individuals in spontaneous communication constitute literally a *biological unit*. [Buck, 1994, p. 266, my italics]

Buck (1994) emphasizes the importance of specifically the right limbic system, and localizes this biologically-based spontaneous emotional communication system to the right hemisphere, in accord with other research that indicates a right lateralization of spontaneous gestures (Blonder *et al.*, 1995) and emotional communication

(Blonder *et al.*, 1991). Earlier I pointed to Bowlby's (1969) speculation that human feelings are recognized through facial expressions, posture, tone of voice, physiological changes, tempo of movement, and incipient action.

Indeed, this right-brain process lies at the heart of the nonverbal relational communications between patient and therapist. Lyons-Ruth (2000), a member of Stern's Study Group (1998 a,b), describes the centrality of the "recognition process" that occurs in the "ordinary moments of change in psychoanalytic treatment":

> [M]ost relational transactions rely heavily on a substrate of affective cues that give an evaluative valence or direction to each relational communication, and these communications are carried out at an implicit level of rapid cueing and response that occurs too rapidly for simultaneous verbal translation and conscious reflection. [Lyons-Ruth, 2000, pp. 91–92]

Recall that the right hemisphere recognizes emotions from visually presented facial cues (Adolphs *et al.*, 2000), is specialized for "implicit learning" (Hugdahl, 1995), and performs rapid (80 msec) valence-dependent, automatic appraisals of emotional facial expressions (Pizzagalli *et al.*, 1999).

Furthermore, the right hemisphere uses an expansive attention mechanism that focuses on global features while the left uses a restricted mode that focuses on local detail (Derryberry & Tucker, 1994), a characterization that fits with Freud's "evenly suspended attention". And in contrast to the left hemisphere's activation of "narrow semantic fields", the right hemisphere's "coarse semantic coding is useful for noting and integrating *distantly* related semantic information" (Beeman, 1998, p. 279), a function which allows for the process of free association. Bucci (1993) has described free association as "following the tracks of nonverbal schemata", by loosening the hold of the verbal system on the associative process and giving the nonverbal mode the chance to drive the representational and expressive systems, that is by shifting dominance from a left to right hemispheric state. In this manner, as Freud describes, the clinician uses "the derivatives of the unconscious which are communicated to him to reconstruct that unconscious, which has determined the patient's free associations" (Freud, 1912, p. 116).

In recent writings I have suggested that if Freud was describing how the unconscious can act as "a receptive organ", Klein's concept of projective identification (Schore, 2000d, 2002a) attempts to model how an unconscious system acts as a "transmitter", and how these transmissions will then influence the receptive functions of another unconscious mind. Klein proposed that although this primitive process of communication between the unconscious of one person and the unconscious of another begins in early development, it continues throughout life. These moments of right-brain to right-brain communication represent an alignment of what Zeddies (2000) calls the "nonlinguistic dimension" of the "relational unconscious" of both the therapist and the patient.

There is now a growing consensus that despite the existence of a number of distinct theoretical perspectives in psychoanalysis, the clinical concepts of transference (Wallerstein, 1990) and counter-transference (Gabbard, 1995) represent a common ground. In my ongoing work I propose that nonverbal transference–counter-transference interactions that take place at preconscious–unconscious levels represent right-hemisphere to right-hemisphere communications of fast acting, automatic, regulated, and dysregulated emotional states between patient and therapist. Transferential events clearly occur during moments of emotional arousal, and recent neurobiological studies indicate that "attention is altered during emotional arousal such that there is a heightened sensitivity to cues related to the current emotional state" (Lane *et al.*, 1999, p. 986).

Current psychoanalytic research highlights the role of "fleeting facial expressions" that act as indicators of transference and countertransference processes (Krause & Lutolf, 1988; Schore, 1994, 1998c; Andersen *et al.*, 1996). These are nonconsciously appraised from movements occurring primarily in the regions around the eyes and from prosodic expressions from the mouth (Fridlund, 1991). Since the transference–countertransference is a reciprocal process, facially communicated "expressions of affect" that reflect changes in internal state are rapidly communicated and perceptually processed within the affectively synchronized thera-peutic dialogue. This finding is relevant to the "reciprocal process", described by Munder Ross, in which the therapist has access to "the subliminal stimulation ... that emanates from the patient" (1999,

p. 95). In fact, these very same spontaneously communicated and nonconsciously perceived visual and auditory cues represent "the intrapsychic edge of the object world, the perceptual edge of the transference" (Smith, 1990, p. 225).

Only in a right hemispheric dominant receptive state in which "a private self" is communicating with another "private self" can a self–selfobject system of spontaneous affective transference–countertransference communications be created. Fosshage (1994), a self psychologist, notes that when the self-object seeking dimension is in the foreground, the analyst must *resonate* at the deepest layers of his/her personality to be sufficiently available to the patient's developmental and self-regulatory needs. In other words, a state of resonance exists when the therapist's subjectivity is empathically attuned to the patient's inner state, one that may be unconscious to the patient, and this *resonance* then interactively amplifies, in both intensity and duration, the affective state *in both members of the dyad*. Sander (1992) states that "moments of meeting" between patient and therapist occur when there are "matched specificities between two systems in *resonance*, attuned to each other". Loewald (1986) describes "resonances between the patient's and the analyst's unconscious".

Resonance phenomena are now thought to play one of the most important roles in brain organization and in CNS regulatory processes (Schore, 2000c, in 2002a). Although this principle is usually applied to the *synchronization* of processes within different parts of a whole brain, I have suggested that it also describes the resonance phenomena that occurs between the two right brains of the psychobiologically attuned mother–infant dyad. So this also applies to the moments within the treatment process when two right brains, two emotion-processing unconscious "right minds" within the therapeutic dyad are communicating and in *resonance*. In a recent issue of the *Journal of the American Psychoanalytic Association*, Kantrowitz (1999, p. 72) suggests that, "It is in the realm of preconscious communication that the interwovenness of intra-psychic and interpersonal phenomena becomes apparent", and emphasizes the importance of "attunement and *resonance*".

This leads to the following proposals: empathic *resonance* results from dyadic *attunement*, and it induces a *synchronization* of patterns of activation of both right hemispheres of the therapeutic dyad.

Misattunement is triggered by a mismatch, and describes a context of stressful *desynchronization* between and destabilization within their right brains. Interactive *reattunement* induces a *resynchronization* of their right-brain states. These brain state shifts occur rapidly at levels beneath awareness. In other words, the two right-brain systems that process unconscious attachment-related information within the co-constructed intersubjective field of the patient and therapist are temporally co-activated and coupled, deactivated and uncoupled, or reactivated and re-coupled. The unconscious minds and bodies of two self systems are connected and co-regulating, disconnected and autoregulating, or reconnected and again mutually regulating their activity. Recall self regulation occurs in two modes, autoregulation, via the processes of a "one-person psychology", or interactive regulation, via a "two-person psychology".

Implications of a psychoneurobiological model of emotional development for clinical practice

Even more specifically, during the treatment, the empathic therapist is consciously attending to the patient's verbalizations in order to *objectively* diagnose and rationalize the patient's dysregulating symptomatology. But she is also listening and interacting at another level, an experience-near *subjective* level, one that processes socio-emotional information at levels beneath awareness. According to Kohut (1971) the empathically immersed clinician is attuned to the continuous flow and shifts in the patient's feelings and experiences. Her "oscillating attentiveness" (Schwaber, 1995) is focused on "barely perceptible cues that signal a change in state" (Sander, 1992), in both patient and therapist, and on "nonverbal behaviours and shifts in affects" (McLaughlin, 1996). The attuned, intuitive clinician, from the first point of contact, is learning the nonverbal moment-to-moment rhythmic structures of the patient's internal states, and is relatively flexibly and fluidly modifying her own behaviour to *synchronize* with that structure, thereby creating a context for the organization of the therapeutic alliance.

Freud asserted that the work of psychotherapy is always concerned with affect. Perhaps the most important clinical advances in this realm have come from those working in "the nonverbal realm of psychoanalysis" (e.g., Jacobs, 1994; Schore, 1994; Schwaber, 1998; Stern *et al.*, 1998a,b; Hollinger, 1999). The current emphasis in developmental studies on "heightened affective moments" and in emotion studies on "actual moments of experience" is mirrored in very recent psychotherapy research which is exploring "significant moments" in the therapeutic hour. And learning research on the importance of the implicit perception of affective information is echoed in the clinical principle that in order for implicit affective learning to take place, the patient must have a vivid affective experience of the therapist (Amini *et al.*, 1996).

Neurobiology is also delving into this theme—studies demonstrate the involvement of the right hemisphere in implicit learning (Hugdahl, 1995) and nonverbal processes (see Schore, 1994) and the orbitofrontal system in implicit processing (Rolls, 1996) and procedural (Rolls, 1996) or emotion-related learning (Rolls *et al.*, 1994). Such structure–function relationships may elucidate how alterations in what Stern and his colleagues (1998b) call nonverbal "implicit relational knowledge" are at the core of therapeutic change. In light of the central role of the limbic system in both attachment functions and in "the organization of new learning", the corrective emotional experience of psychotherapy, which can alter attachment patterns, must involve unconscious right-brain limbic learning.

But a dyadic-transactional perspective entails not only more closely examining the patient's emotion dynamics, but also bringing the *therapist's emotions* and personality structure more into the picture. During a therapeutic affective encounter, the therapist is describing his psychobiological state of mind and the counter-transference impressions made upon it by the patient's unconscious transference communications. These are expressed in clinical heightened affective moments when the patient's internal working models are accessed, thereby revealing the patient's fundamental transferential modes and coping strategies of affect regulation (Schore, 1997c).

Gans describes the "ever-deepening grasp of the patient's essence that can result from therapists' ongoing efforts to distil meaning from reactions caused or evoked in them by their patients" (1994, p. 122). These countertransferential reactions include the clinician's "visceral reactions to the patient's material" (Loewald,

1986, p. 278). Recall that attachment is fundamentally the right-brain regulation of biological synchronicity between organisms, and thus the empathic therapist's resonant synchronization to the patient's activated unconscious internal working model triggers, in the clinician, the procedural processing of his autonomic visceral responses to the patient's nonverbal, nonconscious communications. In rupture and repair transactions (Beebe & Lachmann, 1994; Schore, 1994; Lewis, 2000) the therapist also utilizes his autoregulatory capacities to modulate and contain the stressful negative state induced in him by the patient's communications of dysregulated negative affect. The psychobiologically attuned therapist then has an opportunity to act as an interactive affect regulator of the patient's dysregulated state (see Schore, 2002a). This model clearly suggests that the therapist's role is much more than interpreting to the developmentally disordered patient either distortions of the transference, or unintegrated early attachment experiences that occur in incoherent moments of the patient's narrative.

We need to go beyond objectively observing the disorganization of left-brain language capacities by dysregulating right-brain states and feeding this back to the patient in insight-oriented interpretations. Rather, we can directly engage and therefore regulate the patient's inefficient right-brain processes with our own right brains. On the part of the therapist, the most effective interpretations are based on the clinician's "awareness of his own physical, emotional, and ideational responses to the patient's veiled messages" (Boyer, 1990, p. 304). On the part of the patient, the most "correct understandings" can be used by the patient "only if the analyst is attuned to the patient's state at the time the interpretation is offered" (Friedman & Moskowitz, 1997, p. xxi). This interactive regulation allows the dyad to interactively hold on-line and amplify internal affective stimuli long enough for them to be recognized, regulated, labelled, and given meaning. This is an interactive context that supports a corrective emotional experience.

In light of the observation that "physical containment by the therapist of the patient's disavowed experience needs to *precede* its verbal processing" (Dosamantes, 1992, p. 362), the interactive regulation of the patient's state enables him or her to now begin to verbally label the affective experience. In a "genuine dialogue" with the therapist, the patient raises to an inner word and then into a spoken word what he needs to say at a particular moment but does not yet possess as speech. But the patient must experience this verbal description of an internal state as heard and felt by an empathic other. In this manner the emotionally responsive aspects of the therapist's interventions are transformative for the patient.

This affectively focused therapeutic experience may literally alter the orbitofrontal system. A functional magnetic resonance imaging study (Hariri *et al.*, 2000) provides evidence that higher regions of, specifically, the right prefrontal cortex attenuate emotional responses at the most basic levels in the brain, that such modulating processes are "fundamental to most modern psychotherapeutic methods", that this lateralized neocortical network is active in "modulating emotional experience through interpreting and labelling emotional expressions", and that "this form of modulation may be impaired in various emotional disorders and may provide the basis for therapies of these same disorders" (p. 48). This process is a central component of therapeutic narrative organization, of what Holmes (1993b, p. 150) calls turning "raw feelings into symbols". Recall that the same "neocortical network" which "modulates the limbic system" is identical to the right-lateralized orbitofrontal system that regulates attachment dynamics.

As a result of such modulation, the patient's affectively charged but now regulated right-brain experience can then be communicated to the left brain for further processing. This effect, which must follow a right-brain then left-brain temporal sequence, allows for the development of linguistic symbols to represent the *meaning* of an experience, *while one is feeling and perceiving the emotion generated by the experience.* The objective left hemisphere can now co-process subjective right brain communications, and this allows for a linkage of the nonverbal implicit and verbal explicit representational domains. This in turn facilitates the "evolution of affects from their early form, in which they are experienced as bodily sensations, into subjective states that can gradually be verbally articulated" (Stolorow & Atwood, 1992, p. 42). The patient can reflect upon not only what external information is affectively charged and therefore personally meaningful, but how it is somatically felt and cognitively processed by his self regulatory system.

The exploration for meaning is thus not in the content but in the very process of sensing and communicating emotional states. In a growth-facilitating therapeutic context, meaning is not singularly discovered but dyadically created. Focusing, at levels beneath and above awareness, not so much on cognitions as on the subtle or abrupt ebbs and flows of affective states, and on rhythms of attunement, misattunement, and reattunement within the therapeutic dyad allows us to understand the dynamic events that occur within what Holmes (1993b) calls "the spontaneous encounter of two solitudes". The essential mechanisms that regulate, in real time, the connections, disconnections, and reconnections of the inner worlds of the patient and the therapist are mediated by the transactions of the nonverbal transference–countertransference.

Brown (1993) asserts that the process of emotional development, as it continues in adulthood, brings the potential to observe and understand the processes of our own minds. "Adult affective development is the potential for self-observation and reflection on the very processes of mental functioning" (p. 42). This involves not simply the affective content of experience but of the very processes by which affect comes into experience—how it is experienced by the self and what informs the self about its relationship to internal and external reality. "Psychotherapy is one medium of adult affective development in the sense that it serves the purpose of disciplined conscious reflection on affective processes" (p. 56).

I suggest that Brown is describing a developmental progression in the patient's internal psychic structures, namely the orbitofrontal system and its cortical and subcortical connections that performs functions central to affect regulation (Schore, 1994; Davidson et al., 2000). This, "the thinking part of the emotional brain" (Goleman, 1995), acts to "integrate and assign emotional–motivational significance to cognitive impressions; the association of emotion with ideas and thoughts" (Joseph, 1996) and in "the processing of affect-related meanings" (Teasdale et al., 1999). Because its activity is associated with a lower threshold for awareness of sensations of both external and internal origin, it functions as an "internal reflecting and organizing agency" (Kaplan-Solms & Solms, 1996). This orbitofrontal role in "self-reflective awareness" (Stuss et al., 1992) allows the individual to reflect on his or her own internal emotional states, as well as others (Povinelli & Preuss, 1995). Furthermore, in light of recent interest of neuroscience in the "mind's eye" (Kawashima et al., 1995), I propose that the psychobiological operations of the right orbitofrontal system represent the "subjective lens of the mind's eye".

It is important to note that the right hemisphere cycles back into growth phases throughout the lifespan (Thatcher, 1994; Schore, 1999a, 2001a, 2002b) and that the orbitofrontal cortex retains a capacity for plasticity in later life (Barbas, 1995), thereby allowing for the continuing experience-dependent maturation of a more efficient and flexible right frontal regulatory system within the growth-facilitating environment of an affect regulating therapeutic relationship. This neurobiological development may, in turn, mediate an expansion of the patient's unconscious right mind and the transformation of an insecure into an "earned secure" (Phelps *et al.*, 1998) attachment.

A psychoneurobiological model of the attachment communications between patient and therapist indicates that, in order to create an optimal working alliance, the therapist must access, in a timely fashion, both her own subjective, unconscious, intuitive, implicit responses, as well as her objective conscious, rational, theory-based explicit knowledge in the work. These very recent applications of the advances in developmental psychoanalysis and neuropsychoanalysis to theoretical and clinical psychoanalytic therapeutic models support Bowlby's assertion, in his last writings, that, "Clearly the best therapy is done by the therapist who is naturally intuitive and also guided by the appropriate theory" (1991a, p. 16).

From a cognitive social neuroscience perspective, intuition is now being defined as "the subjective experience associated with the use of knowledge gained through implicit learning" (Lieberman, 2000, p. 109). Recall that right hemispheric processes are central to implicit learning and that psychotherapy essentially alters and expands implicit relational knowledge. But in light of the intrinsic dyadic nature of attachment, this expansion occurs in the brain/mind/bodies of both the patient and therapist. In his last work, Bowlby (1991b) described the therapeutic process as a "joint exploration". An attachment model grounded in both biology and psychoanalysis thus accounts for how a successful therapeutic relationship can act as an interactive affect regulating context that optimizes the growth of two "minds in the making", that is increases in complexity in both the patient's and the therapist's continually developing unconscious right minds.

References

Adolphs, R., Damasio, H., Tranel, D., Cooper, G., & Damasio, A. R. (2000). A role for somatosensory cortices in the visual recognition of emotion as revealed by three-dimensional lesion mapping. *Journal of Neuroscience*, 20: 2683–2690.

Ainsworth, M. D. S. (1967). *Infancy in Uganda: Infant Care and the Growth of Love*. Baltimore: Johns Hopkins University Press.

Ainsworth, M. D. S. (1969). Object relations, dependency and attachment: a theoretical review of the infant-mother relationship. *Child Development*, 40: 969–1025.

Amini, F., Lewis, T., & Lannon, R. *et al.* (1996). Affect, attachment, memory: contributions toward psychobiologic integration. *Psychiatry*, 59: 213–239.

Anders, T. F., & Zeanah, C. H. (1984). Early infant development from a biological point of view. In: J. D. Call, E. Galenson & R. L. Tyson (Eds.), *Frontiers of Infant Psychiatry, Volume 2*. New York: Basic Books.

Andersen, S. M., Reznik, I., & Manzella, L. M. (1996). Eliciting facial affect, motivation, and expectancies in transference: significant-other representations in social relations. *Journal of Personality and Social Psychology*, 71: 1108–1129.

Anderson, S. W., Bechara, A., Damasio, H., Tranel, D., & Damasio, A. R. (1999). Impairment of social and moral behaviour related to early damage in human prefrontal cortex. *Nature Neuroscience*, 2: 1032–1037.

Atchley, R. A., & Atchley, P. (1998). Hemispheric specialization in the detection of subjective objects. *Neuropsychologia*, 36: 1373–1386.

Barbas, H. (1995). Anatomic basis of cognitive–emotional interactions in the primate prefrontal cortex. *Neuroscience and Biobehavioural Reviews*, 19: 499–510.

Bechara, A., Damasio, H., Tranel, D., & Damasio, A. R. (1997). Deciding advantageously before knowing the advantageous strategy. *Science*, 275: 1293–1295.

Beebe, B. & Lachmann, F. M. (1994). Representations and internalization in infancy: three principles of salience. *Psychoanalytic Psychology*, 11: 127–165.

Beeman, M. (1998). Coarse semantic coding and discourse comprehension. In: M. Beeman & C. Chiarello (Eds.), *Right Hemisphere Language Comprehension*. Mahweh, NJ: Erlbaum.

Bion, W. R. (1962). The psychoanalytic study of thinking: II. A theory of thinking. *International Journal of Psycho-Analysis*, 43: 306–310.

Blonder, L. X., Bowers, D., & Heilman, K. M. (1991). The role of the right hemisphere in emotional communication. *Brain, 114*: 1115–1127.

Blonder, L. X., Burns, A. F., Bowers, D., Moore, R. W., & Heilman, K. M. (1995). Spontaneous gestures following right hemisphere infarct. *Neuropsychologia, 33*: 203–213.

Bowers, D., Bauer, R. M., & Heilman, K. M. (1993). The nonverbal affect lexicon: Theoretical perspectives from neuropsychological studies of affect perception. *Neuropsychology, 7*: 433–444.

Bowlby, J. (1969). *Attachment and Loss, Volume 1: Attachment*. New York: Basic Books.

Bowlby, J. (1978). Attachment theory and its therapeutic implications. In: S. C. Feinstein & P. L. Giovacchini (Eds.), *Adolescent Psychiatry: Developmental and Clinical Studies*. Chicago: University of Chicago Press.

Bowlby, J. (1981). *Attachment and Loss, Volume 3: Loss, Sadness, and Depression*. New York: Basic Books.

Bowlby, J. (1991a). The role of the psychotherapist's personal resources in the therapeutic situation. *Tavistock Gazette*, autumn.

Bowlby, J. (1991b). *Charles Darwin*. New York: Norton.

Boyer, L. B. (1990). Countertransference and technique. In: L. B. Boyer & P. L. Giovacchini (Eds.), *Master Clinicians on Treating the Regressed Patient*. Northvale, NJ: Jason Aronson.

Bradley, S. (2000). *Affect Regulation and the Development of Psychopathology*. New York: Guilford.

Brenner, C. (1980). A psychoanalytic theory of affects. In: R. Plutchik & H. Kellerman (Eds.), *Emotion: Theory, Research, and Experience, Volume 1*. New York: Academic Press.

Brothers, L. (1995). Neurophysiology of the perception of intention by primates. In: M. S. Gazzaniga (Ed.), *The Cognitive Neurosciences*. Cambridge, MA: MIT Press.

Brothers, L. (1997). *Friday's Footprint*. New York: Oxford University Press.

Brown, D. (1993). Affective development, psychopathology, and adaptation. In: S. L. Ablon, D. Brown, E. J. Khantzian & J. E. Mack (Eds.), *Human Feelings: Explorations in Affect Development and Meaning*. Hillsdale, NJ: Analytic Press.

Bucci, W. (1993). The development of emotional meaning in free association: a multiple code theory. In: A. Wilson & J. E. Gedo (Eds.), *Hierarchical Concepts in Psychoanalysis*. New York: Guilford Press.

Buck, R. (1994). The neuropsychology of communication: spontaneous and symbolic aspects. *Journal of Pragmatics, 22*: 265–278.

Carmichael, S. T., & Price, J. L. (1995). Limbic connections of the orbital and medial prefrontal cortex in macaque monkeys. *Journal of Comparative Neurology, 363*: 615–641.

Cavada, C., & Schultz, W. (2000). The mysterious orbitofrontal cortex. Foreword. *Cerebral Cortex, 10*: 205.

Cavada, C., Company, T., Tejedor, J., Cruz-Rizzolo, R. J., & Reinoso-Suarez, F. (2000). The anatomical connections of the macaque monkey orbitofrontal cortex. A review. *Cerebral Cortex, 10*: 220–242.

Chiron, C., Jambaque, I., Nabbout, R., Lounes, R., Syrota, A., & Dulac, O. (1997). The right brain hemisphere is dominant in human infants. *Brain, 120*: 1057–1065.

Cooper, A. M. (1987). Changes in psychoanalytic ideas: transference interpretation. *Journal of the American Psychoanalytic Association, 35*: 77–98.

Craik, F. I. M., Moroz, T. M., Moscovitch, M., Stuss, D. T., Winocur, G., Tulving, E., & Kapur, S. (1999). In search of self: a positron emission tomography study. *Psychological Science, 10*, 26–34.

Critchley, H. D., Elliott, R., Mathias, C. J., & Dolan, R. J. (2000a). Neural activity relating to generation and representation of galvanic skin conductance responses: a functional magnetic resonance imaging study. *Journal of Neuroscience, 20*: 3033–3040.

Critchley, H., Daly, E., Philips, M., Brammer, M., Bullmore, E., Williams, S., Van Amelsvoort, T., Robertson, D., David, A., & Murphy, D. (2000b). Explicit and implicit neural mechanisms for processing of social information from facial expressions: a functional magnetic resonance imaging study. *Human Brain Mapping, 9*: 93–105.

Damasio, A. R. (1994). *Descartes' Error*. New York: Grosset/Putnam.

Davidson, R. J., Putnam, K. M., & Larson, C. L. (2000). Dysfunction in the neural circuitry of emotion regulation—a possible prelude to violence. *Science, 289*: 591–594.

Derryberry, D., & Tucker, D. M. (1994). Motivating the focus of attention. In: P. M. Niedentahl & S. Kiyayama (Eds.), *The Heart's Eye: Emotional Influences in Perception and Attention*. San Diego: Academic Press.

Dobbing, J., & Sands, J. (1973). Quantitative growth and development of human brain. *Archives of Diseases in Childhood, 48*: 757–767.

Dolan, R. J. (1999). On the neurology of morals. *Nature Neuroscience, 2*: 927–929.

Dosamantes, I. (1992). The intersubjective relationship between therapist and patient: a key to understanding denied and denigrated aspects of the patient's self. *The Arts & Psychotherapy, 19*: 359–365.

Dozier, M., Cue, K. L., & Barnett, L. (1994). Clinicians as caregivers: role of attachment organization in treatment. *Journal of Consulting and Clinical Psychology, 62*: 793–800.

Edelman, G. (1989). *The Remembered Present: A Biological Theory of Consciousness*. New York: Basic Books.

Eisenberg, L. (1995). The social construction of the human brain. *American Journal of Psychiatry, 152*: 1563–1575.

Emde, R. N. (1988). Development terminable and interminable. I. Innate and motivational factors from infancy. *International Journal of Psycho-Analysis, 69*: 23–42.

Emde, R. N. (1990). Mobilizing fundamental modes of development: Empathic availability and therapeutic action. *Journal of the American Psychoanalytic Association, 38*: 881–913.

Falk, D., Hildebolt, C., Cheverud, J., Vannier, M., Helmkamp, R. C., & Konigsberg, L. (1990). Cortical asymmetries in frontal lobes of Rhesus monkeys (*Macaca mulatta*). *Brain Research, 512*: 40–45.

Feldman, R., Greenbaum, C. W., & Yirmiya, N. (1999). Mother–infant affect synchrony as an antecedent of the emergence of self-control. *Developmental Psychology, 35*: 223–231.

Field, T., & Fogel, A. (1982). *Emotion and Early Interaction*. Hillsdale, NJ: Erlbaum.

Fink, G. R., Markowitsch, H. J., Reinkemeier, M., Bruckbauer, T., Kessler, J., & Heiss, W-D. (1996). Cerebral representation of one's own past: neural networks involved in autobiographical memory. *Journal of Neuroscience, 16*: 4275–4282.

Fonagy, P., & Target, M. (1997). Attachment and reflective function: their role in self-organization. *Development and Psychopathology, 9*: 679–700.

Fosshage, J. L. (1994). Toward reconceptualising transference: theoretical and clinical considerations. *International Journal of Psycho-Analysis, 75*: 265–280.

Freud, S. (1895). *Project for a Scientific Psychology. S.E., 1*.

Freud, S. (1900). *The Interpretation of Dreams. S.E., 4 and 5*.

Freud, S. (1912). *Recommendations to Physicians Practicing Psycho-analysis. S.E., 12*.

Freud, S. (1913a). *On Beginning the Treatment. S.E., 12*.

Freud, S. (1913b). *The Claims of Psycho-analysis to Scientific Interest. S.E., 13*.

Freud, S. (1915a). *Repression. S.E., 14.*

Freud, S. (1915b). *Instincts and Their Vicissitudes. S.E., 14.*

Freud, S. (1915c). *The Unconscious. S.E., 14.*

Freud, S. (1920). *A General Introduction to Psycho-analysis. S.E., 16.*

Freud, S. (1923). *The Ego and the Id. S.E., 19.*

Fridlund, A. (1991). Evolution and facial action in reflex, social motive, and paralanguage. *Biological Psychology, 32:* 3–100.

Friedman, N., & Moskowitz, M. (1997). Introduction. In: M. Moskowitz, C. Monk, C. Kaye & S. Ellman (Eds.), *The Neurobiological and Developmental Basis for Psychotherapeutic Intervention.* Northvale, NJ: Jason Aronson.

Gabbard, G. O. (1995). Countertransference: the emerging common ground. *International Journal of Psycho-Analysis, 76:* 475–485.

Galin, D. (1974). Implications for psychiatry of left and right cerebral specialization: a neurophysiological context for unconscious processes. *Archives of General Psychiatry, 31:* 572–583.

Gans, J. S. (1994). Indirect communication as a therapeutic technique: a novel use of countertransference. *American Journal of Psychotherapy, 48:* 120–140.

Garavan, H., Ross, T. J., & Stein, E. A. (1999). Right hemisphere dominance of inhibitory control: an event-related functional MRI study. *Proceedings of the National Academy of Sciences of the United States of America, 96:* 8301–8306.

Gedo, J. (1979). *Beyond Interpretation.* New York: International Universities Press.

Goleman, D. (1995). *Emotional Intelligence.* New York: Bantam Books.

Groddeck, G. (1977). *The Meaning of Illness.* London: The Institute of Psychoanalysis/Hogarth Press.

Hariri, A. R., Bookheimer, S. Y., & Mazziotta, J. C. (2000). Modulating emotional responses: effects of a neocortical network on the limbic system. *NeuroReport, 11:* 43–48.

Henry, J. P. (1993). Psychological and physiological responses to stress: the right hemisphere and the hypothalamo–pituitary–adrenal axis, an inquiry into problems of human bonding. *Integrative Physiological and Behavioural Science, 28:* 369–387.

Hess, E. H. (1975). The role of pupil size in communication. *Scientific American, 233:* 110–119.

Hollinger, P. C. (1999). Noninterpretive interventions in psychoanalysis and psychotherapy. A developmental perspective. *Psychoanalytic Psychology, 16:* 233–253.

Holmes, J. (1993a). Attachment theory: a biological basis for psychotherapy? *British Journal of Psychiatry, 163*: 430–438.

Holmes, J. (1993b). *John Bowlby and Attachment Theory*. London: Routledge.

Hoppe, K. D. (1977). Split brains and psychoanalysis. *Psychoanalytic Quarterly, 46*: 220–244.

Horvath, A. O., & Greenberg, L. S. (1994). *The Working Alliance: Theory, Research, and Practice*. New York: Wiley.

Hugdahl, K. (1995). Classical conditioning and implicit learning: the right hemisphere hypothesis. In: R. J. Davidson & K. Hugdahl (Eds.), *Brain Asymmetry*. Cambridge, MA: MIT Press.

Jackson, J. H. (1931). *Selected Writings of J. H. Jackson, Volume I*. London: Hodder and Stoughton.

Jacobs, T. J. (1994). Nonverbal communications: some reflections on their role in the psychoanalytic process and psychoanalytic education. *Journal of the American Psychoanalytic Association, 42*: 741–762.

Joseph, R. (1996). *Neuropsychiatry, Neuropsychology, and Clinical Neuroscience* (2nd edn). Baltimore: Williams & Wilkins.

Kantrowitz, J. L. (1999). The role of the preconscious in psychoanalysis. *Journal of the American Psychoanalytic Association, 47*: 65–89.

Kaplan-Solms, K., & Solms, M., (1996). Psychoanalytic observations on a case of frontal-limbic disease. *Journal of Clinical Psychoanalysis, 5*: 405–438.

Kawashima, R., O'Sullivan, B. T., & Roland, P. E. (1995). Positron-emission tomography studies of cross-modality inhibition in selective attentional tasks: closing the "mind's eye". *Proceedings of the National Academy of Sciences of the United States of America, 92*: 5969–5972.

Keenan, J. P., McCutcheon, B., Freund, S., Gallup, G. C. Jr., Sanders, G., & Pascual-Leone, A. (1999). Left hand advantage in a self-face recognition task. *Neuropsychologia, 37*: 1421–1425.

Keenan, J. P., Wheeler, M. A., Gallup, G. G. Jr., & Pascual-Leone, A. (2000). Self-recognition and the right prefrontal cortex. *Trends in Cognitive Sciences, 4*: 338–344.

Kohut, H. (1971). *The Analysis of the Self*. New York: International Universities Press.

Krause, R., & Lutolf, P. (1988). Facial indicators of transference processes within psychoanalytic treatment. In: H. Dahl & H. Kachele (Eds.), *Psychoanalytic Process Research Strategies*. New York: Springer-Verlag.

Lane, R. D., Chua, P. M-L., & Dolan, R. J. (1999). Common effects of emotional valence, arousal and attention on neural activation during visual processing of pictures. *Neuropsychologia, 37*: 989–997.

Lester, B. M., Hoffman, J., & Brazelton, T. B. (1985). The rhythmic structure of mother–infant interaction in term and preterm infants. *Child Development, 56*: 15–27.

Levin, F. (1991). *Mapping the Mind.* Mahweh, NJ: Analytic Press.

Lewis, J. M. (2000). Repairing the bond in important relationships: a dynamic for personality maturation. *American Journal of Psychiatry, 157*, 1375–1378.

Lieberman, M. D. (2000). Intuition: a social neuroscience approach. *Psychological Bulletin, 126*: 109–137.

Loewald, H. (1986). Transference–countertransference. *Journal of the American Psychoanalytic Association, 34*: 275–287.

Lyons-Ruth, K. (2000). "I sense that you sense that I sense ...": Sander's recognition process and the specificity of relational moves in the psychotherapeutic setting. *Infant Mental Health Journal, 21*: 85–98.

Main, M., Kaplan, N., & Cassidy, J. (1985). Security in infancy, childhood and adulthood: A move to the level of representation. *Monographs of the Society for Research in Child Development, 50*: 66–104.

Marcus, D. M. (1997). On knowing what one knows. *Psychoanalytic Quarterly, 66*: 219–241.

Matsui, M., Gur, R. C., Turetsky, B. I., Yan, M. X.-H., & Gur, R. E. (2000). The relation between tendency for psychopathology and reduced frontal brain volume in healthy people. *Neuropsychiatry, Neuropsychology, & Behavioural Neurology, 13*: 155–162.

McLaughlin, J. T. (1978). Primary and secondary processes in the context of cerebral hemispheric specialization. *Psychoanalytic Quarterly, 47*: 237–266.

McLaughlin, J. T. (1996). Power, authority, and influence in the analytic dyad. *Psychoanalytic Quarterly, 63*: 201–235.

Mesulam, M.-M. (1998). From sensation to cognition. *Brain, 121*: 1013–1052.

Miller, L. (1991). *Freud's Brain: Neuropsychodynamic Foundations of Psychoanalysis.* New York: Guilford Press.

Mlot, C. (1998). Probing the biology of emotion. *Science, 280*: 1005–1007.

Morris, J. S., Ohman, A., & Dolan, R. J. (1998). Conscious and unconscious emotional learning in the human amygdala. *Nature, 393*: 467–470.

Munder-Ross, J. (1999). Once more on the couch: consciousness and preconscious defences in psychoanalysis. *Journal of the American Psychoanalytic Association*, 47: 91–111.

Ornstein, R. (1997). *The Right Mind: Making Sense of the Hemispheres*. New York: Harcourt Brace.

Papousek, H., & Papousek, M. (1995). Intuitive parenting. In: M. H. Bornstein (Ed.), *Handbook of Parenting, Volume II. Ecology and Biology of Parenting*. Hillsdale, NJ: Erlbaum.

Petrovich, S. B., & Gewirtz, J. L. (1985). The attachment learning process and its relation to cultural and biological evolution: proximate and ultimate considerations. In: M. Reite & T. Field (Eds.), *The Psychobiology of Attachment and Separation*. Orlando, FL: Academic Press.

Phelps, J. L., Belsky, J., & Crnic, K. (1998). Earned security, daily stress, and parenting: a comparison of five alternative models. *Development and Psychopathology*, 10: 21–38.

Pizzagalli, D., Regard, M., & Lehmann, D. (1999). Rapid emotional face processing in the human right and left brain hemispheres: an ERP study. *NeuroReport*, 10: 2691–2698.

Polan, H. J., & Hofer, M. A. (1999). Psychobiological origins of infant attachment and separation responses. In: J. Cassidy & P. R. Shaver (Eds.), *Handbook of Attachment: Theory, Research, and Clinical Applications*. New York: Guilford Press.

Povinelli, D., & Preuss, T. M. (1995). Theory of mind: evolutionary history of a cognitive specialisation. *Trends in Neuroscience*, 18: 418–424.

Price, J. L., Carmichael, S. T., & Drevets, W. C. (1996). Networks related to the orbital and medial prefrontal cortex; a substrate for emotional behaviour? *Progress in Brain Research*, 107: 523–536.

Reite, M., & Capitanio, J. P. (1985). On the nature of social separation and attachment. In: M. Reite & T. Field (Eds.), *The Psychobiology of Attachment and Separation*. Orlando, FL: Academic Press.

Rolls, E. T. (1996). The orbitofrontal cortex. *Philosophical Transactions of the Royal Society of London B*, 351: 1433–1444.

Rolls, E. T., Hornak, J., Wade, D., & McGrath, J. (1994). Emotion-related learning in patients with social and emotional changes associated with frontal lobe damage. *Journal of Neurology, Neurosurgery, and Psychiatry*, 57: 1518–1524.

Ryan, R. M., Kuhl, J., & Deci, E. L. (1997). Nature and autonomy: an organizational view of social and neurobiological aspects of self-regulation in behaviour and development. *Development and Psychopathology*, 9: 701–728.

Sable, P. (2001). *Attachment and Adult Psychotherapy*. New York: Jason Aronson.

Sander, L. W. (1992). Letter to the Editor. *International Journal of Psycho-Analysis*, 73: 582–584.

Schore, A. N. (1994). *Affect Regulation and the Origin of the Self: The Neurobiology of Emotional Development*. Mahwah, NJ: Erlbaum.

Schore, A. N. (1996). The experience-dependent maturation of a regulatory system in the orbital prefrontal cortex and the origin of developmental psychopathology. *Development and Psychopathology*, 8: 59–87.

Schore, A. N. (1997a). A century after Freud's Project: is a rapprochement between psychoanalysis and neurobiology at hand? *Journal of the American Psychoanalytic Association*, 45: 841–867.

Schore, A. N. (1997b). Early organization of the nonlinear right brain and development of a predisposition to psychiatric disorders. *Development and Psychopathology*, 9: 595–631.

Schore, A. N. (1997c). Interdisciplinary developmental research as a source of clinical models. In: M. Moskowitz, C. Monk, C. Kaye & S. Ellman (Eds.), *The Neurobiological and Developmental Basis for Psychotherapeutic Intervention*. Northvale, NJ: Aronson.

Schore, A. N. (1998a). The experience-dependent maturation of an evaluative system in the cortex. In: K. Pribram (Ed.), *Brain and Values: Is a Biological Science of Values Possible*. Mahweh, NJ: Erlbaum.

Schore, A. N. (1998b). Early shame experiences and infant brain development. In: P. Gilbert & B. Andrews (Eds.), *Shame: Interpersonal Behaviour, Psychopathology, and Culture*. New York: Oxford University Press.

Schore, A. N. (1998c). Affect regulation: a fundamental process of psychobiological development, brain organization, and psychotherapy. Unpublished address, Baby Brains: Psychobiological Development of the Infant and its Implications for Therapy Practice Conference. Tavistock Clinic, London, July 1998.

Schore, A. N. (1998d). The right brain as a neurobiological substrate of Freud's dynamic unconscious. Unpublished keynote address, Conference, "Freud at the Millennium", Georgetown University. Washington, DC, October, 1998.

Schore, A. N. (1999a). Commentary on emotions: neuro-psychoanalytic views. *Neuro-Psychoanalysis*, 1: 49–55.

Schore, A. N. (1999b). Psychoanalysis and the development of the right brain. Unpublished address, The First North American International

Psychoanalytic Association Regional Research Conference, "Neuroscience, Development & Psychoanalysis". Mount Sinai Hospital, New York, December, 1999.

Schore, A. N. (2000a). Foreword to the reissue of *Attachment and Loss, Volume 1: Attachment* by John Bowlby. New York: Basic Books.

Schore, A. N. (2000b). Attachment and the regulation of the right brain. *Attachment & Human Development, 2*: 23–47.

Schore, A. N. (2000c). The self-organization of the right brain and the neurobiology of emotional development. In: M. D. Lewis & I. Granic (Eds.), *Emotion, Development, and Self-organization*. New York: Cambridge University Press.

Schore, A. N. (2000d). Projective identification—an interface of developmental psychoanalysis, neuropsychoanalysis, and clinical psychoanalysis. Scientific Meeting, Tavistock Society of Psychotherapists, Tavistock Clinic, London, March 2000.

Schore, A. N. (2000e). Attachment, the right brain, and empathic processes within the therapeutic alliance. *Psychologist Psychoanalyst, 20*(4): 8–11.

Schore, A. N. (2001a). The right brain as the neurobiological substratum of Freud's dynamic unconscious. In: D. Scharff (Ed.), *Freud at the Millennium: The Evolution and Application of Psychoanalysis* (pp. 61–88). New York: Other Press.

Schore, A. N. (2001b). The effects of a secure attachment relationship on right brain development, affect regulation, and infant mental health. *Infant Mental Health Journal, 22*: 7–66.

Schore, A. N. (2001c). The effects of relational trauma on right brain development, affect regulation, and infant mental health. *Infant Mental Health Journal, 22*: 201–269.

Schore, A. N. (2002a). Clinical implications of a psychoneurobiological model of projective identification. In: S. Alhanati (Ed.), *Primitive Mental States, Volume III: Pre- and Peri-natal Influences on Personality Development* (pp. 1–65). London: Karnac.

Schore, A. N. (2002b). Disregulation of the right brain: a fundamental mechanism of traumatic attachment and the psychopathogenesis of post-traumatic stress disorder. *Australian and New Zealand Journal of Psychiatry, 36*, 9–30.

Schore, A. N. (2002c). Advances in neuropsychoanalysis, attachment theory, and trauma research: implications for self psychology. *Psychoanalytic Inquiry, 22*: 433–484.

Schore, A. N. (2003a). *Affect Regulation and Disorders of the Self*. New York: W. W. Norton.

Schore, A. N. (2003b). *Affect Regulation and the Repair of the Self*. New York: W. W. Norton.

Schwaber, E. A. (1995). A particular perspective on impasses in the clinical situation: Further reflections on psychoanalytic listening. *International Journal of Psycho-Analysis, 76*: 711–722.

Schwaber, E. A. (1998). The non-verbal dimension in psychoanalysis: "state" and its clinical vicissitudes. *International Journal of Psycho-Analysis, 79*: 667–679.

Semrud-Clikeman, M., & Hynd, G. W. (1990). Right hemisphere dysfunction in nonverbal learning disabilities: social, academic, and adaptive functioning in adults and children. *Psychological Bulletin, 107*: 196–209.

Siegel, D. J. (1999). *The Developing Mind: Toward a Neurobiology of Interpersonal Experience*. New York: Guilford Press.

Smith, H. F. (1990). Cues: The perceptual edge of the transference. *International Journal of Psycho-Analysis, 71*: 219–227.

Snow, D. (2000). The emotional basis of linguistic and nonlinguistic intonation: implications for hemispheric specialization. *Developmental Neuropsychology, 17*: 1–28.

Solms, M. (1996). Towards an anatomy of the unconscious. *Journal of Clinical Psychoanalysis, 5*: 331–367.

Sroufe, L. A. (1996). *Emotional Development: The Organization of Emotional Life in the Early Years*. New York: Cambridge University Press.

Stern, D. N. (2000). Foreword to the reissue of *Attachment and Loss, Volume III: Loss: Sadness and Depression* by John Bowlby. New York: Basic Books.

Stern, D. N., Sander, L., Nahum, J. P., Harrison, A. M., Lyons-Ruth, K., Morgan, A. C., Bruschweiler-Stern, N., & Tronick, E. Z. (1998a). Non-interpretive mechanisms in psychoanalytic therapy. *International Journal of Psycho-Analysis, 79*: 903–921.

Stern, D. N., Bruschweiler-Stern, N., Harrison, A. M., Lyons-Ruth, K., Morgan, A. C., Nahum, J. P., Sander, L., & Tronick, E. Z. (1998b). The process of therapeutic change involving implicit knowledge: some implications of developmental observations for adult psychotherapy. *Infant Mental Health Journal, 19*: 300–308.

Stolorow, R. D., & Atwood, G. E. (1992). *Contexts of Being: The Intersubjective Foundations of Psychological Life*. Hillsdale, NJ: Analytic Press.

Stone, M. H. (1977). Dreams, free association, and the nondominant hemisphere: an integration of psychoanalytical, neurophysiological, and historical data. *Journal of the American Academy of Psychoanalysis*, 5: 255–284.

Stone, V. E., Baron-Cohen, S., & Knight, R. T. (1998). Frontal lobe contributions to theory of mind. *Journal of Cognitive Neuroscience*, 10: 640–656.

Stuss, D. T., Gow, C. A., & Hetherington, C. R. (1992). "No longer Gage": frontal lobe dysfunction and emotional changes. *Journal of Consulting and Clinical Psychology*, 60: 349–359.

Sullivan, R. M., & Gratton, A. (1999). Lateralized effects of medial prefrontal cortex lesions on neuroendocrine and autonomic stress responses in rats. *Journal of Neuroscience*, 19: 2834–2840.

Taylor, G. J., Bagby, R. M., & Parker, J. D. A. (1997). *Disorders of Affect Regulation: Alexithymia in Medical and Psychiatric Illness*. Cambridge, UK: Cambridge University Press.

Teasdale, J. D., Howard, R. J., Cox, S. G., Ha, Y., Brammer, M. J., Williams, S. C. R., & Checkley, S. A. (1999). Functional MRI Study of the cognitive generation of affect. *American Journal of Psychiatry*, 156: 209–215.

Thatcher, R. W. (1994). Cyclical cortical reorganization: origins of human cognitive development. In: G. Dawson & K. W. Fischer (Eds.), *Human Behaviour and the Developing Brain*. New York: Guilford Press.

Trevarthen, C. (1990). Growth and education of the hemispheres. In: C. Trevarthen (Ed.), *Brain Circuits and Functions of the Mind*. Cambridge, England: Cambridge University Press.

Tronick, E. Z., & Weinberg, M. K. (1997). Depressed mothers and infants: failure to form dyadic states of consciousness. In: L. Murray & P. J. Cooper (Eds.), *Postpartum Depression and Child Development*. New York: Guilford Press.

Tronick, E. Z., Bruschweiler-Stern, Harrison, A. M., Lyons-Ruth, K. Morgan, A. C., Nahum, J. P., Sander, L., & Stern, D. N. (1998). Dyadically expanded states of consciousness and the process of therapeutic change. *Infant Mental Health Journal*, 19: 290–299.

Wallerstein, R. S. (1990). Psychoanalysis: the common ground. *International Journal of Psycho-Analysis*, 71: 3–19.

Watt, D. F. (1990). Higher cortical functions and the ego: explorations of the boundary between behavioural neurology, neuropsychology, and psychoanalysis. *Psychoanalytic Psychology*, 7: 487–527.

Westen, D. (1997). Towards a clinically and empirically sound theory of motivation. *International Journal of Psycho-Analysis*, 78: 521–548.

Wexler, B. E., Warrenburg, S., Schwartz, G. E., & Janer, L. D. (1992). EEG and EMG responses to emotion-evoking stimuli processed without conscious awareness. *Neuropsychologia, 30*: 1065–1079.

Winnicott, D. W. (1971). *Therapeutic Consultations in Child Psychiatry*. New York: Basic Books.

Winson, J. (1990). The meaning of dreams. *Scientific American, November*: 86–96.

Wittling, W. (1997). The right hemisphere and the human stress response. *Acta Physiologica Scandinavica, Supplement, 640*: 55–59.

Wittling, W., & Roschmann, R. (1993). Emotion-related hemisphere asymmetry: Subjective emotional responses to laterally presented films. *Cortex, 29*: 431–448.

Yamada, H., Sadato, N., Konishi, Y., Muramoto, S., Kimura, K., Tanaka, M., Yonekura, Y., Ishii, Y., & Itoh, H. (2000). A milestone for normal development of the infantile brain detected by functional MRI. *Neurology, 55*: 218–223.

Zald, D. H., & Kim, S. W. (1996). Anatomy and function of the orbital frontal cortex, II: function and relevance to obsessive–compulsive disorder. *Journal of Neuropsychiatry, 8*: 249–261.

Zeddies, T. J. (2000). Within, outside, and in between: the relational unconscious. *Psychoanalytic Psychology, 17*: 467–487.

CHAPTER TWO

Neuroscience and intrinsic psychodynamics: current knowledge and potential for therapy

Colwyn Trevarthen

I am going to talk mainly about new ideas we have gained in the last few years concerning how communication with infants works, with particular reference to its timing—the rhythms and narrative melodies that we have been able to reveal by musical analysis.

Two or three years ago I had the great fortune to be offered collaboration by Stephen Malloch, a young Australian musical acoustics expert who was completing a PhD in Music and Physics at the University of Edinburgh. Stephen had developed computer analysis of the sounds of musical instruments to explore how a composer had crafted them to create a beautiful piece of music. He is a violin teacher and has studied conducting. As a practising musician he has a sensitive ear for the collaboration required between players, and he has discovered a latent talent for science too. Now he is working in a first rate acoustics laboratory in Sydney, where they are focusing attention on the infant's perception of emotion in speech, and on the nature of musical expression, combining this with the analysis of gestures of dance. The idea of looking at both the choreography and the music of communication together is turning out to be very helpful in unravelling how infant and mother can coordinate their expressions so precisely, and with such ease. We find that a young baby may be expressing itself more with delicate hand movements than with its voice. So we have to pay attention to the baby's dance while the mother is speaking or singing.

I hope I will have time to talk in more detail about the development of the brain. But first, before I start to describe communication with babies, I want to situate the period that interests me, where it is in the life story of the human brain. I will talk mainly about behaviour in the first year after birth, but, in trying to understand the psychology of an infant, we must not forget that during gestation, before birth, there have been nine busy months of brain development. A newborn brain may be only one third the size of an adult brain, but it has all the structures, all the nerve cell nuclei and fibre tracts, that a neuroanatomist could want to find. True, some of its tissues, cells, and connections are immature, and the proportions of the cerebral hemispheres are different. The temporal lobes are proportionally very short, the frontal lobes are flat rather than bulging as they are in a toddler or adult, the parietal cortex is smaller, too. But those are changes in cortical volume and complexity that are stuck on top of a very elaborate subcortical brain that is well formed before birth. We will have to trace developments in this core brain back down to the embryo stage, the first two months of life, because many of the structures that are going to be important in early communication are functioning in the brain long before the cerebral cortex is even beginning to be formed. And, in fact, as we come to understand the spontaneous activity and self-regulation of mind functions, the question arises—what on earth does the cortex do? No doubt it is very good at storing information: keeping the fruits of experience, polishing skills. I am inclined to imagine it as a kind of library, and I am becoming much more interested in the librarian and the readers than in the books, but we will come back to that.

How the infant's self finds human companionship

Let me give you some examples of the first communications of infants.

Thirty years ago, when I began to look at mother and infant

interaction, I was at Harvard, in a marvellous small research group set up by the visionary psychologist and educator Jerome Bruner, working with an ethologist Martin Richards and the famous Boston paediatrician Berry Brazelton. Neither Martin nor I had any particular axe to grind concerning infant intelligence and its development. Martin had been analysing maternal behaviour of hamsters, I had been using ciné film to research eye–hand coordination in monkeys and their visual learning. Berry Brazelton was a sensitive doctor very interested in the physiological state control of newborn babies and assessment of their well-being, and this involved him in observations of how the baby accepted holding by the mother. I had become intensely interested in finding out what babies were like because my wife had just had her first baby and I was very impressed with what our little son could do, how well coordinated he was and how purposeful. Martin and I agreed that we would start as explorers, and just describe events in the first six months. We looked at visual attention and tracking and reaching for objects, but very quickly we discovered that young infants were seeking conversation.

Our infants were showing amazing skill at engaging their mothers in chat. Proto-conversation is a very elaborate and bafflingly sophisticated behaviour between a mother and a baby that occurs in the first three months. At first the newborn reacts sensitively to the mother's voice, but is vague about looking at her. After about six weeks it is very easy to engage the baby in eye contact, and the mother and the baby can chat with well focused attention to one another's moves.

The term "proto-conversation" was first used by Mary Catherine Bateson, a most interesting person. She is the daughter of Margaret Mead and Gregory Bateson, two world-famous anthropologists, and she herself was an anthropologist and a linguist. At the same time as we were beginning our project, in 1968, she was working only three miles away at the MIT Electronics Laboratory, looking at films of a baby and a mother chatting together. She noticed this delicate interaction and she said it was the foundation not only for the development of speech and language, but also for "ritual healing practices". So she was making a connection both with linguistics and anthropology. Now I am sure you will be interested in her ideas about the ritual healing; what she refers to is the rhythmic participation and the obvious emotional involvement of the mother and baby, which, in certain respects, resembles the ceremonies and rituals of comforting and healing in all cultures. As it happens, we did not know anything about Bateson's work for several years, not until 1979, when her friend and the source of the films she studied, Margaret Bullowa, edited an excellent book, *Before Speech*, reviewing new work on the beginnings of human communication, and she invited us to contribute.

We have since published many papers and I will give some references to recent ones that review what we have found. Today I want to focus on the new musical analysis which has enormously enriched our understanding. But before I do that I want to make a couple of points with one picture.

Here is a picture of a lively newborn baby, 20 minutes old, in a hospital in Hyderabad in India. The baby's attention is focused on a red ball that is being held by a nurse. The baby is tracking the ball with its nose, its mouth, its hands, and its feet, and as the ball is moving around, the baby's body is pulled with it as a completely coherent whole intentional agent. There is no question of this being a loosely connected bundle of reflexes. The baby is alive with a one-time, one-space mind. The object is perceived by the baby to be located outside his or her body and it is tracked. Now, we can infer another thing that is very important. This is also a communication game, because the baby's interest in the ball is not just because it is a

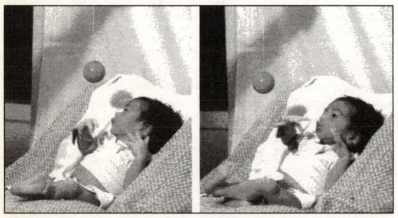

Figure 1. Newborn infant, less than one hour after birth, in a hospital in Hyderabad, tracking, with all of his body and senses, a red ball moved by a person. Photo by Kevin Bundell.

red sphere, which is an abstract mathematical concept anyway. The ball is a highly visible thing that is being *moved*, and it's going to be moved *contingently*. That is, if the baby moves, the ball will immediately move too. It will move because the nurse, who is holding the ball by a thread, is fixing her attention on the baby, watching every response. They are playing a game together. This little person, 20 minutes old, is involved in a game with an adult, demonstrating coherence of its intentionality and its awareness of a world outside the body, and especially a world that offers live company. Now there is a whole stack of precious theories disproved.

What one baby girl and her mother have to say to each other

At Harvard we developed the one-camera filming technique that uses a mirror to photograph the mother's face while the camera is aimed to see the whole baby clearly. Here we see a six-week-old baby Scottish girl, Laura, smiling at her mother, cooing and raising her right arm. The mother follows every expression and replies with sympathetic speech. We have found that when two-month-olds are

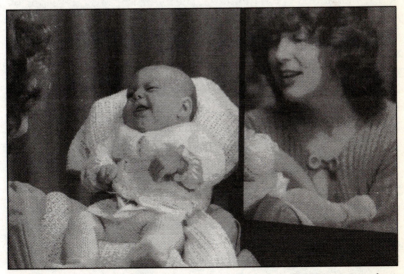

Figure 2. Laura, 6 weeks old, in the laboratory at the University of Edinburgh, 1979. She smiles to her mother who is chatting with her. Photo by Colwyn Trevarthen.

expressive, making their turn in the proto-conversational exchange, they usually move their right arm more than their left. It is very interesting that this asymmetry of gesture, already present at birth, can be related to the cerebral asymmetry of language. In toddlers the cortex of the left cerebral hemisphere, which senses and moves the right side of the body, begins a great development related to the learning of speech and language. In the two-month-old, the preference for right hand expressions of communication is certainly more subcortical. It has got something to do with a one-sided motivation for expression to another person that is arising from deep in the brain, a motivation that occurs a year and a half or two years before any speech. So it is an asymmetric communicative impulse, which is anticipating development of asymmetry in the cerebral cortex.

This sound recording was made of Laura and her mother in 1979 with good quality equipment, but it wasn't studied in detail until three years ago when Stephen Malloch applied his musician's awareness to it. You can see the spectrographic curves he produced of the mother's speech sounds, the frequency of which is plotted vertically while the horizontal dimension is time in seconds. The horizontal dotted line is middle C. The mother begins this section by saying, with typical measured "motherese" speech, "Come on. Again. Come on then. That's clever". And then the baby does two coos, "Ooo Ooo", and the mother responds, "Oh yes, is that right?" Now what Stephen noticed is that if you mark a vertical red line exactly where there is a stress in the mother's speech, a very regular bar structure is revealed. The "C" in "come on", the "G" in "again", the "C" in "come on" and the "TH" in "that's clever" are very evenly spaced at 1.53 and 1.50 seconds. He was able to extend the measure, that bar structure, right through 30 seconds, and he showed that the mother and baby were collaborating to use that time base.

Everything about this typical proto-conversation is interesting musically. First of all, there are these graceful fluctuations in pitch creating a melody. Melodic fluctuations of voicing are characteristic of motherese. "Come on" has a rising–descending curve, and then "Come on then" has the same shape, but slower. Over the whole exchange the pitch of both the mother's speech and the baby's coos descend to middle C, after exploring the octave above, which, again, is typical.

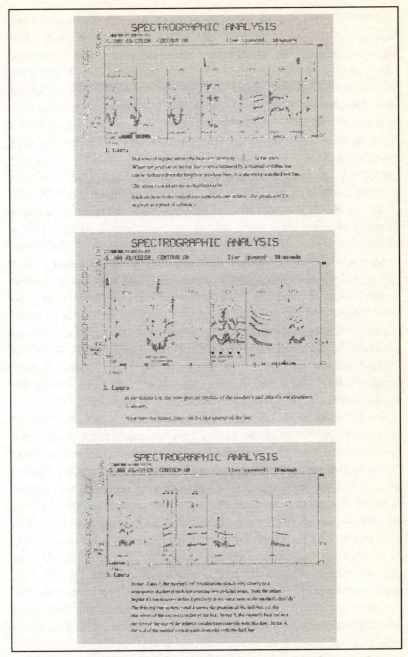

Figure 3. Sonographic diagrams of the protoconversation between Laura and her mother made by Stephen Malloch, twenty years later.

The next 10 seconds get more exciting. They collaborate on the beat in one bar where the mother, using a rapid speech, says, "Tell me/some more/then" with three even undulations. The baby coos, "Ah", at exactly the right moment at the end of the bar to complete a four-note group on a good "allegro"; and then the mother says a long "Aaaah" with falling pitch, which is a kind of celebration of how clever the baby is. In the last 10 seconds they first get into a jazzy sort of duet, which is really rather nice. The mother says enticingly, "Come on" then, "Ch ch ch ch ... ch ch", These are unpitched very short hissing sounds in two fast bursts. She is holding the baby's foot and bouncing it in synchrony with "Ch ch ch ch ... ch ch". It sounds just like timpani—maracas or a snare drum. The baby, at exactly the same moments, is cooing like a clarinet, so that is not a bad dance band. A percussion, like drum, castanets, a bodhrán combined with pitched instrument like a flute, a violin or clarinet makes a perfect dance band and something like this is often heard in folk music, as well as in jazz or ballroom dancing. So what Laura and her mother are doing together is a little piece of improvised music. Throughout 30 seconds they both respect the bar structure set up by the mother, sometimes leaving a bar silent. At the end the mother makes two long gentle sounds, "Egoo ... Egoo" separated by a blank bar. In each of these utterances she brings the fundamental frequency of her voice down to middle C (C4).

In addition to this spectrographic analysis, which permits an accurate examination of the timing, Stephen made pitch plots of the voices, converting the melodious sounds into tones as we hear them, with their correct musical pitch measured in psychophysical units called "sones", accurate to a quarter tone and with the octaves of equal size. Mother and baby explore the space in the two octaves either side of middle C, most of their sounds moving above C4. The mother's voice plays with large graceful gestures, sometimes rising or falling over most of an octave. Though smaller, the infant's coos are melodious too, usually rising a few notes above C4. As their conversation progresses the range of pitch explored by the mother increases and the level rises until about two thirds through, after which she slowly descends until, with her last two utterances, she is gently falling from E or D and coming to rest on C.

A compressed summary graph, showing the whole conversation as a single display of pitch curves shows clearly how the variations of the mother's pitch form a wave, swelling and then fading away over a period of 27 seconds. And Laura's little contributions seem to fit appropriately in the whole piece. After analysing several proto-conversations we have found that something close to a 30-second cycle is a consistent feature. Similar cycles of excitement are common in music, and 20 to 30 seconds is the usual length of a verse or stanza in a baby song, the stanza being made up of four phrases each lasting about five seconds. Interestingly, this same period, around 30 seconds, is an autonomic cycle known by physiologists for 150 years, a spontaneous change in the brain's regulation of internal processes in the body. If you measure heart rate and respiration in people when they are asleep there is a cycle of speeding up and slowing down over around 30 seconds. It is one manifestation of "time in the mind".

"Dynamic narrative envelopes" and "intermodal fluency"
(Stern, 2000)

So, what we have found by looking at this longer time scale of tens of seconds is a modulation of excitement and we are calling it a *narrative cycle*. The whole transcript of vocalizations between Laura and her mother goes like this:

- Introduction
  Come on. Again. (*pause*)
  Come on then. [baby gesture]
  That's clever! [Two Coos by Laura]
- Development
  Oh yes! Is that right? (*pause*)
  Well, tell me some more then. (*pause*)
- Climax
  Tell me some more then [Coo] Aaaah! (*pause*)
  Come on. *Duet*: Ch-ch-ch-ch+[Coo].
- Resolution
  Ch-ch+[Long coo].
  Egoo (*pause*) Egoo.

The classical three phases of a narrative—Introduction, Develop-ment, Climax, and Resolution—are indicated. The analysis shows

UNIVERSITY OF HERTFORDSHIRE LRC

that the bars are combined in pairs, which make linguistic and musical phrases, and the mother's rate of speech (syllable rate) speeds up when she says, "Well, tell me some more then. Tell me some more then" and Laura coos; that is, she coos at the climax.

Music, with its changing mood or colour, does seem to be telling us something. We often get the impression that a piece of music without words is telling a story. You can hear the narrative of melody in the cyclic episodes of both folk songs and classical music.

Another feature that merits much further attention is the form of the vocal gestures at different points in the "story of feeling". If we take the case of a slightly older baby, a 12-week-old, a pitch plot shows both mother and baby making elegant rising and falling curves of sound, joining perfectly together. At the end the mother extends the fall from D above C5 down to B below C4, well over an octave. These curves have exactly the same dynamic characteristics as spontaneous hand gestures we all make in conversation. You can easily imitate these vocal curves with your hand. We think that the two kinds of expression, with voice and with hands, are generated by the same dynamic process in the brain. I believe that the "language" of gesture, its moods and energy, should be seen as related to the kind of expression that has powerful communicative significance in therapeutic work.

Unhappiness and loss of expressive musicality: an experiment with the melody and timing of responses in human company

We have begun to look at this question by comparing the expressions of happy mothers with those of mothers who are not happy. Professor Lynne Murray of the Winnicott Unit in Reading University gave us some recordings of a depressed mother and a happy mother for analysis by Malloch's methods. The recordings of both cases had been made when the babies were eight weeks and six months old. In the earlier recording the depressed mother was very unhappy and unable to communicate well with her infant, but four months later her depression had cleared. When she was depressed the pitch range of her talk with her baby dropped to the octave below middle C, and, moreover, she says things like "It's not really interesting at all is it? Oh dear!" When she is feeling well and she can chat happily with her six-month-old, she is saying playfully, "Ooh! can you catch my finger?" and now her speech is much higher pitched, well above C4. The voice is an instrument of emotion and its tones and level of energy clearly portray the feelings of communication. All of the parameters of the expression of the mother change in depression; the tempo, the pitch, and the whole communicative structure change, and it has immediate effects on the baby.

You may know that Lynn Murray pioneered experiments with "still face" and "double video". The double video technique involves making proto-conversation mediated through video, with the mother and baby communicating with each other while in different rooms. In the most advanced version of the apparatus, they see each other as full-sized and in colour on the video screen in front of them, and they are each photographed through this image. The recordings obtained show that mother and baby are communicating with very vivid expressions and the baby makes many different expressions in response to the mother. And at the end of a minute and a half this baby is extremely happy.

Now, what the double video system allows you to do is to immediately replay one minute of the mother's happy communication to the baby. This recording is physically identical with the real-life happy communication of the mother. It is a perfect copy, but it has no responsivity, it can't react, and that depresses the baby. The replayed tape makes the baby confused and disturbed. The baby is not seeking a particular kind of expression from the mother, it is not behaving like a stimulus–response system reacting to stimuli, but is making predictions about a good conversation, and if the conversation is not live the baby does not like it. This test proves that an eight-week-old is motivated to join in proto-conversation by very well-coordinated behaviours involving the whole of the baby's body interacting sensitively and immediately with the mother's behaviour. The baby expects the mother to do the same.

A newborn, two months premature, already knows how to communicate

A few moments of one of Saskia Van Rees's beautiful films shows a baby, Naseera, who was two months premature, with her father.

The baby is inside the father's shirt against his chest and they are vocalizing together. You hear on the video Naseera "coo", and the father imitates the sound, and then after a pause there is a very nice even rhythmic exchange: "baby–father", short pause, "baby–father–baby–father–baby–father". This is followed by a pause for five seconds, and then the father calls, followed about three seconds later by the baby and immediately the father. After this, while the father's attention has wandered, Naseera calls three times at precisely four-second intervals. That is, she makes three vocalizations on her own; her first call is weak and when he doesn't reply the next one is louder. Now these four-second silences equal phrase length intervals—the duration of a standard linguistic phrase, or a phrase in music, or a line in simple poetry. It looks like the baby has the same sense of time passing, the same rhythmic sense of hierarchy as an adult, of time at least up to four seconds. The fast exchange between Naseera and her father is extremely regular and the beat is *andante*. It is about 0.7 of a second. It is also clear that the father is imitating the baby's coos and he is being taught how to communicate by his premature daughter.

How baby songs tell tales of mutual adventure

What we have learned from these examples is that a baby begins life with a tremendous sensitivity to the rhythmic processes going on inside the mind of a mother or father. These measures of time and the expression of impulses to move are incorporated into traditional baby songs. We have been collecting and analysing baby songs in many languages. Examples from Greek, Italian, and Scottish English are typically made up of stanzas, each with four simple phrases, with the exception that the Greek ones often have a characteristic double phrase line, so that the stanzas are twice as long as English or Italian ones. There is a very characteristic pattern of rhyming vowels at the end of the second and fourth lines. For example, in the Scottish song, "well" and "bell" rhyme.

Clappa, clappa handies,
Mummy's at the **well**,
Daddy is away to London,
To buy Leanne a **bell**.

Babies become very expert by four to six months at predicting the timing and rhyming features of the baby songs. For example, when a mother was singing, "Round and round the garden like a teddy bear", to her five-month-old Leanne, eagerly watched by her daughter, the baby vocalized exactly on top of the long vowel of "bear", and matched the sound of the vowel.

The spectrograph and pitch-plot for "Rock-a-bye baby on a tree top" show the emphasized vowels "top" and "rock" and "fall" and "all" and the overall narrative form of the pitch-plot rising to a climax at "fall" and tumbling down to "all". It is uncannily like a silhouette of Edinburgh City with St Giles Cathedral in the middle and the castle rock at the right end. The point is that the melody has a dramatic shape, which is evident in the pitch changes. The singer's voice rises and falls over the first line, "Rock-a-bye baby on a tree top", and then rises a little higher for, "When the wind blows the cradle will rock", and then the wind gets up, and the baby falls. Use of rhyming and of pitch to create a narrative melody is what baby songs are all about.

Knowing songs and games is a source of pride, because it is shared

Participation in baby songs is a matter of intense pride. A picture of six-month-old Emma sitting on her father's knee in her home at Edinburgh shows how absolutely thrilled she is to show a stranger "clap-a-handies", She has spent the last weeks visiting my laboratory with her mother and they often played this game with great enjoyment. In contrast, with a stranger in the laboratory, she tries to show "clap-a-handies" but it does not work. He hasn't a clue what she is trying bravely to show him, he seems so "stupid", and she is extremely worried and unhappy. We have a lot of detailed evidence from this kind of behaviour with six-month-old babies and we are convinced we are right to call their feelings "pride" and "shame". We are now convinced that these are primary, intuitive emotions. We do not think that they are constructed out of simpler reactions by social experience. We think that pride and shame are absolutely foundational in developing human relations.

You may have seen a photograph in the press, of 18-month-old

Figure 4. Emma, six months old, with her father at home in Edinburgh, proudly showing her mother "Clappa clappa handies", following her mother's request, "Clap handies!". Photo by Penelope and John Hubley, 1979.

Tiger Woods, practising golf strokes on the carpet, looking up to the camera with an enormous grin of pride. This is what his father says about him, "Even as a toddler Tiger was able to identify the swing flaws of adult players. 'Look Daddy that man has a reverse pivot'".

I am sure that the main motivation for cultural learning is something that is quite separate from what is described by attachment theory as the motivation for seeking proximity to a mother. That is why we have developed what we call the Theory of Companionship. We are not suggesting that attachment theory is wrong, it is just that it is certainly not an adequate account of the emotions that normally operate in the development of a baby's self-confident possession of knowledge. The emotions of attachment have to do with regulating the needs of one's own body by communication with another person, soliciting their help and support. Cognitive learning, and so forth, relates one's own body to objects. Cultural learning and everything to do with education and shared artificial knowledge and skills involves communication in relation to a joint experience of the world of objects, and that is where you get these very powerful emotions of pride—pride in knowledge and pride in skill, and shame in not being thought master of such things, to be thought unskilled or ignorant. These emotions of companionship are very important in the development of happy self-confidence, at any age. I believe they should be attended to in therapy, especially for children.

Our evidence shows that the baby has a well-integrated self at birth, an effective self. But it has to work out what to do with this motivated life it has, and one of the first things to learn is the meaning of the world: to learn the meaning of other older persons' actions, first in proto-conversation and imitation games, then in action games and baby songs, and later in the use of objects that have been conceived as tools. The meaning of the world can only be acquired in communication and collaboration with other people. There is no such thing as meaning found entirely by a single self. Meaning has to be communicated, or communicable. As we observe the development of infants over the first year, we see a steady progression towards integration in a joint understanding of objects and actions. By the end of the first year the baby has achieved this understanding and can share in the world's meaning. With luck and affectionate support, this becomes a source of great pleasure and pride.

Infants have complex "moral" emotions that regulate their learning in relationships

Several of us in Developmental Psychology now believe that the idea of the "construction" of complex moral emotions, the progressive assembly of proper social sensibilities from simple categories of feeling that name an individual person's experience, such as "joy", "sadness", "anger" and so on, is mistaken. We think that this is a false analysis produced by a categorical description, particularly of static facial expressions in photographs. Most of the research on emotions analyses perception of photographs or drawings of facial expression. We have learned to describe our feelings as these named types.

But, in everyday experience, emotions are transient and volatile, sensitive to company. Feelings vary in their rate of change and they vary in intensity, and this is particularly clear in the voice. Voices express emotion by tempo, loudness, and by what is called "timbre" or "voice quality". Spectral analysis of voice sounds gives you information about the degree of tension or relaxation or harmoniousness of the motor system in the throat where those sounds are being made. Information about the intensity, dynamics and so on of emotion is also carried in any body movement. You can tell the emotions of a person just by watching them move. You can tell a lot about a person's state of mind from listening to them walking. There has, I believe, been inadequate study of emotional dynamics, the ways emotions move.

The psychiatrist and developmental psychologist Daniel Stern makes a distinction between "categorical emotions" and what he calls "dynamic emotions", and he makes a further important distinction. He talks about "relational emotions". These are emotions that are *between* people rather than in an individual.

Observation of the behavioural reactions of people in dynamic social situations indicates that their contact is regulated by rapidly changing complex blends of emotion, and there are configurations of expression that combine evidence about the way a person is directing their attention to others and the way they show pleasure and sadness or anger. These combinations may also suggest that they are experiencing states of pride and shame depending upon the relationship between their experience and other people's estimation of their knowledge of that experience. Both pride and shame are signalled by a combination of where the person is looking in relation to other persons, and their expression of joy or discomfort. We have many recordings of babies who are trying to perform some trick that they have learned, such as a clap-a-handies baby song, in which they appear to show emotional evaluations of this kind of self-and-other awareness. In some cases, they look to a familiar person with a beaming smile of pride. In other cases, the baby looks away from a stranger, or stares, with an expression of sadness or distress, the whole pattern of expression indicating embarrassment or shame.

Two people in Britain who have done interesting work on the more subtle states of interpersonal emotion are Dr Vasudevi Reddy in Portsmouth, who has been studying coyness and flirtatious expressions of three-month-old babies and Dr Ricardo Draghi-Lorenz who has been looking at jealousy and other complex emotions in babies under one year.

This, I know, is in some disagreement with developmental psychologists and child psychiatrists, including Alan Schore for example, with regard to the emotion of "guilt", and I know we must be prepared for that challenge. There is an active debate now, but I think what we see in the descriptive account of infants' more complex expressions is that the simple social construction theory is wrong. We do not agree with Michael Lewis and the other constructivists who perceive emotions as products of rational response to the other person's sanctions and rewards. A powerful idea in European and many other complex cultures is that emotions are educated into people in society, by the kind of constraints that are put on naïve feelings by authority of various kinds. That as you learn to behave in society, you learn to be polite, you learn to be well mannered, you learn to control cognitively the wild emotions that you are born with which are animal like. I believe this looking at young persons' behaviour from the outside, and from the perspective of adult convenience, is misleading, and I think that it ought to be questioned.

My impression is that babies have much more morality and much more dignity than they are credited with, especially when they are confident. Obviously an unhappy baby will fall apart, and will behave in an emotionally grotesque way and suffer extremes of emotion, which resist being controlled. But that can be true of adults, too. You only need to suffer an unexplained insult from a colleague to know what I mean by shame.

I think it is interesting to consider that pride and shame have evolved in a species that is very much involved in cultural learning, because these are the emotions that regulate success in achieving knowledge and skills. That is why I showed Tiger Woods, a toddler, absolutely thrilled with himself because he knows something and because everybody else knows he knows it. That appraisal by others is extremely important. We have many photos of babies "showing off". After six months they may be, when confident at home, incredible show-offs. If they are happy they are showing off most of the time. And it goes on to University. Perhaps the ultimate show-offs are academic professors.

Videos show there is an intrinsic motive pulse or IMP moving all the body

I will describe three videos which illustrate the talents of young infants for communication.

Video I: A Greek mother sings a patriotic song
(Film by Katia Mazakopaki of The University of Crete)

Jasonas, an eight-week-old in Crete is enthralled as his mother sings a Greek political song, a rousing tale that the baby loves. If you watch the baby's right hand, you see it waving with the melody, and Jasonas is moving his mouth in sympathy with the mother's singing. He tracks the phrases of the song, keeping with its changing energy.

Video II: A Turkish father and his 10-week-old daughter Hande
(Film by Saskia van Rees)

The voice-over explains what we see:

> *"About two months later Hande is 10 weeks old. She can stay awake and play with her father for quite a long time now. Daddy says Hande's name over and over again. He talks to her and looks for eye contact. Daddy starts the game off in his way. At 10 weeks old, babies are capable of joining in actively, looking, greeting [her eyebrows flash up], laughing and making noises. Daddy watches and listens to Hande's initiatives attentively. He takes her very seriously and attunes himself to her baby level".*

He is talking in time with the music playing in the room.

> *"Daddy takes his turn in the game, and then lets the baby have her turn".*

We see her hand move to the music.

> *"Not only is Hande making little noises, but she is also practising speech movements with her mouth and tongue. This is preparation for the actual babbling and talking, which will come at a much later stage. When the music stops you can hear the exchange of noises clearly".*

It is clear from the way the father imitates Hande's sounds that babies teach adults to talk.

Video III: Naseera, who was two months premature, with her father
(Film by Saskia van Rees)

> *"Naseera's father takes over the contact. The next time he is also going to kangaroo with Naseera".*

This is the baby we have already described, who was two months premature.

We are starting to do research in intensive care units inspired by this film. There can be a lot of communication in this intimate situation. Premature babies do not show their communicative talents unless they are in an intimate contact with a sympathetic human being.

> *"Naseera's father is completely absorbed in her. He talks to her and imitates her facial expressions. Naseera enjoys this and a real interchange of feelings is set in motion".*

He takes the baby very seriously. He really thinks she is a person, that he is talking to a person. He sighs when the baby moves her hand.

> *"Naseera's father imitates not only noises and facial expressions but also her hand movements".*

Premature babies have very elaborate hand movements which have never been studied.

> *"Naseera's mother is still too weak after the operation to come and visit but father comes every day and kangaroos with Naseera. Here she is three weeks older and already has plump cheeks. She is under her father's t-shirt and can already converse well with him".*

Here follows the vocal exchange between Naseera and her father that we have analysed already.

Video IV: A blind baby conducts her mother's song
(Film by Gunilla Preisler of Stockholm University)

A film of a blind Swedish baby girl of five months shows how clever a baby can be at feeling the impulse of a song in her body. She was born totally blind, yet she is able to "conduct" the rhythms and melodies of her mother's song with her left hand.

This poses difficult questions for brain science. It is difficult to imagine where in the brain the unified "intermodal" sense of time and space in movement can be. What central motive process can so immediately and precisely couple the impulse and melody of the mother's song as heard, to the dance of the baby's hands she has never seen, up and down parallel to the axis of her body, and to the side or to the centre.

The Professor of Music at Edinburgh, Nigel Osborne, saw the behaviour of the baby, and he said she is conducting very well with fairly conventional conducting principles, up for high pitch and down at the end of the phrase. Nobody knew that the baby was doing this until the video was seen; the mother had not noticed. Professor Osborne said that not only was the baby conducting well, but with some slight anticipation like a real conductor, and he's right. We have made precise analysis of the gestures the baby made. It is clear that the hand moves a fraction of a second ahead of the melody of the song at several points. The baby knows the song and is performing it with the mother, like a dancer to an orchestra, and this means that the baby has inside its brain somewhere a system that can create a musical narrative for the body and express it and remember.

How the shape of the brain relates to its purposes

The classical way of diagramming the human cerebral cortex indicates that it processes sensory information coming in at the back and sends it forward to the "pre-central" motor system. In fact, all information that is perceived is *expected* by the brain. There is a process seeking in the other direction, first setting up a motor plan, then looking for the sensory information needed. The motor or "executive" action is leading to the cognitive experience, so the initiative is actually frontal in origin. It has got to do with initiating voluntary activity and then the experience comes about. We should remember that the proper meaning of the word "experience", from its Latin derivation, is "from *trying* to do something". It refers to the *intention* to know something, like the French word "experience" which means "an experiment". In the English language this original meaning has been degraded to mean just the information that comes in, and that is a comment on English rational empiricism, which is a philosophy going back about 400 years. It is strong now, bolstered by a belief in science as a search for facts.

Other parts of the brain beneath the cortex that have to do with emotions, integrate with the inner state of the body, and with the impulses to move the body. Inevitably, they also have a lot to do with communication. The self-regulation of the body and its motivation involves the core of the brainstem and the hypothalamus and many other parts that are outside the cortex that is so conspicuous on the outside of the cerebral hemispheres. The nuclei in the brainstem that motivate voluntary action and attention project up into the cerebral cortex and they modulate the activity of the cortical cells, changing their communication with each other and with the rest of the brain. The cerebral cortex is not the site of consciousness, nor really the only place where memories are formed, although it may be the biggest store of memory.

The structures that make the signals of communication, that is the muscle systems that are moved in vocalization and speech, or in facial expression, are all innovated from nerves that come from the cranial nerves and those nerves originally evolved for self-regulation of visceral functions, like circulation of the blood, breathing, eating, and digestion. In social animals, the same cranial efferent nerves have more and more components that serve in communication and the regulation of relationships.

Moreover, the anatomy of that brainstem system, the cranial nerve system, is well-formed in a seven-week-old embryo human, long before the cerebral cortex has even begun to form neurons. The brainstem neurons project up into the forebrain and their products regulate the migration and development of cortical cells and the connections that form between them. The evidence from brain embryology is that the emotional system or the brainstem motivating mechanism has the role of morpho–genetic regulator of cortical growth. The same neuronal systems continue to be regulators of cortical function throughout life. They motivate attention, selective awareness, and the shaping of motor actions. This finding fits with evidence coming from neuropsychology, or the effects of brain damage, that emotional systems have a formative influence on cognitions, rather than the other way about.

Cognitive Psychology, insofar as it attempts to explain psychological processes as the processing of sensory information, may now really be at a dead end. There are two fundamental principles of mental life that it does not deal with: it leaves intentions and emotions unexplained, and it forgets time. In the recently published *MIT Encyclopaedia of Cognitive Science*, there are 473 entries, and only one mentions time. This one is an entry on "time in the mind" by Ernst Pöppel, a German psychophysicist. We know from the way infants behave that temporal coordination of brain activity and temporal coordination of body movements, generated from inside the brain, are absolutely fundamental to everything that we do psychologically, whether the perceptual guidance of our own intentional movements, or internal self-regulation of the body, or communication with another body and mind. All depend upon regulation of time, on neural generation of time.

My colleague Professor David Lee, an expert on human perceptuo-motor performance, argues from mathematical analysis of movements and of the neural activity that accompanies or precedes a movement that the brain does not "process" information it "makes" it, or "generates" it. He makes one further argument. We know that the brain loses a lot of cells, that cell death is going on all the time. If the brain were an information-processing network, processing information in a linear way, stage by stage, loss of neurons would be a serious threat to its function. Every now and again something would be lost at a crucial point, and a function would be lost. But the mathematical evidence for motor images generated in the brain as time–space functions in populations of neurons suggests how the brain can be very resistant to damaging effects of cell death. It keeps its sense of the essential information for action even when parts are shut down. This may explain why the brains of even senile old people and very severely mentally handicapped children can have temporal coherence and can respond to music therapy, for example, even when their pick-up of perceptual information is confused and their attention is weak.

I believe we are still searching for a good theory of how the brain works. I think the evidence is that we are about to find out how little we know, and I am not as optimistic as some people are about the benefits of findings in the "decade of the brain" just finished. I have been reviewing books on cognitive neuroscience recently, especially the newer "developmental cognitive neuroscience", and the picture does not quite hang together, at least that is my impression. I am sure we will still have to pay sensitive and sympathetic attention to ordinary everyday expressions of pleasure and displeasure, curiosity and doubt, comradeship and mistrust between people meeting in their community life, especially those people who are too young to speak, but who seem to understand us, and what our impulses and feelings are, so well.

The vexed question of when does a baby get a coherent sense of self

I believe that the 20-minute-old newborn baby I showed you, has a self. It is quite clear that he or she was a coherent agent, moving in a single time. And moving in space, knowing where left and right were.

Any baby involved in sharing a song is, as my musician colleague puts it, "sharing the sense of purpose in passing time". So you are doing something with your sense of existing self when you listen to a narrative. You are being a protagonist. You are involved. That blind Swedish baby was using its body to express a sense of the song or the dance shared with the mother. There is some narrative component that is common to both the body movement and the sound of the voice. It is something a-modal, not related to any particular sensory modality or part of the body. The dance of the hands is not dependent on sight at all. All babies move their hands to music in subtle ways. They make graceful conducting movements with their hands. We think that the blind baby may, at this age, move her hands even more than is usual, to enrich the experience of the song.

We do not know where the self is in the brain, but we do know that all the places and levels of the brain are fantastically interconnected and integrated. And, of course, the brain and the body are inseparably linked at every stage. That wholeness of the functioning being is what I understand by the self.

The inner sense of time and the rhythm of moving, the secret of communication and of language

Even insects have quite well formed selves and a tremendous sense of rhythm, which some species share. There is beautiful work on synchronous chorusing among cicadas in tropical forests, for example. I heard multi-species orchestral concerts of cicadas in the trees of Tokyo this summer. Absolutely marvellous. They are very much mutually aware, and sharing the beat.

Biologists know about the importance of rhythm in both intrinsic coordination of the individual and in communication, formation of social groups, and so on. I think that psychology is still battling with the rational, reductive, linguistic, verbal explanation of mental life of the socially approved, and socially educated, person. The mistakes that were made about babies' minds, to which I have referred, all come from extrapolation from the problems of adult thought, what psychologists call "declarative" awareness.

In Edinburgh our Computational Linguists seem to have lost all interest in communication. The study of grammar cannot progress that way. It just gets more and more complex. But, as soon as you start to relate grammar to these spontaneous rhythmic characteristics of mother and baby communicating, then grammatical syntax gains a new meaning, a new vitality and usefulness. What we are studying is dynamic emotional syntax; phrases and narrative sequences of feeling that are certainly foundational for the structure of verbal sentences, and their messages.

Stephen Pinker, the linguist, has explicitly scoffed at music. He says that it is nothing but biological cheesecake of no adaptive use whatsoever. I believe he has lost track of the principal and first function of language, which is to bring people into intimate mental engagement—a task for which music has magical power.

References

Bråten, S. (1992). The virtual other in infant's minds and social feelings. In: A. H. Wold (Ed.), *The Dialogical Alternative* (pp. 77–97) (*Festschrift for Ragnar Rommetveit*). Oslo/Oxford: Scandinavian University Press/Oxford University Press.

Draghi-Lorenz, R., Reddy, V., & Costall, A. (2001). Re-thinking the development of "non-basic" emotions: a critical review of existing theories. *Developmental Review, 23*: 263–304.

Malloch, S. (1999). Mother and infants and communicative musicality. In: *Rhythms, Musical Narrative, and the Origins of Human Communication.*

Musicae Scientiae, Special Issue, 1999–2000 (pp. 13–28). Liège: European Society for the Cognitive Sciences of Music.

Panksepp, J. (1998). The periconscious substrates of consciousness: affective states and the evolutionary origins of the self. *Journal of Consciousness Studies, 5*: 566–582.

Papousek, M., & Papousek, H. (1981). Musical elements in the infant's vocalization: their significance for communication, cognition, and creativity. In: L. P. Lipsitt & C. K. Rovee-Collier (Eds.), *Advances in Infancy Research, 1*: 163–224.

Papousek, H., & Papousek, M. (1987). Intuitive parenting: a dialectic counterpart to the infant's integrative competence. In: J. D. Osofsky (Ed.), *Handbook of Infant Development* (2nd edn) (pp. 669–720). New York: Wiley.

Reddy, V. (2000). Coyness in early infancy. *Developmental Science, 3*(2): 186–192.

Schore, A. N. (1994). *Affect Regulation and the Origin of the Self: The Neurobiology of Emotional Development*. Hillsdale, NJ: Erlbaum.

Stern, D. N. (1999). Vitality contours: The temporal contour of feelings as a basic unit for constructing the infant's social experience. In: P. Rochat (Ed.), *Early Social Cognition: Understanding Others in the First Months of Life* (pp. 67–80). Mahwah. NJ: Erlbaum.

Stern, D. N. (2000). *The Interpersonal World of the Infant: A View from Psychoanalysis and Development Psychology* (Second Edition with new Introduction). New York: Basic Books.

Trehub, S. E. (1990). The perception of musical patterns by human infants: the provision of similar patterns by their parents. In: M. A. Berkley & W. C. Stebbins (Eds.), *Comparative Perception; Volume 1, Mechanisms* (pp. 429–459). New York: Wiley.

Trevarthen, C. (1998). The concept and foundations of infant inter-subjectivity. In: S. Bråten (Ed.), *Intersubjective Communication and Emotion in Early Ontogeny* (pp. 15–46). Cambridge: Cambridge University Press.

Trevarthen, C. (1999). Musicality and the intrinsic motive pulse: evidence from human psychobiology and infant communication. In: *Rhythms, Musical Narrative, and the Origins of Human Communication. Musicae Scientiae, Special Issue, 1999–2000* (pp. 157–213). Liège: European Society for the Cognitive Sciences of Music.

Trevarthen, C. (2001a). Intrinsic motives for companionship in under-standing: their origin, development and significance for infant mental health. *Infant Mental Health Journal, 22*(1–2): 95–131

Trevarthen, C. (2001b). The neurobiology of early communication: intersubjective regulations in human brain development. In: A. F. Kalverboer & A. Gramsbergen (Eds.), *Handbook on Brain and Behaviour in Human Development* (pp. 841–882). Dordrecht, The Netherlands: Kluwer.

Trevarthen, C. (2002). Origins of musical identity: evidence from infancy for musical social awareness. In: R. MacDonald, D. J. Hargreaves & D. Miell, (Eds.), *Musical Identities* (pp. 21–38). Oxford: Oxford University Press.

Trevarthen, C., & Aitken, K. J. (1994). Brain development, infant communication, and empathy disorders: intrinsic factors in child mental health. *Development and Psychopathology, 6*: 597–633.

Trevarthen, C., & Aitken, K. J. (2000). Intersubjective foundations in human psychological development. *Annual Research Review. The Journal of Child Psychology and Psychiatry and Allied Disciplines, 42*(1): 3–48.

Trevarthen, C., Aitken, K. J., Papoudi, D., & Robarts, J. Z. (1998). *Children with Autism: Diagnosis and Interventions to Meet their Needs* (2nd edn). London: Jessica Kingsley.

Tronick, E. Z. (1989). Emotions and emotional communication in infants. *American Psychologist, 44*(2): 112–126.

van Rees, S., & de Leeuw, R. (1987). *Born Too Early: The Kangaroo Method with Premature Babies*. Video by Stichting Lichaamstaal, Scheyvenhofweg 12, 6093 PR, Heythuysen, The Netherlands.

CHAPTER THREE

Psychotherapy in an age of neuroscience: bridges to affective neuroscience

Douglas F. Watt

A basic question for this entire conference that we have to address first is, "Why integrate affective neuroscience with psychotherapeutic approaches?" That is not a trivial question, and until recently, was not assumed in many venues to be either a meaningful or a necessary one. Although one could spend many pages on this question alone, I would heuristically focus on a few basic points summarized as follows:

- The most important reason is that affective neuroscience is in a real renaissance. Emotion has been a neglected topic in neuroscience for decades, not even thought of as worth serious study by many neuroscientists. Fortunately, that prejudice has melted and we have seen an explosion of interest in this topic, with a leading edge of major summary statements by Damasio (1999), Panksepp (1998), LeDoux (1996) and others.
- The second reason is also far from trivial: the legacy of Freud's Project. Freud was certainly right in trying to ground any viable metapsychology in neuroscience, but there was just not enough fundamental neuroscience, in his days, to make it feasible to do so. However, we do know enough now to attempt to more

fully ground (meta)psychology in neuroscience. The previous "ideological" separation of psychotherapeutic approaches and neurobiology is softening and, although many prejudices are still quite active, it is at least intellectually respectable to try to bridge these domains.

● Another important development is that psychiatry has moved away from its "phrenology of neuromodulators" phase of the 1970–1980s towards more neurodynamical notions about monoamines as key modulators for global state control, concomitant with clinical neuroscience moving towards a deepening integration with other aspects of neuroscience. The field of psychiatry is finally moving past decades of stagnation associated with the notion that disorders were either "functional or organic". Certainly, "top down" psychological and "bottom up" biological approaches must meet somewhere in the middle, suggesting that a most crucial development will be a deeper empirical understanding, based on more research, into the neurobiology of psychotherapy.

● The progress that has been made in understanding primary or prototype emotion from a neuroscientific viewpoint also makes preliminary bridging more feasible, and there is an increasing focus also on understanding cognition–emotion interactions, as these are obviously the crucible in which psychotherapy and, for that matter, much of human consciousness, takes place.

● Finally, interdisciplinary work is now widely seen as a *sine qua non* in neuroscience, particularly in work on the "hard problems" of consciousness and emotion, and this makes bridging between disciplines more traditionally segregated, in general, a more attractive and viable enterprise.

Bridging neuroscience and psychodynamic points of view involves melding traditions that are very old on the one hand, with a science that is still in its infancy on the other. Therefore, a basic question would be to ask, "What happens when a mature (if evolving) discipline (psychotherapy) meets an exploding science?" The mature discipline contributes best by being clear what its established principles are. A major ongoing issue in psychotherapy, of course, is trying to establish anything in the way of fundamental principles that would garner any version of universal consensus.

One might readily, if a bit cynically, respond with the observation that psychotherapists have never been able to agree on anything. An open question about the domain of psychotherapy would be whether there can be any real consensus on any framework, or technical, or process issue, given the contentious nature of the field over many decades.

With that in mind, I'm offering the following as possible established principles with the obvious caveat that these principles apply more to long- and mid-term therapy approaches and less to very short-term and technically focused approaches. It is also worth emphasizing that these are just my sense of a set of basic integrative principles, and other clinicians, investigators, and theorists might have a very different set of suppositions.

— The psychotherapeutic alliance is foundational, and indeed in a real sense the alliance is virtually the whole ball game in any kind of exploratory or supportive psychotherapy, in that basic failure of a trusting alliance means that any putative advantage to one technical approach over another is in some sense "voided" or cancelled out.

— Every therapeutic relationship becomes a container and activator for affects experienced in all other relationships, with the degree of this determined by the degree of attachment and intimacy experienced in the therapy relationship. This, of course, is the principle underlined in the concepts of transference and the repetition compulsion (Freud, 1920; Watt, 1986, 1990).

— There is no avoiding the pain, either old or new, but timing and the titration of pain within psychotherapy is everything. It is not dissimilar to the timing and titration of frustration that a well-attuned parent does with a child. Certainly, confronting severe early hurt or emotional trauma requires a correspondingly strong psychotherapeutic alliance.

— The depth of change in psychotherapy is presumably quite multifactorial, but this is still poorly understood and researched. The major factors influencing depth of change would be very hard to comprehensively outline or operationalize but my list of such therapeutic factors would include the following.

1. The motivation for change.
2. The degree of empathic connection to therapist.

3. The amount of time spent on core affective–behavioural issues and especially the degree of primary affect that is mobilized *in the sessions*; that is, not just talked about but experienced in the therapy sessions.

4. An assessment of the patient's native talents for affective work is important but is also very poorly defined (for instance, introspective, in touch with, and able to talk about affects versus blunted, alexithymic, etc).

5. The use of various technical approaches putatively optimizing change and repair, that rest on foundations of a trusting relationship (e.g. EMDR, hypnosis, free association, etc.).

— Successful empathic work on trauma improves the patient's baseline affective state and mastery, and deepens and strengthens the therapeutic alliance.

— It is much harder to repair severe early damage to the self stemming from early abuse or neglect, probably because this damages the very processes of attachment (Bowlby, 1969) and possibilities for a trusting engagement with others which still seem to be basic keys to any successful psychotherapy. It is easier in therapy to repair problems of excessive guilt or "triangular competitive" problems (which used to be called "neurotic" problems) than if the basic attachment mechanisms are either atrophied or severely pathologically inhibited.

— However, failures at "early stages" of development are not all-or-nothing in nature, and early issues can be reactivated and recapitulated at later stages, in therapy. Every event is potentially in the service of repetition and eventual mastery. However, psychological difficulties exist on a smooth continuum of severity which means that there is no existing clear-cut typology of psychological difficulties (or "problems in living"). An additional implication is that their interdigitation with Axis I conditions is still quite unclear, although some notion of psychosocial stressors is typically assumed contributory to exacerbations of many Axis I conditions.

Certainly, there is in all probability an extremely complex epigenetic developmental landscape involving interactions between poorly researched neurobiological and less poorly researched psychological developmental factors in the creation of every Axis I disorder. In the psychological literature, there have been various proposals along the line of multi-axial personality factor matrices that presumably load on various "constitutional" factors (these may reflect various neurobiological predispositions, and the manner in which the genome may set "thresholds" for the activation of various systems in the brain). I do not have the time to go into the various factor analytic approaches to personality, but it is safe to say that research outlining genetic predispositions in the brain and their interactions with environmental factors is certainly in its infancy. Perhaps the prototype work here has been the beginning of systematic research into shyness and amygdaloid complex activation.

Given the truism that there is still a basic lack of fundamental bridgework between the two disciplines of neuroscience and psychotherapy, several basic points can be made here about the nature of the missing bridgework, and about the resulting obstacles to the bridging of the disciplines.

● In many ways, a most critical nexus for bridging psychotherapy and neuroscience is an understanding of the fundamental nature of primary or prototype emotions, or what I would call "prototype affective states". Arising from this is a second fundamental question: *the implications of prolonged activation of negative states for the creation of psychopathology and neuropsychiatric disorders*. I am referring here centrally to the prolonged activation of fear, rage, and separation distress. We do not know what "too long" and "too frequent" mean in a specific way in terms of potential long-term effects on the brain, but this is a most crucial matter. What does it do to a person's psychological and neurobiological system to have these proto-type negative emotional states activated for "too long", and/or "too frequently"? How much does this predispose to various Axis I and Axis II disorders? This fundamental nexus has been largely neglected in neuropsychiatry, excepting for the work on PTSD (post-traumatic stress disorder).

● Another problem in bridging the disciplines is that it is not only psychotherapy that is fragmented and ideologically divided, but neuroscience itself is badly fragmented. Work in various neuroscience disciplines related to both emotion and Axis I and

II disorders is still quite fragmented with grossly insufficient "cross talk" between various contributing disciplines. As a cardinal example, there is in general little appreciation within the human clinical neuropsychological tradition of the fundamental neuroscience work that has been done on animal models for emotion.

- Perhaps as a consequence of this fragmentation, cortical and cogno-centric conceptions of human emotion are dominant in most of the literature on emotion, rather than more ethologically grounded typologies for emotion. Here, too, there has been a serious neglect of animal models and a very species-centric conception of emotion. (I will not elaborate on this in detail here for reasons of space.)

- Another problem in bridging the disciplines comes from the insulation of psychotherapy training and theory from neuroscience, particularly affective neuroscience.

- Lastly, but definitely not least, another obstacle to bridging the gap between the two disciplines comes from the oversimplified or trivialized views of the neurobiological correlates of Axis I disorders. To describe depression, for example, as a "chemical imbalance" grossly oversimplifies what we understand about monoamines and state control.

Neuroscience has hardly been without its own distorting biases on the subject of emotion. I would outline the following long-standing biases in neuroscience that, at least historically, have hampered bridging between the various psychotherapy disciplines and neuroscience.

- There has been a long-standing neglect of emotion and consciousness from within a largely positivistic neuroscience, although as mentioned above this is now softening and changing substantially in the context of the major momentum achieved by neuroscience investigators such as Joseph LeDoux, Antonio Damasio, and Jaak Pansksepp.

- The strongly molecular and behaviourist bias in neuroscience hampers bridging to psychotherapy. Molecular genetics is obviously revolutionizing every biological domain, and it does give us the promise of a much more fine grained understanding of foundational mechanisms in any biological domain, but it cannot by itself answer the fundamental issue of how the brain integrates large-scale networks, how it is that the many structures involved in emotion are working not in isolation but as part of a concerted functional system. Thus, we are still left with the challenge of how to potentially bridge from an understanding of micro-system variables to deciphering the daunting problem of "macro-system" states of the functional integration large-scale or global neural networks. Everything that psychotherapists and others interested in emotions are focusing on requires large-scale brain activity and neural network integrations, given the focus on subjective affective states.

• Many misconceptions about what really might be fundamentally constitutive of emotion, still hampers bridging the disciplines. I would argue that emotion refuses to be reduced to any simple one or two elements, but remains stubbornly multifactorial, involving facial and other motor system changes and motor primings, a subjective feeling state or "valence", and physiological/autonomic changes, along with frequent (but not invariant) "top-down" cognitive drives or appraisals. Additionally, since it seems to require highly distributed systems including large portions of the reticular activating system, it exists in close interdigitation with behavioural organization, with executive functions, and with an equally close interdigitation with attentional functions. These are three slices of the consciousness pie, three fundamental psychological concepts that require, again, large-scale neural network integrations. These functional concepts cannot be meaningfully understood from a neuroscience point of view unless we assume underpinnings in large-scale integrated activity in the brain. Emotion has tended to also be modelled in terms of its tie in humans to higher cognitive functions, instead of its tie to mammalian prototypes or emotional "primitives", such as the prototype states of fear, rage, lust, separation distress, play, bonding and nurturing, and other basic social emotions that are part of the matrix of attachment.

• Many typologies for emotion are grossly deficient and ignore ethologically derived categories, failing to distinguish primary versus secondary emotions. Secondary emotions reflect modulated activation of prototype states, with cognitive aspects (particularly a "self-image") and "blends" or partial activations of the prototype states (for example, the crucially important and powerfully pathogenic affect of shame reflects activation of a sense of oneself as exposed and defective in the eyes of significant others, and depends on the underlying prototype state of separation distress.).

● There has been a general lack of interest in early developmental processes within neuroscience, and a general neglect of the whole process of attachment in terms of its neural substrates (we will see later on just how pivotal this question is for the venture of bridging neuroscience and psychotherapy).

Like many failures in communication, both parties share a fundamental responsibility, and there are many basic problems contributed from the psychological side of the border. At the top of the list would be the legacy of the isolation of psychoanalysis, its defensive management of borders with neighbouring disciplines, and its abandonment of empirical research (with a few notable, but lonely, exceptions). There has also been a long-standing reification of metapsychology in psychoanalysis that has badly atrophied potential empirical research and bridge building. Partly as a consequence of this, in the context of the re-medicalization of psychiatry, psychiatry discovered "monoamine tweaking", and has largely decided (for the most part) that it doesn't need psychoanalysis any more and maybe not even psychodynamics. One might ask, "does this gap need to change?" If the answer to that is, yes, and I would assume that most people at this conference would answer that question in the affirmative, then the next and more difficult question becomes, "HOW will this change"?

Depression and obsessive compulsive disorder (OCD) as paradigmatic disorders for bridging affective neuroscience and psychotherapy disciplines

The slide (*Figure 1*) is taken from the famous study in the 1980s that showed that both psychotherapy and selective serotonin reuptake

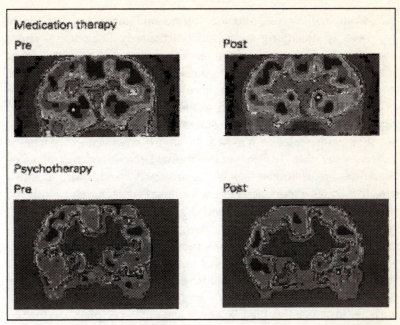

Figure 1. Changes in orbital frontal activity in OCD patients after medication or psychotherapy.

inhibitors (SSRIs) normalized excessive activity in the right caudate orbitofrontal thalamocorticolimbic–corticostriatal loop systems, in patients with OCD. Although the study itself garnered its fair share of attention in the neuropsychiatric press, no one has ever come up with an experimental paradigm for investigating how psychotherapy might achieve the same thing as a SSRI, in calming down a revved-up orbitofrontal contingency system where the person was always catastrophizing. This striking finding, comparing biological and psychological therapies, as largely equivalent in outcome, thus remains largely unexplained. But it is hopefully a prototype for much more work to come that will move us into an era of a better integrated mind–brain language.

Part of the basic problem, in terms of generating a comprehensive theory of depression, has been our somewhat "monocular" focus on monoamines in psychiatry (serotonin, dopamine, norepinephrine, acetylcholine, etc.), and the tendency to reify these important, but also quite general, global state control systems as the be-all-and-end-all regulatory systems in the brain. Nothing reinforces behaviour like success, and the "monoaminization" of psychiatry has been spectacularly successful (particularly financially). However, this emphasis on monoamines has encouraged neglect of other lines of neuroscience evidence, outside of clinical psychiatry, that neuropeptides are really much more specific control systems for the brain, particularly with respect to the induction and modulation of primary or prototype affective states. The prototype affective states would include states such as sadness (our human version of what is called "separation distress" in the animal behavioural neuroscience literature), fear, anger, sexual desire, play, and other positive affective states experienced in the context of attachments, with the positive affective states experienced in attachments being, of course, one of the deepest and most basic source of value for humans, indeed, probably for many if not most mammals.

The evidence from much behavioural neuroscience suggests that multiple neuropeptides, including several key neuropeptides referenced later in this chapter (see *Table 1* on prototype emotion), such as substance P (a big player not just in the peripheral induction and modulation of pain, but also in the central modulation of rage states, interestingly enough), corticotrophin releasing factor (CRF), along with oxytocin, and various endogenous opioids (which are probably among the most essential modulators for positive affective states) are critical regulators of affective states. The emerging research does not support anything like a "neuropeptide phrenology" in which affective states can be reduced to the activity of one or two simple brain chemicals, but instead, consistent with many other findings about complex functions, suggests that these primary or prototype affective states reflect concerted activations of perhaps a small collection of peptidergic control systems. All of this, of course, begs a crucially unanswered question about which we know strikingly little: the nature of the complex interplay between monoamines and neuropeptides, which is no doubt varied and very complicated. As just a small slice of this large problem, we know for example that there are extensive interactions between the opioids and dopamine systems, not surprising in that dopamine supports a generalized motivational arousal and seeking (from Jaak Panksepp's work) and such a system certainly must follow and somehow encode the contingencies of social reward very closely.

As a critical example, a basic problem in depression research has been generating an adequate model for the cascade of events that leads to a major or clinical depression, a model that would of necessity involve a number of oversimplifying assumptions, but such a model is essential to reduce the confusing buzz of interacting variables affecting an adult brain in a complex social milieu. There are many such models, but I would argue that the best model is provided by the reaction of small mammals (including small humans) to long periods of separation from primary caretakers. We know that in both humans, and in primates and other mammals, such an unfortunate separation generates an intense reaction of separation distress and grief, which, if not relieved by the reappearance of the nurturing caretaker, ushers in a massive behavioural, affective, and even homeostatic shutdown. In other words, I think the evidence suggests the best candidate model for depression centres on its potential role in quelling intolerable grief and separation panic (or other hugely painful stimuli which the organism is helpless to fend off). This initial reaction of separation distress, panic, and agitation—if it were allowed to go on indefinitely—would probably kill the small and relatively helpless creature, and depression in this sense is protective, and not an "illness". Depression thus has to be conceptualized as reflecting a fundamental adaptive mechanism conserved across millions of years of evolutionary time, with this adaptive mechanism presumably developing coincident with the creation of increasingly complex social relations and deepening dependence of many species in our evolutionary line on attachments to con-specifics. Clearly this depressive mechanism(s) can be *disinhibited*, particularly in individuals with certain genetic constitutions and unfortunate life histories, setting the stage for repetitive and chronic depressive states.

In the context of such prolonged separation reactions for the helpless infant mammal, there are presumably huge shifts in the peptidergic state of the brain, with presumably crashing opioid levels, similar changes in oxytocin and prolactin systems, dramatic elevations of CRF, and many other rapid and powerful changes that we have barely started to map. It is certainly possibly, but by no means empirically, established that such huge changes in the peptidergic modulatory state of the brain *then initiate compensatory shifts in monoaminergic systems*, including serotonin, norepinephrine, and dopamine, all of which have been implicated in depression. It is entirely possible that virtually all of our existing antidepressants therefore address this secondary and probably compensatory reaction by monoamine systems in the cascade of processes leading to a clinical depression. This is consistent with emerging models in medicine in which *illnesses reflect derailments driven by compensatory efforts of the body and brain to deal with frequently prolonged stresses that are outside of its envelope of adaptive capacities*. Also associated with this animal model for depression, would be much old clinical wisdom that depression for all its complexities and despite all its flavours, has fundamental connections to the loss of love (and to the internalization of these important experiences in our sense of self-esteem). All of these many considerations suggest, in turn, that the current treatment model ("monoamine tweaking"), which dominates managed care and primary care medicine, is simply not adequate a fair percentage of the time. It also raises a strong suspicion that the refractory nature of some depressions is not simply due to some undiscovered "biochemical fault line" (although that may also be a factor), but also to unacknowledged psychosocial and psycho-dynamic dimensions to many if not most depressions.

The above considerations strongly suggest that depression is not simply an "illness", and as we have already learned through trial and error, certainly cannot be modelled in terms of some kind of simple shortage of monoamines in the brain, but more of complex dysregulation of multiple monoaminergic systems. However, the conceptualization of depression (particularly echoed in the popular media unfortunately) has been of some kind of "chemical imbalance" (death is also caused by a "chemical imbalance" so this is trivial and not an explanation). Thus, it becomes concep-tualized as an illness, like cancer or heart disease, when the research really does not support such a simplistic model, and frankly this notion is most aggressively presented in the service of drug companies selling drugs. While managed care also has its own financial reasons for fostering such a model, most researchers, even within biological psychiatry, have been increasingly forced to embrace a more complex view of depression as reflecting interdependent derailments in *multiple* monoaminergic systems. But if we really want to get a better handle on this very common malady, surely one of the central ills that our mortal flesh is heir to, our future research and clinical efforts hopefully will include closer and more consistent consideration of some of these issues: (1) that animal models will be critical to untangling the biological cascades that lead to major depression; (2) that a simple model of one neurobiological alteration for one disorder is very unlikely; (3) that interactions between organism and environmental stressors will have to be better integrated into neurobiological models and research; and (4) that depression may be a final common pathway that can be arrived at through a "sufficient number" of critical variables that are poorly outlined at present, instead of one set of invariant "causes" or any single neurobiological derailment. Instead the literature supports the concept of a poorly outlined but presumptive biological cascade, with regulatory and adaptive failures at each step of any possible cascade sequence.

Basic evolutionary assumptions about emotion and cognition

Virtually all of our concepts in psychology and neuroscience that attempt to bridge the various mind–brain disciplines can be evaluated in terms of their fundamental conformity with basic evolutionary principles. These basic evolutionary principles at the level of neural systems can be represented in terms of fundamental relationships between homeostasis, emotion, and cognition with the following graphic:

HOMEOSTASIS ↔ EMOTION ↔ COGNITION

As the encephalization of the brain preceded outward from a primitive brainstem/reticular core early in our phylogenesis, evolution appears to have created a seamless integration of homeostasis, emotion, and cognition. An evolutionarily informed approach would assume that emotion is an evolutionary extension of homeostasis, and cognition an extension of emotion, and that the brain is adaptively organized to achieve the seamless integration of homeostasis, emotion, and cognition. Deep interpenetration of these three basic phenomena reflects evolutionary refinement of the brain's processing ability, as encephalization proceeded outward from a primitive brainstem/reticular core from quite early in our phylogenesis. The interpenetration of these functions within the brain's neural networks reflects the evolutionary refinement of the brain's processing ability, and a fundamental evolutionary conservatism, not that the brain has three architecturally different processing levels.

Homeostasis, as the preservation of multiple complex somatic functions within generally narrow parameters necessary for the sustaining of life, is a fundamental ventral brain function largely organized by the brainstem and hypothalamus, although there are also important modulations of this provided in more dorsal and later developing "limbic" systems. Emotion can be understood as an evolutionary extension of homeostasis, providing basic and behavioural and body tuning paradigms that help maintain homeostasis in the context of prototypic adaptive challenges (Panksepp, 1998), such as dealing with predators, securing food and territory, and the structuring of fundamental relationships with conspecifics. Emotion also includes fundamental aspects of a subjective state typically experienced along an intrinsic pain–pleasure axis. Cognition can be understood analogously as an evolutionary refinement of our ability to deal with prototypic adaptive challenges that are fundamentally affective, such as how to better secure a mate, protect and nurture young, defend territory, secure necessary supplies, select appropriate social behaviours, etc., etc. Obviously in humans, the explosion of the neocortex and of the prefrontal systems allows for an extremely rich overlay of complex higher cognitive operations involving working memories, semantic memories, complex behavioural organizations informed by conscious planning, and so forth. These cognitive extensions potentially allow increasingly subtle and adaptive fine-tuning of behaviour and subjective state consonant with basic emotional pushes and pulls.

These basic evolutionary principles, perhaps best represented above graphically as homeostasis ⟺ emotion ⟺ cognition, are expressed in the fundamental interactivity and rich connectivities between thalamocortical (more dorsal) brain systems and many subcortical (basal forebrain, diencephalic, and midbrain–reticular) systems. Although the later arriving "higher" cognitive functions have a certain partial autonomy if development proceeds "well enough", any version of full independence is illusory. One needs only to be in a life-threatening situation, struggling with terrible hunger or thirst, or in great pain to appreciate this fact. In all of these situations, homeostatic mandates dominate any and all cognitive processing and conscious focus.

There is also the important principle of Jacksonian partial dependence of "lower" functions on more cognitive dorsal brain systems, and this dependence appears to consistently increase with both progressive encephalization and ontogenesis. Thus, as development proceeds both in ontogeny and phylogeny, lesions of cortical systems can affect affective and even sometimes homeostatic regulation, as these functions have become increasingly dependent on "supervision" and modulation by the more dorsal thalamocortical systems. Extremely rich connectivities between thalamocortical (more dorsal) brain systems and multiple subcortical and brainstem systems instantiate these fundamental principles. Rather than the brain having anything like three discrete processing levels for homeostasis, emotion, and cognition (which would be fundamentally phrenological), brain regions often participate in several of these interactive functions, and mediate their deep interactions. A clinical example of this Jacksonian principle might be cingulate lesion cases (Mesulam, 2000). In some of these patients, one can have neuroendocrine, autonomic, and other homeostatic disturbances (due to disruption of cingulate projections into ventral limbic and hypothalamic systems), frequent affective–motivational disturbances, and cognitive deficits, typically in aspects of higher attentional and executive functions, classically indexed by troubles with the Stroop or "Go–No–Go" paradigm.

The fundamental dependence of cognitive processes on the subcortical integrity of the brain is graphically visualized in various syndromes affecting reticular–thalamocortical relations that globally devastate cognitive processes (outstanding examples are confusional states, and akinetic mutism, AKM). Rather than any kind of neat dividing line between systems that subserve homeostasis, emotion, and cognition, one instead finds evidence of distributed processing in which systems at multiple levels of the neuroaxis potentially contribute to the adaptive regulation of homeostasis by emotion, and of emotion by cognition. One might, in fact, argue that the processing of any one functional task shades gradually and imperceptibly into the processing of the tasks of the next level, and strict or neat separations between the tasks of homeostasis, emotion, and cognition are simply not observable in the brain's deeply re-entrant architecture. Thus, relatively more automatic, inflexible patterns of response (both around management of the internal milieu and of behaviour) are, over phylogenetic and ontogenetic development, integrated and subsumed by systems that allow more adaptive flexibility and fine tuning of organism response (a seminal insight of John Hughlings Jackson roughly a century ago). Cognition and emotion thus become deeply inter-penetrating, hierarchically-positioned activities in which emotion provides the motivational foundations for all directed cognitive activity, while cognition allows for modulation, blending, and especially *adaptive inhibition* of prototype affective states. Thought, as Freud so cogently put it so many years ago, is trial (affective) action. This is not a picture of *opposed functions* (as the simplistic and from my point of view pointless *emotion versus cognition* debates that dominated psychology for decades might have one believe). Cognitive appraisal becomes a very frequent top-down driver in the activation of emotion, this in turn helping to form new cognitive–affective associations (complex affective meanings).

Bridging the domains of psychotherapy and affective science in an age of distributed network models: "global state" functions of attention, executive functions, and emotion

Neuroscience has ambivalently moved towards gradual acceptance of the seminal insights of Luria, who was one of the first to articulate the hypothesis that complex psychological functions in the brain could only be instantiated in distributed networks, and not in simple "centres" for a particular function in a particular structure. Consciousness theory is increasingly drawn to such models to explain fundamental aspects of consciousness such as attentional function, organized behaviour or intention, and increas-ingly, emotion, including its manifestations in consciousness (feelings). As I suggested earlier, I have argued in other work that these complex functions of attention, organized behaviour or executive functions, and affective functions are global state functions (GSF), nothing less than "differential slices of the consciousness pie". Jointly, attention, organized or purposeful behaviour, and emotion constitute what Damasio (1999) calls "tests for core consciousness". These GSF have the following basic properties: (1) they all show an intrinsic functional interpenetration with one another (i.e. attention has intrinsic executive aspects closely paralleling the organization of behaviour, emotion informs salience and underpins attentional mechanisms and virtually all of the goals for behavioural organization, etc); (2) their foundations are putatively mapped to unconscious processes; (3) they do not show neat localization in discrete neocortical structures, but instead require highly distributed networks running from the ventral brainstem to many thalamocortical regions; and (4) these inter-digitating global state functions of attention, executive function, and emotion are foundational for all higher cognitive operations in the brain. Indeed, the most critical foundations for these complex functions appear to be consistently in subcortical areas and in the mesodiencephalic areas of the upper brainstem. Experimental work on the neural correlates of affect, attention, and volition show hugely overlapping architectures. Although dorsal portions of processing chains can be distinguished, the lines of traffic support-ing these GSF become increasingly crowded and difficult to distinguish in the ventral brainstem and mesodiencephalic regions. Diseases that "ablate" emotion also profoundly derail (empty or even end) consciousness [AKM, persistent vegetative state (PVS)— see later discussion of AKM].

Of course all this begs the basic question, "How and why are attention, executive function, and emotion so intimately related?" A comprehensive answer to this would put us much closer to the currently highly desired Holy Grail in neuroscience, an under-standing of the neural mechanisms for sentience itself. However, several basic points could be offered tentatively here as hypotheses.

- Much of this fundamental relatedness is probably mediated by reticular and other mesodiencephalic structures, particularly in the upper brainstem (midbrain to pons) including the hypo-thalamus, and periaqueductal gray (PAG), and also in the so-called "non-specific" thalamus (the intralaminar nuclei of the thalamus and the "reticular thalamus" or nRt). (There are also likely to be paralimbic and cerebellar contributions to these functional integrations of attention, purposeful behaviour, and emotion.)
- These mesodiencephalic regions (including the ventral dien-cephalon or hypothalamus) contain basic structures that

organize homeostasis, and that differentially arouse, "prime" and "gate" the thalamocortical forebrain. This means that these systems can move the "state space" of the whole brain in particular directions consonant with biological and perhaps even social needs.

- These brainstem regions generate both many of the "primi- tives" for survival behaviours (supported in the cranial nerves and brainstem nuclei) and the primitives for attentional functioning also, including eye movement, which is virtually paradigmatic for attentional control in highly visual animals.
- It is not a coincidence that the basic foundations for attention, emotion, cortical forebrain arousal, and homeostasis are all in contiguous regions in the upper brainstem (Damasio, 1999).
- These mesodiencephalic regions, when lesioned bilaterally, show consistently the greatest disruption of core consciousness for the smallest amount of lost brain tissue. Neocortical lesions do not.

Chemoarchitectures and neuroanatomy of prototype emotions

From all this one could readily ask how it is that the meaningful localization of emotion in the brain is even possible. As we will see, related problems involve the concept of a "limbic system" that has recently become increasingly controversial, with some investigators suggesting that term be scrapped altogether. Additionally, in discussing emotion, one has to offer a basic typology or taxonomy for emotion or else the question of the neural substrates of emotion becomes virtually impossible to research or explore empirically. What is contained in the limbic system varies from source to source, but one representation of these structure and connectivities might be from Mesulam. This particular graphic (*Figure 2*) includes many basal forebrain systems, ventral portions of the basal ganglia, all of the paleocortex, with the hypothalamus as an epicentre for the system. This representation does not include the monoaminergic projection systems, and PAG, which many would include as the most ventral portions of the "limbic system" underneath the hypothalamus. The fact that the two classical subcortical components in this system (the hippocampus and the amygdala) are both heavily involved in

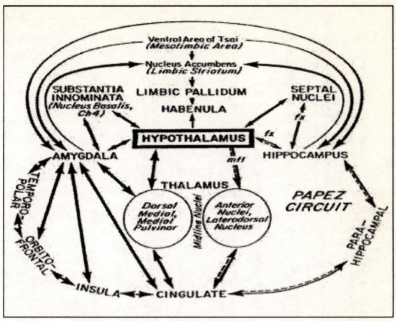

Figure 2. Paleocortical versus archicortical trends within limbic system,
two subcortical structures functioning as multimodal correlators
(from Mesulam's *Principles of Behavioural and Cognitive Neurology*, 2000, with
permission). Both HC and AMYG project to hypothalamus, thalamus, basal
forebrain, and paralimbic cortex. AMYG supports affective valence tagging
and emotional conditioning (mostly negative?). HC supports spatiotemporal
mapping of serial, clustered, cortical encodings to create episodic memory.

cognition, and really are sitting more at the cognition–emotion
border in the brain, has further muddied the limbic system concept.

*The current party line: amygdala drives ventral brainstem
systems, instantiating the "primitives" of affect (Figure 3)*

So, what's wrong with this? I would offer four fundamental
concerns about this formulation.

1. Parallel distributed processing is not equivalent to neatly linear
   top-down causalities like this, and the actual connectivities are
   much more re-entrant and massively parallel, especially regarding the various brainstem regions referred to here.

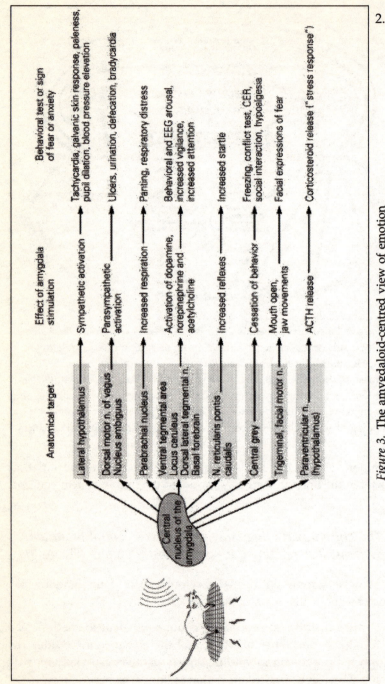

Figure 3. The amygdaloid-centred view of emotion
(from Principles of Neural Science (Kandel, Schwarz, Jessel, 2000) with permission).

Lesion studies show cessation of emotion only with PAG and VTA (ventral tegmental area) lesions (raising the question, "why do behaviourists neglect a structure that appears to organize all prototype affective behaviours?").

3. The coherent instantiation of all these "primitives" of affect is still quite possible *despite total absence of the amygdala* (individuals lose only fear conditioning and related operations), further underlining that the amygdala is hardly the master conductor here, only one of several possible conductors that can instantiate a coherent response.

4. Imaging studies paint a very different picture about the regions activated and deactivated in prototype emotion (more on this later). This suggests quite clearly that the integration of the "primitives" of affect, the creation of the composite that constitutes emotion, is not dependent on the amygdala.

There are some major unacknowledged and fundamental theoretical conundrums in the current amygdaloid centred views of emotion. Evidence suggests that the amygdala is more involved in negative affect than positive, more involved in organism defence than in organism attachment and social gratifications. "Valence tagging" (aka fear conditioning) by amygdala, and other kinds of emotional learning requires a base for value in the brain. Can "valence tagging" systems supply "primitives" for value? I think, on this point, that the research suggests that a telencephalic correlator system like the amygdala must depend on more primitive systems for a base of value. So what is "valence"? (what do the higher, particularly cortical, encodings get associated with?) What is primary organismic value? Those core "value generating" systems are in the diencephalon and midbrain, and brainstem, long viewed as passive output targets for the amygdala. Work on these regions has been largely, but not entirely, neglected in thinking about the neural correlates of emotion, where little attention is paid to the midbrain or even the hypothalamus.

"Unpacking" valence into prototype affective states

Part of the problem is that the emotions literature has been satisfied with a typology that emphasizes simple dimensional variables such as level of arousal, valence, and approach-avoidance. Simple notions of valence, in particular, may be too global to attack the problem or parse out the experimental space. This is not an adequate typology to parse the problem space of emotion, and a different approach to taxonomy, informed by more fundamental ethological concepts, is needed.

Jaak Panksepp's work makes major contributions on this point in terms of unpacking valence into core prototypes of social–biological relationships to other species and conspecifics—what Panksepp calls "grade A blue ribbon emotions:" social bonding/ attachment, sexuality, nurturance, sadness/separation distress, playful affection, rage/anger, fear, and a non-specific seeking system. His summary of this work (1998) emphasizes that there are distributed neural architectures, with dominant neuropeptidergic modulation, that underpin emotional primitives or prototypes. There is no neat phrenology for the neuropeptide systems; prototype emotion is not controlled neatly by one peptide for each state, but rather a likely cluster of these modulators that have the capacity to induce these states with MUCH more specificity than the monoamines. These architectures show a fundamental basal forebrain–diencephalic–midbrain organization, and sit underneath the thalamocortical architectures evolved for higher cognitive processes (there are functionally three clusters of systems here— can you spot the 3 clusters?) (The following table, *Table 1*, is taken from Watt, 1998). The three basic clusters would be: (1) a non-specific seeking system that supplies the general gain for the system (a dopaminergic projection system running from the ventral tegmental area up through lateral hypothalamus with diffuse mesolimbic and mesocortical projections; (2) an organism defence system subserving fear and rage states; and (3) an attachment system, regulating bonds with con-specifics and other living things.

Peri-Aqueductal Gray revisited

PAG is a "peri-reticular" region, one of Damasio's "proto-self" structures (Damasio, 1999), essential for both emotion and consciousness, but frankly poorly understood, with research into PAG function often quite fragmented and looking at small pieces of

Table 1. Prototype emotion.

Affective Behaviour	Distributed Neural Networks	Neuromodulators
Seeking and Exploratory Behaviour	Ventral Tegmental Area (VTA) to more dorsolateral hypothalamic to periaqueductal gray (**PAG**), with diffuse mesolimbic and mesocortical "extensions". Nucleus accumbens as basal ganglia processor for emotional "habit" systems.	DA (+), glutamate (+), many neuropeptides including opioids, neurotensin, CCK
Rage— ("Affective Attack")	medial amygdala to bed nucleus of stria terminalis (BNST) to anterior and ventromedial and perifornical hypothalamic to more dorsal **PAG**	Substance P (+) (? Ach, glutamate (+) as non-specific modulators?)
Fear	central & lateral amygdala to anterior and medial hypothalamic to more dorsal **PAG** to nucleus reticularis pontine caudalis	Glutamate (+) ACTH, and neuropeptides (DBI, CRF, CCK, alpha MSH, NPY)
Sexuality	BNST and corticomedial amygdala to preoptic and ventromedial hypothalamus to lateral and more ventral **PAG**	Steroids (+), vasopressin and oxytocin. LH-RH, CCK.
Nurturance/ maternal care	Anterior cingulate to bed nucleus of stria terminalis (BNST) to preoptic hypothalamic to VTA to more ventral **PAG**	Oxytocin (+), prolactin (+), dopamine, opioids (both + in mod. amounts)
Separation Distress/ Social Bonding	Anterior cingulate/anterior thalamus to BNST/ventral septum to midline & dorsomedial thalamus to dorsal preoptic hypothalamic to more dorsal **PAG** (close to circuits for physical pain)	Opioids (–/+) oxytocin (–/+), prolactin (–/+) CRF (+) for separation distress, ACh (–)
Play/Joy/ Social Affection	Parafascicular/centromedian thalamus, dorso-medial thalamus, posterior thalamus, projecting to more dorsal (? dorsomedial) **PAG** (septum inhibitory re: play, and role of other basal forebrain and hypothalamic systems is still not clear at all.)	Glutamate (+) Opioids (+ in modest amounts, –in large amounts), ACh (muscarinic +) ACh (nicotinic –) DA, NE and 5-HT all appear to be (–)

the functional puzzle and not so much a big picture view of its functional importance for emotion and forebrain/behavioural arousal (see Bandler and Depaulis, 1991). Full caudal rostral lesions of PAG are devastating to both emotion and consciousness, generating the syndrome of AKM, reviewed below in detail. PAG's connectivities are almost entirely with other components of the reticular activating system, the hypothalamus, the amygdala, and anterior limbic cortex in cingulate and orbitofrontal regions. The PAG is thought to contain probably at least four and possibly more columnar structures with slightly different connectivities from column to column, with the current literature identifying a dorsal medial, a dorsolateral, a lateral, and a ventrolateral column.

The connectivities of the dorsomedial column are relatively unmapped as this column has just been more recently identified. The dorsolateral column is thought to be largely an active defensive system, with extensive connections to medial cortex (10, 25, 32), anterior and ventromedial hypothalamus, and centrolateral and paraventricular ILN (these are key intralaminar nuclei in the thalamus involved in cortical activation and arousal). Dorsolateral PAG is also re-entrant with the amygdala and PB (parabrachial nucleus) areas, apparently like all the columns in PAG, although the evidence suggests that different regions of the parabrachial nucleus map to the differential columnar architecture of PAG. (This is consistent with the remarkable specificity of connectivities of these regions such as PAG and other midbrain and pontine structures essential for GSF. They certainly do not show anything that one could consider to be a kind of helter-skelter "connection to everything".) The lateral PAG column is also thought to reflect a more active defensive system. The lateral PAG column has bilateral projections with areas 9 and cingulate 24b, and dorsal hypothalamus. Thalamic ILN efferent targets are not mapped yet for this portion of PAG (as far as I know). (See Cameron, 1995a/b for details.)

The ventrolateral PAG has been conceptualized by Bandler and Depaulis (1991) and others as a more "passive coping" (versus a more positive affective system?). Projections to and from older portions of orbital cortex (14c, 13a, 12o, Iai), posterior lateral hypothalamus, with projections to parafascicular and centromedian portions of thalamic ILN. Both lateral and ventrolateral PAG are bilaterally connected to the amygdala and parabrachial nuclei (PB).

Like the classical reticular activating system (RAS), PAG has widespread afferents and efferents—including with multiple RAS, midbrain, diencephalic, and paleocortical regions. Basal forebrain and paleocortical systems involved in the appraisal of affective significance all project to differential columns in PAG. There are extensive differential reciprocal projections of various columns in PAG to different paleocortical areas, to basal forebrain systems (not just amygdala, but also BNST—bed nucleus of stria terminalis), and septum. There are also differential projections to hypothalamic, parabrachial, and reticular systems (the various monoamine systems in the RAS: dopamine—DA, norepinephrine—NE, serotonin —5-HT) and differential ILN targets for these PAG columns. Several functional correlates may emerge from these connectivities, although this system has not been as closely studied as its more famous "relatives" higher in the neuroaxis, particularly the amygdala.

- PAG would seem to generate a "global value map" representing relative activation states of prototypes, organizing motor and visceral tunings consonant with the prototype states.
- Many in neuroscience have accepted the doctrine that PAG is a passive "step and fetch it" for the amygdala. This view of PAG ironically is most promoted by neuroscientists with a strong behaviourist orientation, who admit that PAG organizes virtually all prototype affective behaviours in animals (see LeDoux, 1996).
- Lesion studies suggest a vital role in consciousness consistent with its peri-reticular connectivities. In primates, PAG lesions have produced a profoundly akinetic, twilight state (see Panksepp, 1998 for summary of the lesion literature). In rats (unfortunately involving SC), PAG lesions have produced an apparently "lights-out" state with total loss of behavioural spontaneity. Thus, global disorders of consciousness (akinetic mutism versus vegetative state) are seen with full rostral–caudal lesions of PAG columns. There has been the discovery of the first relatively restricted PAG lesions in an adult human (Schiff & Plum, 1999; Watt, 2000.) This case, discussed later, showed severe and unremitting AKM.
- Rather than a simple neo-phrenology in which the primary activation of each column in PAG corresponds to a particular prototype affective state, the more likely foundations for the

prototype states involve differential degrees of activation of the four (or possibly five?) columns in PAG across the different prototype affective states. PAG may thus run competitions between the relative activation levels of primary states, computing agonism and antagonism between prototypes, distributing a resulting global value mapping to both higher and lower portions of the neuroaxis. This competition may be instantiated through extensive bilateral radial connectivities between the columns, mediated by inhibitory interneurons using GABA as a modulator (Jansen *et al.*, 1997).

● This competition may be one substrate for fundamental Darwinian mechanisms to shut down positive states quickly in survival situations: the competitive bias in PAG may be of necessity "against the positives". Negative affective states would need to get control of the motor apparatus quickly and decisively. On the other hand, organisms could afford to have positive aspects shut down immediately, and also afford for those positive affective states to take longer to "come back online". Put more graphically, evolutionary pressures would make selection of these properties very likely, as it much worse to get eaten than it is to miss out on a little fun. This may explain why most of the work on PAG has focused on defence, stress, negative affects—the activation bias in PAG (assuming a competitive gating model of PAG columnar interactions/function) is probably against the positive affects.

Varieties of Akinetic Mutism (AKM)—
clues to neural "minimums" for emotion/motivation

● Hypervigilant AKM (the classical version of AKM) associated with disease/damage to:
   Bilateral anterior cingulate, medial frontal cortex.
● "Slow" AKM syndrome or showing mixed motor slowing/vigilant features associated with disease/damage to:
   1. Bilateral mesodiencephalic injury.

      A. ILN and MRF (midbrain reticular formation, mostly the cuneiform nucleus and superior colliculi).

    B. posterior ILN (intralaminar nuclei)—these are critical for corticostriatal thalamocortical loops that underpin habit systems and skill learning.

    C. PAG (extremely rare—only few closely studied cases).

    D. VTA (the ventral tegmental dopamine system).

    E. Pontine lesions affecting other monoamine reticular systems rarely produces AKM, but it has been reported.

2. Medial forebrain bundle (quite rare, but reported).

3. Bilateral caudate nucleus/nucleus accumbens or globus pallidus.

A full caudal–rostral PAG lesion: akinetic mutism and the emptying out of consciousness (case materials from Schiff & Plum (1999))

The following case study may help to clarify basic aspects of the argument.

This patient was a male in his early thirties with HIV/AIDS but with no pre-existing clinical evidence of extensive white matter encephalopathy or AIDS-related dementia complex, who was found unresponsive, and in a deep stupor. Initial structural imaging with CT showed a large expanding mass lesion of the midbrain. The patient was treated with steroids to reduce swelling and had a marked, rapid regression of the mass lesion in the midbrain. After the mass lesion of the midbrain resolved following the steroid pulse, his stupor improved, and he was then found to demonstrate a classic akinetic mute state: vigilant appearance, relatively intact ocular tracking, some quite limited spontaneous movements of the left arm with stimulation, but following no commands or showing any reliable signs of interaction, affect, or other motivated behaviour, and certainly no demonstrated evidence of any adaptive higher cognitive function. The MRI that followed the CT showed high signal abnormalities in the midbrain, pretectum around the aqueduct, and some involvement into the paramedian thalamus on the left, probably affecting various midline and intralaminar systems, but no other discernible structural pathology. A SPECT scan showed diffuse hypometabolism widely affecting association cortices bilaterally, including frontal, parietal, and temporal association cortices, consistent with the supposition that higher cognitive and executive functions were all "off-line". The patient died several months later secondary to pneumonia, but without any clinical change in his neurological or akinetic mute mental status. At autopsy, pathology confirmed a lymphoma that had regressed through and subsequently destroyed the paramedian tegmental mesencephalon, tracked through the aqueduct to the thalamus, and into the anterior intralaminar region on left side, with the preservation of the right intralaminar region possibly allowing for some movement of the left upper extremity, although the movements appeared purposeless and without clear intention.

As far as we know, no other case of full caudal–rostral PAG involvement with relative sparing of the other mesodiencephalic areas has been correlated with this much structural imaging, functional imaging, and neuropathological data. The case is fully consistent with animal work in which extensive caudal–rostral lesions of PAG consistently produce a severe akinetic mute state with little progress towards any resolution or generation of visible affect or spontaneous motivated behaviour. This functional loss is consistent with the extensive reticular connectivities of PAG, which receives telencephalic projections restricted to limbic and paralimbic systems such as the central nucleus of amygdala, and anterior paleocortices (cingulate/orbital frontal), and with the apparently close relationship between this structure and the largely DA (dopamine) mediated "seeking system" (Panksepp, 1998). PAG has extensive reciprocal projections to these systems, and with the hypothalamus, multiple monoamine nuclei, and the thalamic ILN systems, the posterior ILN group in particular (centromedian/ parafascicular).

PAG contains several (dorsomedial, dorsolateral, lateral, and ventromedial) columnar structures that appear differentially activated across different affective states. Animal work suggests that it plays an essential role in making emotion an active motoric process, as most prototype affective behaviours (fleeing, freezing, copulating, affective vocalizations, possibly many attachment behaviours, etc.) appear to be organized by PAG–hypothalamic–brainstem motor system networks. Its role in the complexity of more cognized human affective states is still poorly outlined empirically, but it may be in a position, by virtue of its extensive reticular and intralaminar connectivities, to widely influence the thalamocortical system consonant with the underlying affective state, and to "gate" or restrict state space of the thalamocortical system. In other words, in play states, certain activities and perceptual states are facilitated, while others are inhibited and not nearly as accessible. Similar organizations would presumably exist in rage, fear, and separation distress states. This notion of affective "gating" of cognitive activity is seen fairly clearly in the phenomenon of state dependent recall in short-term memory, in which sad or happy experiences are better recalled in sad or happy states.

The syndrome of AKM of course always begs the question, "well, gee, aren't these patients still conscious?" Lesser versions of the syndrome seen in bilateral cingulate disease have shown enough recovery that patients have been able to clearly report experiencing events, but having absolutely no desire or motivation to respond or initiate activity, leading to a deepening of the suspicion that this is not a "true" disease of consciousness, and seeming to offer evidence of the independence of consciousness from an emotional underpinning. I would have a different conclusion. Lesser versions of AKM (classically associated with bilateral cingulate disease) may allow some phenomenal content, while the more severe versions (associated with very extensive lesions of PAG, or VTA, and subcortical bilateral basal ganglia presentations) may show a virtual "emptying out" of consciousness, that events simply "don't matter" any more. It may be an essential requirement that stimuli have at least some potential affective significance, or else they don't gain access to conscious workspace. This suggests that mesodiencephalic emotional and homeostatic systems in the ventral brain (PAG in particular) may function to "gate" stimuli into thalamocortical systems as meaningful, and in turn PAG activations may "gate" or selectively restrict the state space of the basal ganglia/prefrontal behavioural systems, consistent with the dominant affective state of the system (i.e. playful behaviours are simply not available when we are very angry, and *vice versa*). With the virtually total loss of affective meaning or salience for most if not all stimuli in very extensive PAG lesions, consciousness may be essentially "greyed out". This suggests that these more severe AKM patients live in a kind of strange, virtually unfathomable netherworld close to the border of a persistent vegetative state.

Irony of cognitive–behavioural view of PAG in
"amygdaloid-centric" views of emotion: valence revisited

As stated earlier, in terms of animal behavioural neuroscience literature, PAG is largely viewed as a passive "step and fetch it" for the amygdala by neuroscientists (see LeDoux, 1996) with a strong behaviourist orientation, who admit that PAG appears to organize virtually all prototype affective behaviours in animals. This may change in primates and humans, due to encephalization, to a more "priming" role in which PAG influences the thalamocortical mantle, tuning the forebrain in a fashion consonant with primary affective state (see Watt, 2000 for summary overview).

There remain most basic questions about the manifestation of emotion in consciousness—*why do emotions feel good or bad*? Certainly we do not have anywhere near a complete answer to this question, but an important clue lies in the basic consideration that emotions are extensions of homeostatic mechanisms and pain/ pleasure. This suggests that emotions within a conscious organism feel good or bad due to primary (pre-emptive) signalling of various body maintenance systems charged with the preservation of the organism, into core or primary consciousness. From this point of view, emotion sits over pain/pleasure foundations as a kind of "proto-qualia".

Additionally, there is the fundamental relationship between emotion and action priming that helps us to understand something about the nature of valence as the fundamental property of emotion. I would argue that no convincing theory about the nature of the affective valence is possible without paying close attention to the implications of action priming, as these action primes "encode" how a certain kind of stimulus is unconditionally positive or negative for an organism, telling the organism unambiguously whether certain kinds of stimulation are biologically desirable or not. For example, running away in fear states, the passive receptivity of infant mammals in receiving nurturance, or fighting against another organism in rage states all provide unambiguous motor "commentary", evolutionarily conserved across many lines and through phylogenesis, about the positive or negative nature of the stimulation for the organism. In other words, put bluntly, nature tells us in these prototype states to "get the hell out of there", "terminate the source of the bad stuff with prejudice", or "stick around", and get some more of the good stuff.

Closing thoughts on the empirical gold mine of attachment

If emotion is the most neglected subject in neuroscience, attachment is the most neglected subject within the large topic of emotion. It is not a coincidence that we use the language of biological damage and pain in talking about the loss of attachments (they "hurt" in a true sense, viscerally). In talking about "narcissistic injuries" that also "hurt", we fear events that disconfirm our worthiness to love, and threaten internal connections to good other(s)—these also cause "hurt". These are important secondary emotions closely related to the prototype state of separation distress. Separation distress, as a prototype state, uses systems close to those in PAG mediating the gating of nociceptive afferents for physical pain: *separation distress probably evolved from those ancient pain circuits* (see Panksepp, 1998). Attachment is a homeostatic mandate for the very young (as for example we see in the syndrome of hospitalism), and how the loss of good attachments affects the brain in a pervasive and profound fashion is both poorly understood but also grossly neglected as a central question by most neuroscientists, even in some of those interested in emotion. Neuroscience badly needs to pay more attention to attachment, since attachment experiences form the neurodevelopmental ground out of which we emerge, and certainly the groundwork for much of cortical development and prefrontal system development. If children grow up with dominant experiences of separation, distress, fear and rage, then they will go down a bad pathogenic developmental pathway, and it is not just a bad psychological pathway but a bad neurological pathway.

Summary of ideas about emotion

To summarize the arguments put forward here concerning emotion and consciousness, I would emphasize the following points:

● Emotions are the vital threads of value that run through the whole neural system. Their primary foundations (the "primitives" of affect, what makes the prototype affect drive us as powerfully as it sometimes does, but not its cognitive elaborations) are supplied by the subcortical brain, in PAG, the hypothalamus, and many other brainstem and reticular regions.

- These threads of value are essential for any attentional function, volition, or consciousness. Organismic value (emotion), allocation of the limited processing resources of consciousness (attention), and the organization of behaviour (the executive function) are three complex integrative domains of CNS function. All three of these domains are the keystones in any viable theory of consciousness. These large-scale GSF "support" each other and are functionally interdigitating.

- Higher systems link to these ventral brain systems defining organismic value, enabling higher cognitive associations to all the basic prototype states (that is, giving "emotional meaning"). The "top down" activation of emotions is often emphasized in the appraisal literature, but emotion is strictly speaking not simply a derivative of appraisal.

- Laterality issues are also important. The right hemisphere is more crucial to GSF, like emotion and attention, and to executive function, than is the left hemisphere. The left hemisphere systems provide inhibition and dampening of right hemisphere mediated arousal, along with all routinized and more analytical cognitive processing. Since the left hemisphere is presumably involved in most if not all consensually validated or routinized coding systems, this underpins its central role in language.

- Again, it is important to draw attention to the basic ignorance in neuroscience, unacknowledged by most neuroscientists, about how attachment experiences in infancy supply the foundations for much of neurodevelopment in mammals.

- The problem of, "what is consciousness?" is as difficult as the problem, "what is emotion and how do things feel either good or bad?" Core consciousness probably rests in correlations of proto-self mappings and object mappings (Damasio), but vast work still lies ahead to understand the specifics of this very general global formulation. I am sure that a strongly neuro-developmental approach has to be taken (for example paying close attention to the neuro-imaging studies in infants), and that highly cortico-centric assumptions about the basis of consciousness in the brain need to be questioned, particularly since the weight of empirical and lesion evidence is that a bunch of mesodiencephalic structures are the most essential players in core consciousness, and that consciousness in general requires a certain kind of integrative communication, possibly indexed by higher frequency oscillatory envelopes between distributed regions in the brain, particularly the critical triad of thalamus, brainstem, and cortex (Llinas, *et al.*, 1994; Baars, 1993; Baars *et al.*, 1998; Freeman, 2001).

A few closing themes

- Emotion evolved to better "routinize" solutions to prototype homeostatic or survival tasks, by providing global somatic and brain tunings consonant with the adaptive load.
- Cognition evolved to enhance the solution of tasks that were prototypically affective: for example, the selection of mates; protection of the young or other con-specifics; protection also of territory; the enhancement of group "fit;" and the social gratification of attachment needs.
- Interactions between our prototype affective states and the vast panoply of human cognition (both language and more gestalt-based right hemisphere modes of cognition) supply most of the content of consciousness once we are past early infancy.
- Mapping these deep interactions is the next great frontier in psychology, with emotion neurodevelopmentally the more primitive function, but providing the motivational foundations for all directed cognitive activity. This could beneficially take the place of the largely pointless debates about "emotion versus cognition" that have dominated psychology for decades. These are basic concepts that Damasio's work (1994) made more visible.
- Neurodevelopment is the great frontier in neuroscience for those of us interested in the "hard problems" (that is, of consciousness, meaning, emotion, personality, social relations, etc.).
- Although neurodevelopment has been modelled in many, many ways in terms of various aspects of an individual's cognitive

growth, from an affective standpoint we need to include the simple ideas that the wisdom of the ages have presented for millennia in virtually all cultures. That is, from an affective standpoint, neurodevelopment is mostly about the progressive and deepening "internalization" of a good, comforting connection to loved others. The biological power of that simple principle has yet to be grasped by more than a tiny minority in neuroscience.

● Those who *do* grasp the primal importance of attachment need to participate in the building of bridges between psychotherapy and neuroscience, or else neuroscience may never do justice to the wisdom of the ages, or give us the "Holy Grail" so eagerly sought these days, which is, understanding the neural nature of sentience and consciousness.

To return to the question I posed at the start of my paper—"what we need to do to bridge the gap between the disciplines and domains of psychotherapy and neuroscience"—I would like to end by proposing the following suggestions.

Psychotherapy training needs to include much more training in neuroscience, especially in clinical and affective neuroscience. We need to see PhD research in clinical psychology that is more neuropsychologically focused on clinical syndromes, and in investigating the interactions of neurobiological and psychological variables. DSM-IV syndromes are a goldmine for bridging the disciplines and for neurodevelopmentally informed research in which we could examine the interactions between nature and nurture, and between brain and social environment. We need less infighting about the virtues of competing technical approaches in psychotherapy, and the mediation of those debates in empirical research on efficacy in specific disorders, and not from the standpoint of metapsychological infighting between schools of psychotherapy and psychoanalysis, which has been the dominant currency in the past. We need to return to Freud's Project, with a *mea culpa* from psychoanalysis about departing from Freud's original goal of grounding psychology in neuroscience. Above all, we need research, and lots more research, towards the goal of an integrated language of mind and brain.

References and Bibliography

Baars, B. J. (1993). How does a serial, integrated and very limited stream of consciousness emerge from a nervous system that is mostly unconscious, distributed, and of enormous capacity? In: G. Bock & J. Marsh (Eds.), *CIBA Symposium on Experimental and Theoretical Studies of Consciousness* (pp. 282–290). London: John Wiley and Sons.

Baars, B. J. & Newman, J. (1994). A neurobiological interpretation of the Global Workspace theory of consciousness. In: A. Revonsuo & M. Kamppinen (Eds.), *Consciousness in Philosophy and Cognitive Neuroscience*. Hillsdale NJ: Lawrence Erlbaum Associates.

Baars, B. J., Newman, J., & Taylor, J. G. (1998). Neuronal mechanisms of consciousness: A relational global workspace framework. In: S. Hammeroff *et al.* (Eds.), *Towards a Science of Consciousness*. Cambridge, MA: MIT Press.

Bandler, R., & Depaulis, A. (Eds.) (1991). *The Midbrain Periaqueductal Gray.* (NATO Asi Series. Series A, *Life Science, Volume 213*). London: Plenum Press.

Blanck, G., & Blanck, R. (1974). *Ego Psychology: Theory and Practice.* New York: Colombia University Press.

Bowlby, J. (1969). *Attachment and Loss, Volume 1: Attachment.* New York: Basic Books.

Bowlby, J. (1973). *Attachment and Loss, Volume 2: Separation, Anxiety and Anger.* New York: Basic Books.

Cameron, A. A., Khan, I. A., Westlund, K. N., Cliffer, K. D., & Willis, W. D., (1995a). The efferent projections of the periaqueductal gray in the rat: a *Phaseolus vulgaris*–leucoagglutinin study. I. Ascending projections. *Journal of Comparative Neurology, 351*(4): 568–584.

Cameron, A. A., Khan, I. A., Westlund, K. N., & Willis, W. D. (1995b). The efferent projections of the periaqueductal gray in the rat: a *Phaseolus vulgaris*—leucoagglutinin study. II. Descending projections. *Journal of Comparative Neurology, 351*(4): 585–601.

Chalmers, D. (1996). Facing up to the problem of consciousness. *Journal of Consciousness Studies, 2*(3): 200–219.

Damasio, A. (1994). *Descartes' Error: Emotion, Reason, and the Human Brain.* New York: Avon Press.

Damasio, A. (1999). *The Feeling of What Happens. Body and Emotion in the Making of Consciousness.* New York: Harcourt Brace & Co.

Freeman, W. J. (2001). *How Brains Make Up Their Minds.* New York: Columbia University Press.

Freud, S. (1920). *A General Introduction to Psycho-Analysis. S.E., 16.*

Heilman, K. M. (1997). Emotion and the brain: a distributed modular network mediating emotional experience. *Journal of Neuropsychiatry*, Winter, 1997.

Kandel, E. R., Schwartz, J. H., & Jessel, T. M. (Eds). *Principles of Neural Science*. New York: McGraw-Hill.

Lane, R. D. (1998). Subregions within the anterior cingulate cortex may differentially participate in phenomenal and reflective consciousness awareness of emotion. http://www.zynet.co.uk/imprint/Tucson/2.htm

LeDoux, J. (1996). *The Emotional Brain. The Mysterious Underpinnings of Emotional Life*. New York: Simon and Schuster.

Llinas, R., Ribary, U., Joliot, M., & Wang, G. (1994). Content and context in temporal thalamocortical binding. In: G. Buzsaki *et al.* (Eds.), *Temporal Coding in the Brain*. Berlin: Springer Verlag.

MacLean, P. D. (1985). Evolutionary psychiatry and the triune brain. *Psychological Medicine, 15*: 219–221.

Mesulam, M. (2000). Patterns in behavioural neuroanatomy: association areas, limbic system, and hemispheric specialization. In: M. Mesulam, (Ed.), *Principles of Behavioural and Cognitive Neurology*. NY: Oxford University Press.

Newman, J. (1997). Putting the puzzle together: Towards a general theory of the neural correlates of consciousness. *Journal of Consciousness Studies, 4*(1&2): 47–66, 101–121.

Newman, J., & Baars, B. J. (1993). A neural attentional model for access to consciousness: a Global Workspace perspective. *Concepts in Neuroscience, 4*(2): 255–290.

Panksepp, J. (1991). Affective neuroscience: a conceptual framework for the neurobiological study of emotions. In: K. Strongman (Ed.), *International Reviews of Emotion Research* (pp. 59–99). Chichester, UK: Wiley.

Panksepp, J. (1998). *Affective Neuroscience*. Oxford University Press.

Papez, J. W. (1937). A proposed mechanism of emotion. *Archives of Neurological Psychiatry, 38*: 725–743.

Schiff, N., & Plum, F. (1999). The neurology of impaired consciousness: global disorders and implied models. Target Article, *Association for the Scientific Study of Consciousness Electronic Seminar*. http://athena.english.vt.edu/cgi-bin/netforum/nic/a/1.

Schore, A. (1994). *Affect Regulation and the Origins of the Self. The Neurobiology of Affective Development*. Hillsdale, NJ: Lawrence Erlbaum Associates.

Watt, D. F. (1986). Transference: a right hemisphere event? An inquiry into the boundary between psychoanalytic metapsychology and neuropsychology. *Psychoanalysis and Contemporary Thought*, 9(1): 43–77.

Watt, D. F. (1990). Higher cortical functions and the ego: the boundary between psychoanalysis, behavioural neurology and neuropsychology. *Psychoanalytic Psychology*, 7(4): 487–527.

Watt, D. F. (1998). Emotion and consciousness: implications of affective neuroscience for extended reticular thalamic activating system theories of consciousness. http://www.phil.vt.edu/ASSC/esem4.html or contact the author at: Quincy Medical Center, Boston University School of Medicine, Boston, Mass. USA.

Watt, D. F. (2000). The centrencephalon and thalamocortical integration. Neglected contributions of periaqueductal gray. *Consciousness & Emotion*, 1(1): 91–114.

CHAPTER FOUR

Early experience, attachment and the brain

Danya Glaser

Introduction

This chapter describes the importance of the child's early years in the light of the growing knowledge about brain development (Zeanah *et al.*, 1997; Shonkoff & Phillips, 2000), and discusses possible practical applications of recent research findings to the protection of children. It is important to note that although the first three years of life are of great importance to the child's later development, continuing and new experiences in childhood and adolescence also influence brain development and there is potential for change even after significant early disadvantage (Nelson, 1999). Brain development is also strongly influenced by prenatal factors, including maternal alcohol (Fitzgerald *et al.*, 2000) and other substance abuse, and significant maternal stress. However, in the absence of a legal mandate not currently available, there are only limited possibilities for protecting the vulnerable foetal brain from adverse circumstances. While the focus in this chapter is on the relationship between the primary caregiver(s) and the young child, this relationship is obviously nested within the family which is, in turn, significantly influenced by the social environment in which the family is located.

Mind–brain equivalents

We are well accustomed to observe and study "mind" functions which include emotion, cognition, perception, and behaviour. There are equivalent neurobiological processes accompanying these mind functions. It is increasingly possible to study brain structures, localization of function and precise timing of brain activity, and neurochemical changes in the brain, simultaneously with observed behaviour and other "mind" functions, by the use of a variety of neurophysiological measures and brain imaging techniques. These include the measurement of:

1. Direct, electrical activity using
   a. electroencephalograms (EEG) which provides crude localization and information about ongoing states (e.g. sleep, epilepsy)
   b. event-related potentials (ERP) which record short, discrete, timed activity in m.seconds, in response to discrete stimuli
2. Indirect, metabolic activity using
   a. Positron emission tomography (PET) which records radio-active labelled oxygen or glucose usage at active sites (1cm localization and timing in 10s of seconds)
   b. Functional magnetic resonance imaging (fMRI) which records deoxygenated haemoglobin levels in active sites (1cm localization and timing in seconds)
3. Structure, in particular the size of particular regions (as well as lesions) using magnetic resonance imaging (MRI) and computerized tomography (CT) scanning.
4. Neurotransmitters, in particular the biogenic amines dopamine and noradrenaline (catechol amines) and serotonin (5HT) which are involved in regulation of emotions and behaviour. Their secretion and usage can be recorded by a variety of means including levels of the neurotransmitters or their metabolites in the blood and urine, and more localized neurotransmitter activity using labelled PET. Dopamine is postulated to mediate the behavioural facilitatory system, activated by rewarding stimuli, or by aversive stimuli when escape or avoidance are possible. Dopamine is thus involved in approach, escape, and active avoidance as well as in predatory aggression (Quay, 1993). It is suggested (Rogeness *et al.*, 1992) that noradrenaline

and serotonin are involved in the mediation of behavioural inhibition in the face of lack of reward, punishment or uncertainty. These two neurotransmitters are therefore involved in *regulating* dopamine dependent behaviour.

The effects of harmful early experience can be considered under three headings:

- Extreme deprivation
- Distorted experiences
- Stress

Brain development

The growing understanding of the process and rate of early brain development lends support to the commonly held belief about the crucial importance of the very early experiences, while emphasizing also the potential for later growth and development. It has become clear that it is the baby's and young child's immediate interpersonal environment which shapes the brain's development. This proceeds very rapidly in the early years of life.

The stepwise *sequence* of brain development is genetically predetermined and cannot be altered by environment and experience. It proceeds from lower to higher brain centres, from the brainstem to the cerebral cortex (Nelson & Bloom, 1997). Areas of the brain subserving different functions mature at different times. Sensory centres serving vision and hearing are the earliest to mature. The process of brain maturation continues into early adolescence.

By birth, most of the brain's 100 billion neurons (nerve cells) are formed and have migrated to their permanent position in the brain. Neurons connect with each other at synapses which are formed between an axon (the extension conveying electrical impulses *from* a neuronal cell body) and a dendrite (one of many fibres leading *into* a neuronal cell body). The signal is transmitted from one neuron to another across the synaptic gap by chemical neurotransmitters. Most post-natal brain growth occurs in the first four years, with the rate being highest in the first year. This post-natal growth is accounted for by a massive, sequential proliferation and over-production of synapses (synaptogenesis) in the brain, the connections

NERVE CELL

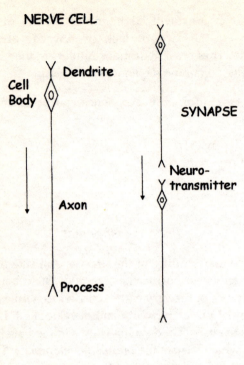

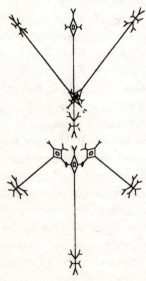

Multiple synapses possible

probably being randomly formed. During early childhood the number of synapses reaches nearly double the number ultimately found in adulthood. The *timing* of synaptogenesis varies between different cortical regions. It is accompanied by the necessary proliferation of glial cells (which modulate neuronal activity by providing structural support and nourishment), and blood capillaries.

Not all the synaptic connections survive, many being subsequently "pruned" due to lack of use. It is environmental input, which includes sensory input and interactions between the primary carers and the baby, which determines which synapses will persist.

> During brain growth there is a constant sorting and juggling of nerve cells and connections. Those that make a match with their environment thrive, and the others wither. [Bownds, 1999, p. 124]

or to quote Courchesne, Chisum and Townsend (1994) "neurons that fire together, wire together". A competitive process operates, determining which neurons and neural connections will survive. One aspect of the competition is for potential binding sites on the receiving neuron. When a neural pathway is activated by a stimulus, the synapses that have become engaged will store a chemical signal, and repetition of the same or similar stimuli will stabilize the neural pattern which will become less susceptible to subsequent change. The circuits that are reinforced and retained in the baby's brain, are determined by the quality and content of the day to day interactions with the primary caregivers. The "instruction" to attend to the primary caregiver is genetic, the outcome depends on the nature of the caregivers' responses. This occurs within emotional communication. Pruning serves to fine-tune synaptic connections. Like synaptogenesis, its timing varies in different areas of the brain. The prefrontal cortex continues to mature into adolescence.

The overproduction of synapses is found especially in brain regions which have been genetically programmed to anticipate and respond to experiences which are part of the expected environment of the infant. These experiences include sensory input, the handling of young infants, responsive gaze by the parent, talking to the infant and responding sensitively to the infant's attachment behaviour (see below). The absence of these inputs and interactions with the infant would be unusual for the majority of infants. This aspect of brain development is called *experience-expectant* (Greenough & Black,

1992). Experience-expectant development implies the existence of critical periods of development. Absence or insufficient input at the appropriate time will lead to an absolute or relative failure of development of particular functions. These include stereoscopic vision, aspects of language, and possibly selective attachments.

The other aspect of brain maturation has been termed by Greenough and Black *experience-dependent*. In this too, environmental inputs actively contribute to brain development. Unlike the experience-expectant process, here the nature of the experiences are not predetermined, and are particular to each individual child and carer–child relationship. The experience-dependent synapses which "wire together" following particular input, do not *anticipate* the experiences at any precise developmental stage, although learning (e.g. acquisition of languages) proceeds much more easily at the appropriate developmental stage, early in life. It is clear that experience-dependent development continues into adulthood, although its rate is greatest in early life. Experience-dependent processes can generate new synapses in response to new experiences.

The brain's ability to change its own structure in response to the environment and experience is termed neuroplasticity. This is a recursive process, since changes in the brain facilitate the incorporation of new experiences. The duration of plasticity is determined by whether the development of a region and function is limited to a critical or sensitive (less precise and more prolonged) period (Nelson, 1999) or is experience-dependent. The latter allows for continuing plasticity. While neural plasticity enables change to continue to occur, it also implies that the child remains vulnerable to the effects of harmful experiences in shaping brain development. Learning continues throughout the life span, although the rate of acquisition slows with increasing maturity. Since brain maturation is an orderly process, learning is initially a sequential process which relies on the development of prior skills for the acquisition of new ones. Moreover, the *nature* of what has previously been learnt will either shape or interfere with subsequent learning.

Implications of the process of brain development

The importance of experiences in infancy and early childhood is, therefore, clear but the mechanisms are complex. We need to consider both the effects of lack of provision of experiences, and the effects of particular undesirable, stressful or traumatic and neglectful experiences.

Extreme neglect

Neglect and failure of environmental stimulation during critical or sensitive periods of brain development may lead to permanent deficits in certain functions. Experience-expectant development has been especially well studied and found in visual and auditory function. The critical period for developing binocular vision ends at about six months. Irreversible reduction in visual acuity (amblyopia) occurs if an eye is deprived of visual input due, for instance, to a cataract or when vision in one eye is repressed in order to avoid double-vision (diplopia) caused by an uncorrected squint beyond the age of eight to ten years (Taylor & Taylor, 1979). Profoundly deaf children do not continue to vocalize in later infancy (Scarr, 1993) because auditory input fails to reach the appropriate brain area during its critical period. Serious deprivation of language in early life will lead to long-term deficits in speech perception and language development.

In the domain of interpersonal development, there is now evidence from work with adoptees from Romanian orphanages for a sensitive period for development of attachments which probably ends at about the age of three (O'Connor *et al.*, 2000) (see below). There are also now indicators suggesting a sensitive period for the development of affect regulation, particularly the regulation of arousal (see below). Other deficits in experience may be compensated for after infancy.

Undesirable, insensitive, and stressful—distorted experiences

Most of the harmful effects of dysfunctional early experience are due to the distortion of normal development rather than to the complete absence of aspects of experience at critical points. Early deleterious experiences can have significant negative effects on the developing brain that may be long-term (Nelson & Bosquet, 2000).

The frontal lobes are connected in a complex circuitry with the limbic system (particularly the amygdala) as well as with the parietal (somato–sensory) and temporal lobes. The frontal lobes play a major role in the expression and regulation of emotion. There are distinct differences between the activities of the left and right frontal lobes. The *left* frontal lobe is involved in *positive* affect including approach, joy, happiness, and interest. It is also specialized for maintaining continuity and stability of the person's interaction with the environment. In contrast, the *right* frontal lobe is involved in *negative* affect including withdrawal, fear, distress, sadness, anxiety, and disgust. The right frontal lobe regulates the processing of novel stimuli that disrupt ongoing activity, such as might occur during the expression of fear or distress (Dawson, 1994). It has been suggested that the left frontal lobe modulates the activity of the right frontal lobe and thereby negative affect (Davidson, 1994). Individual differences between right and left activation are (at least in part) related to experiential rather than to innate temperamental differences and can change in response to experience.

Affect regulation includes the modulation of internal feeling states and arousal, as well as the regulation of the intensity and duration of affect expression, according to the needs of the person at a particular time. There is an innate contribution to emotional reactivity and the capacity to regulate one's affect which is, however, poorly developed at birth. Face recognition develops very early in life, and from birth, through intimate face-to-face sensitive and vocal interaction, the mother who "for the developing infant (...) essentially *is* the environment" (Schore, 1994), begins to help the infant to regulate his/her affect by alleviating distress and reinforcing positive affect. This is a recursive reciprocal process whose efficacy for the infant's development depends on the mother's sensitivity and attunement (Stern, 1995) to the infant cues. This includes an accurate appraisal of the infant's feeling state, synchronicity with the infant and the appropriate intensity of the mother's response. Regulated affect allows the infant to engage in exploration of their environment and in learning.

Davidson (1994) has suggested that exposure of the young child to particular affective interactions could lead to enduring structural changes in the prefrontal brain with a change in the asymmetry between the two lobes, which would carry significant consequences for later behaviour and affect. This has been found in infants and young children of depressed mothers. The EEGs of the children show hyperactivation of the right frontal lobe (Jones *et al.*, 1997) and relatively decreased left frontal activity (Dawson *et al.*, 1997). It is possible to explain the evolution of these EEG changes on the basis of observations of the interactions between depressed mothers and their infants. These show the mothers to be negative, emotionally unavailable or unresponsive to the infant's communications and affective state, or out of synchrony and consequently intrusive with the infant, who becomes more aroused and distressed. These experiences lead to amplification of synapses and neuronal networks associated with negative affect, and the under-use and pruning of those involved in positive affect and approach behaviour. Infants are particularly susceptible to these effects between six and 18 months of age (Dawson *et al.*, 1994), suggesting a sensitive period for this aspect of frontal lobe development. Enduring changes have been found in their behaviour and emotional state, including social withdrawal, negativity and distress. Reduced cognitive verbal abilities in the pre-school years of boys, whose mothers had been depressed before the boys were 18 months old (Murray, 1997; Sinclair & Murray, 1998), have also been found.

Children who have been abused in early life have been found to have higher amplitude of ERPs when instructed to respond to angry, rather than happy, faces presented to them (Pollak *et al.*, 1997). Moreover, they have been found to interpret facial expressions which are ambiguously sad/angry or frightened/angry as angry. Moreover, both boys and girls who had been physically abused before the age of five years, have been found to be aggressive and have difficulty with externalizing behaviour and peer relationships in later childhood and into adolescence, even when the abuse had ceased. The implication is that being presented with negative affect carries a different meaning to maltreated children and elicits a physiologically measurable different response. For a child in danger, it is adaptive for their survival to construe possible signals of danger as such. This predisposition becomes maladaptive when used indiscriminately and outside abusive situations.

The stress response

The body's response to stress is a physiological coping response necessary for survival, and involves several body systems. They include the hypothalamic–pituitary–adrenal axis (HPA), the autonomic nervous system, the neurotransmitter system, and the immune system. There are individual variations in the threshold above which an individual perceives an experience to be stressful. These individual differences in stress responsiveness are partly innate (genetically determined) and partly based on prior experience. There are costs to the stress response, and individual children who are innately more reactive to stress are therefore more vulnerable to its consequences.

The end result of the HPA axis response to stress is the increased secretion of cortisol, and this response commences in early infancy. Serum cortisol acts in a number of different ways and on most tissues and organs. Its actions include suppressing the immune response, increasing the level of circulating glucose and dampening of fear responses to the stressor, as well as adverse effects on the hippocampus, which is particularly involved in the processing of memory for events. Children who show raised levels of cortisol during normal days at nursery, have greater difficulty in focusing and sustaining attention.

The response of the sympathetic nervous system to stress results in secretion of adrenaline and noradrenaline by the medulla of the adrenal gland. The effects of these hormones include raising the heart rate, blood pressure, sweating, and activation of the fight or flight response. There is also an increase in neurotransmitter secretion in the brain in response to stress, which includes noradrenaline and dopamine. Significantly raised levels of these neurotransmitters in the prefrontal cortex interfere with its functions (Arnsten, 1999) which include the planning and organizing of actions using "working memory" and the inhibiting of inappropriate responses and attention to distractions ("executive functions"), a disturbance not unlike Attention Deficit Hyperactivity Disorder (ADHD).

What are the specific effects on the developing child of early stressful events and activation of the stress response? Early stress which is mediated by the young child's interpersonal experiences is often the beginning of an enduring pattern, which may include neglect, abuse or exposure to inter-parental violence. The stressful experiences are, therefore, repeated. Predictability and a sense of control which are based on previous experience or sensitive preparation of the child, modulate the cortisol response to potentially threatening experiences (Gunnar & Barr, 1998). The infant's sense of predictability is entirely dependent on the primary caregiver's reliability. The only control which the (immobile) infant can exert is in the dyadic synchronous and reciprocal interactions with the mother and other primary carers. Both predictability and the sense of control are compromised in the face of abuse and neglect.

Children who have been abused and neglected have been found to show dysregulated cortisol responses as well as other evidence of neurobiological changes, alongside the well documented "mind" difficulties (Glaser, 2000). It is not, however, clear how these difficulties relate to the age and developmental stage of the child at the time when the maltreatment commenced. One recent study, showing some decrease in brain volume in children who had been abused and who suffered from post-traumatic stress disorder, found that the duration of the abuse was inversely related to the volume of their brains. This suggests that the reduction of brain volume might have been related to earlier onset of the abuse (De Bellis *et al.*, 1999).

Over activation of the stress response early in life with over-stimulation of the noradrenergic system may lead to a long lasting reactive repression of noradrenaline. "Normal" children show improvement with increasing age in their capacity to avoid responses which have negative consequences, mediated by nor-adrenaline in the brain. Children who have been abused show a diminished capacity to avoid these responses. This is postulated to be related to a diminished noradrenergic behavioural inhibition system (Mezzacappa *et al.*, 2001).

Attachment

Attachment is a biological instinct (Bowlby, 1969). Attachment behaviour is defined as proximity-seeking behaviour by a dependent infant or child, when (s)he senses discomfort of any sort, which includes fear, pain, cold or hunger. The child seeks to get closer to the attachment figure (parent or primary carer) in the (innate) "belief" that the parent will deactivate the attachment system by removing or dealing with its cause, and restore the child's equanimity. The child requires the caregiver's response to be sensitive to the child's particular need, to be benign, appropriate in its intensity and for the responses to be predictable. On the basis of the nature and pattern of the mother's (or the primary caregiver(s)') responses to the child's attachment needs, the child constructs internal working models of self and parent (Bowlby, 1988). These models are beliefs of the child about her/himself and predictions about how the child will be treated by others.

There are well validated measures of the nature of infants' and young children's attachment organization, which begins to be formed from the middle of the first year of life. The child's attachment organization reflects the strategies which the child develops to deal with fear and discomfort in the light of the mother's responses and thus reflects the child's internal working models. Attachment security is measured in infancy and early childhood by the Strange Situation Test (Ainsworth *et al.*, 1978), which yields a secure category (B), two insecure categories—anxious/avoidant (A) and anxious/resistant (C)—and a disorganized/disoriented category (D) (Main & Solomon, 1990). The D category has been repeatedly found in association with physical and emotional abuse and neglect.

The long-term outcome of disorganized attachment

Disorganized attachment is believed to be the infant's and young child's response to an attachment figure who is the cause of the distress, who is frightening and who is unable to deactivate the attachment system, and instead either escalates it by an angry response to the child's need, or withdraws from the child when the child seeks proximity in distress (Solomon & George, 1999). Long-term follow-up studies of children who had shown disorganized attachment in the early years continues to show a likelihood for this pattern either to endure or to evolve into a compulsive-caregiving or compulsive-punitive relationship between the child and the mother. A significant majority of these children show behaviour problems in the pre-school and later school years and more emotional and behavioural difficulties in adolescence. These difficulties are a reflection of a maladaptive process of development which has evolved following early experiences.

Neurobiological correlates of attachment

On the basis of empirical evidence, Gunnar (1998) postulates that a secure attachment relationship buffers or protects the developing brain from the potential deleterious effects of elevated cortisol on the brain during the protracted post-natal brain development. She has shown this in a number of situations in which secure infants respond to stressful stimuli without elevation of cortisol.

Children adopted from institutions

Children who have experienced extreme privation in institutions in which they were placed in early life, for instance in Romania, and who have been adopted subsequently, have been extensively followed up. They have offered a unique opportunity for the study of the effects of early stress as well as severe neglect. It has been found that many (although not all) of those children placed in adoptive families after the age of six months have not shown the formation of attachments. This has been expressed by a lack of differentiation between adults, lack of checking back with the (adoptive) parent in anxiety-provoking situations, and a clear indication that the child would go off with a stranger. The likelihood of this disinhibited attachment disorder (ICD 10) developing is related to the length of time the children had spent in the institution rather than the time spent in their adoptive family (O'Connor et al., 2000). For these children, security or insecurity of attachment is, therefore, not measurable. These findings indicate the likelihood of critical period for the formation of an attachment. This is in contrast to a group of children who were raised in institutions offering good care and stimulation, but no attachment figure. Those children who were adopted before the age of two were able, over time, to form attachments with their adoptive parents (Hodges, 1996).

Conclusions

Although there is evidence that some deficits of experience during critical periods can lead to the absence of development of some functions, this is rarely the case in human infancy. Sensitive periods are commoner and a young child who lacks appropriate interactions during particular stages of development, such as the opportunity for forming an attachment before the age of three, may not develop the normal aspects of these functions. However, harm most commonly follows stressful, inappropriate early experiences which are incorporated into the neural networks at the time of synapse formation, as part of experience-dependent brain maturation and the effects of the stress response on the developing brain. Although later experience will be incorporated and added on to past connections, they cannot undo established patterns, only modify them over time. Moreover, significant changes in the developing child requires change in the interpersonal relationships with him or her. In younger children, these rely on changes in the interactions with the child and their parents and other significant persons in their immediate environment. The primary focus for early inter-vention, therefore, needs to be with the primary carers and the carer–child relationship (Osofsky & Fitzgerald, 2000; Zeanah, 2000). Later, direct therapeutic work with the child who is in a more optimal environment will also be required. The most effective intervention is undoubtedly the prevention, or very early recogni-tion, of inappropriate parent–child interactions when effects on the young child may not yet be apparent.

References

Ainsworth, M., Blehar, M., Waters, E., & Wall, S. (1978). *Patterns of Attachment: A Psychological Study of the Strange Situation*. Hillsdale, NJ: Erlbaum.

Arnsten, A. (1999). Development of the cerebral cortex: XIV. Stress impairs prefrontal cortical function. *Journal of the American Academy of Child & Adolescent Psychiatry*, 38: 220–222.

Bowlby, J. (1969). *Attachment*. Harmondsworth: Penguin Books.

Bowlby, J. (1988). *A Secure Base*. London: Routledge.

Bownds, M. D. (1999). *The Biology of Mind.* Bethseda: Fitzgerald Science Press.

Courchesne, E., Chisum, H., & Townsend, J. (1994). Neural activity-dependent brain changes in development: implications for psychopathology. *Development and Psychopathology, 6:* 697–722.

Davidson, R. (1994). Asymmetric brain function, affective style and psychopathology: the role of early experience and plasticity. *Development and Psychopathology, 6:* 741–758.

Dawson, G. (1994). Frontal electroencephalographic correlates of individual differences in emotion expression in infants: a brain systems perspective on emotion. In: N. Fox (Ed.), *Emotion Regulation: Behavioural and biological considerations. Monographs of the Society for Research in Child Development, 59:* 135–151.

Dawson, G., Hessl, D., & Frey, K. (1994). Social influences on early developing biological and behavioural systems related to risk for affective disorder. *Development and Psychopathology, 6:* 759–779.

Dawson, G., Frey, K., Panagiotides, H., Osterling, J., & Hessl, D. (1997). Infants of depressed mothers exhibit atypical frontal brain activity: a replication and extension of previous findings. *Journal of Child Psychology and Psychiatry, 38:* 179–186.

De Bellis, M., Keshavan, M., Clark, D., Casey, B., Giedd, J., Boring, A., Frustaci, K., & Ryan, N. (1999b). Developmental traumatology Part II: Brain development. *Biological Psychiatry, 45:* 1271–1284.

Fitzgerald, H. E., Puttler, L. I., Mun, E. U., & Zucker, R. A. (2000). Prenatal and postnatal exposure to parental alcohol use and abuse. In: J. D. Osofsky & H. E. Fitzgerald (Eds.), *WAIMH Handbook of Infant Mental Health. Volume 4. Infant Mental Health in Groups at High Risk.* New York: John Wiley & Sons.

Glaser, D. (2000). Child abuse and neglect and the brain—a review. *Journal of Child Psychology and Psychiatry, 41*(1): 97–116.

Greenough, W., & Black, J. (1992). Induction of brain structure by experience: substrate for cognitive development. In: M. R. Gunnar & C. A. Nelson (Eds.), *Minnesota Symposia on Child Psychology 24: Developmental Behavioural Neuroscience* (pp. 155–200). Hillsdale NJ: Lawrence Erlbaum.

Gunnar, M. (1998). Quality of early care and buffering of neuroendocrine stress reactions: potential effects on the developing human brain. *Preventative Medicine, 27:* 208–211.

Gunnar, M., & Barr, R. (1998). Stress, early brain development and behaviour. *Infants and Young Children, 11:* 1–14.

Hodges, J. (1996). The natural history of early non-attachment. In: B. Bernstein & J. Brannon (Eds.), *Children: Research and Policy*. London: Taylor & Francis.

Jones, N., Field, T., & Fox. (1997). EEG stability in infants/children of depressed mothers. *Child Psychiatry and Human Development*, 28: 59–70.

Main, M., & Solomon, J. (1990). Procedures for identifying infants as disorganized/disoriented during the Ainsworth strange situation. In: M. Greenberg, D. Cicchetti & E. Cummings (Eds.), *Attachment in the preschool years* (pp. 121–160). Chicago: University of Chicago Press.

Mezzacappa, E., Kindlon, D., & Earls, F. (2001). Child abuse and performance task assessments of executive functions in boys. *Journal of Child Psychology and Psychiatry*, 42: 1041–1048.

Murray, L. (1997). Postpartum depression and child development. *Psychological Medicine*, 27, 253–260.

Nelson, C. (1999). How important are the first 3 years of life? *Applied Developmental Science*, 3: 235–238.

Nelson, C., & Bloom, E. (1997). Child development and neuroscience. *Child Development*, 68: 970–987.

Nelson, C., & Bosquet, M. (2000). Neurobiology of fetal and infant development: implications for infant mental health. In: C. H. Zeanah (Ed.), *Handbook of Infant Mental Health* (2nd edn) (pp. 37–59). New York: The Guilford Press.

O'Connor, T., Rutter, M., & the English and Romanian Adoptees Study Team. (2000). Attachment disorder behaviour following early severe deprivation: extension and longitudinal follow-up. *Journal of the American Academy of Child and Adolescent Psychiatry*, 39: 703–712.

Osofsky, J. D., & Fitzgerald, H. E. (Eds.) (2000). *WAIMH Handbook of Infant Mental Health. Perspectives on Infant Mental Health; Early Intervention, Evaluation and Assessment; Parenting and Child Care; Infant Mental Health in Groups at High Risk*. New York: John Wiley & Sons.

Pollak, S., Cicchetti, D., Klorman, R., & Brumaghim, T. (1997). Cognitive brain event-related potentials and emotion processing in maltreated children. *Child Development*, 68: 773–787.

Quay, H. (1993). The psychobiology of undersocialized aggressive conduct disorder: a theoretical perspective. *Development and Psychopathology*, 5: 165–180.

Rogeness, G., Javors, M., & Pliszka, S. (1992). Neurochemistry and child and adolescent psychiatry. *Journal of the American Academy of Child & Adolescent Psychiatry*, 31: 765–781.

Scarr, S. (1993). Biological and cultural diversity: The legacy of Darwin for development. *Child Development, 64*: 1333–1353.

Schore, A. (1994). *Affect Regulation and the Origin of the Self: The Neurobiology of Emotional Development*. New Jersey: Lawrence Erlbaum.

Shonkoff, J., & Phillips, D. (2000). *From Neurons to Neighborhoods*. Washington, DC: National Academy Press.

Sinclair, D., & Murray, L. (1998). The effect of postnatal depression on children's adjustment to school. *British Journal of Psychiatry, 172*: 58–63.

Solomon, J., & George, C. (1999). The place of disorganization in attachment theory. In: J. Solomon & C. George (Eds.), *Attachment Disorganization*. New York: Guilford Press.

Stern D. (1995). *The Interpersonal World of the Infant*. New York: Basic Books.

Taylor, V., & Taylor, D. (1979). Critical period for deprivation amblyopia in children. *Transactions of the Ophthalmological Societies of the UK, 99*: 432–439.

Zeanah, C. H. (Ed.) (2000). *Handbook of Infant Mental Health* (2nd edn). New York: Guilford Press.

Zeanah, C. H., Boris, N. W., & Larrieu, J. A. (1997). Infant development and developmental risk: a review of the past ten years. *Journal of the American Academy of Child and Adolescent Psychiatry, 36*: 165–178.

CHAPTER FIVE

Emotion, false beliefs, and the neurobiology of intuition

Oliver Turnbull

I t seems that every contemporary piece written on the relationship between neuroscience and psychotherapy should begin with a statement to the effect that we are living in an incredible period—a period in which two polar extremes, two separate views of the world, are finally coming together. Experimental psychology (which for our purposes can be regarded as having transformed itself into modern cognitive neuroscience) has long stressed the importance of "rationality" in mental life. However, as Panksepp (2000) points out: "The one thing all might agree upon is that the experimental psychology that emerged during the past century has yet to give us a lasting or coherent science of the human mind" (p. 240). The problem arose because experimental psychology (read: neuroscience) has held an interest in just *one* part of the mental apparatus. These days we call that part "cognition"—so that by the end of the twentieth century the neuroscience of the mind was a *cognitive* neuroscience.

Simultaneously, psychotherapists have been interested in an entirely different aspect of the mental apparatus, stressing the importance of affect, irrationality, and intuition. In the last decade or so, we have seen a coming together of these two fields (or groups of fields). This shift has not arisen primarily because the psychotherapies have changed in any dramatic way. However, neuroscience certainly *has* changed. Amongst other things, cognitive neuroscience has become interested in emotion, and that has led to all sorts of interesting developments—some of which form the basis of this paper.

At the beginning of this piece it seems appropriate to give a grand overview of some of the thinking of those of us involved in neuropsychoanalysis (most especially Mark Solms and Karen Kaplan-Solms)—without spending too much time on detail. This will allow me to outline our position on grand issues, such as the neurobiology of the internal world (see Kaplan-Solms & Solms, 2000, or Solms & Turnbull, 2002 for more detail). This paper will then discuss false beliefs: people who believe things that are patently not true about the external world and whom, when confronted on these beliefs, argue against the evidence of external reality. In doing so, I will suggest a possible role for affect in false belief, and I will suggest that affect is really much more important for cognition than many people believe—certainly than most cognitive neuroscientists believe. In the process, the paper will discuss some data from our group.

Two perspectives on the mental apparatus

I would like to begin with a quote from Sigmund Freud:

> There is no choice for us in psychoanalysis but to assert that mental processes are in themselves unconscious and to liken the perceptions of them by means of consciousness to the perception of the external world by means of sense organs. [Freud, 1915, p. 171]

The first part of this quote, about the importance of the unconscious and the magnitude of its influence on mental life, is not especially important for this paper. I think that virtually all the readers of this piece more or less agree with that proposition. Many cognitive psychologists are arriving at this conclusion too (e.g. Bargh & Chartland, 1999). However, the second part of the quote is either something that one takes for granted, or is something people are *very* unhappy to agree with. The latter part of the quote suggests that the perception of the internal world can be likened to the perception of the external world, by means of "sense organs". What do we mean, then, by sense organs? For more detail I highly recommend Mark Solms' (1997a) original paper on this argument (see also Solms and Turnbull, 2002, Chapters 1–3 review), but I will try and briefly outline some of the core issues relating to the quote, and its relationship to the general field of psychotherapy. Everyone is familiar with the classic five Aristotelian senses: smell, taste, touch, hearing, and vision. One might add them up in a different way (for example by adding vestibular sensation) and perhaps reach a number different from five,[1] but everyone agrees that these senses constitute various ways of observing the external world. Simultaneously, there is *another* world of which the developing mind must become aware—a world constituted by the *inside* of the body. This is the world of the viscera—made up of a number of different organs: which run respiration, blood supply, digestion, and other processes vital for the body's survival (and for the continued survival of our species). These "internal" processes are represented in the brain, primarily, in the brainstem structures that are discussed in more detail in Doug Watt's chapter in this book.

This is a world of fluctuations in glucose levels, and variations in core body temperature, that represent the essence of the motivational drives. The extent to which we are able to meet these drives in early development (and hence keep ourselves alive and satisfied) forms the essence of what we might regard as the internal world. However, the classic psychoanalytic position (and perhaps also the modern neuroscientific position) is that we cannot experience the drives directly (see Panksepp, 1998). The drives are extraordinarily important for mental life, but somehow we can never directly *know* them. Indeed, we can never directly know objects in the *external* world either. I can never truly know whether this table is real. I can touch it, and look at it, but I cannot know its essence. For example, the fact that the whirring of electrons around atomic nuclei means that this apparently solid table consists mostly of empty space, or the fact that its brown appearance results from an amalgamation of three classes of electromagnetic radiation detector in my retina, which I perceive as colour. Intellectually, I can understand all of these things, and I can know more about this external world by the use of additional perceptual aids (such as microscopes and telescopes). However, I am always bounded by the filter of my perceptual organs.

Similarly, we cannot directly know our drives. However, we can perceive them by means of special sense organs that are directed internally. These internally directed sense organs have been labelled by us as "emotions": which we experience as feelings of anger, fear, sadness, and happiness etc. Thus, for Freud, the drives are perceived as fluctuations in emotion systems. Satisfaction of the drives (or objects linked with the drives through experience) leads to feelings of pleasure, and frustration of the drives leads to its opposite. Thus, we might well say that affect is an internally directed perceptual modality—allowing us to perceive the essential (visceral) part of the world that keeps us alive. We might also say that the neurosciences have been focusing on the mental apparatus by observing it through the *external* sense organs. What you see when you look at the mental apparatus through the external sense organs is a *brain*—something you can see and touch (and taste and smell and hear if you were that way inclined). However, readers of this book are concerned with another class of experience, a class of experience achieved when we look internally, and are concerned with the subjective. Again, we can perceive the mental apparatus (the *same* mental apparatus), by virtue of looking at it through a different set of sense organs. Here, it *appears* to be a different thing altogether: it is no longer a brain, it is a mind.

This is the general philosophical position of our group in neuropsychoanalysis, and it stands in a very interesting relationship to developments in modern neuroscience. For example, Antonio Damasio (1994, 2000) appears to have rediscovered Freud's view of the dual nature of consciousness. Damasio argues that consciousness is the relationship between two great classes of knowledge: on the one hand, we see (and hear etc.) things in the outside world with our external sense organs: for example a dog. Simultaneously, we experience an emotion through the second class of sense organ: our emotions. Our emotional response is built from a lifetime's experience of the emotional consequences of encountering dogs, including encountering different types of dog (dobermann versus poodle), under different circumstances (family pet versus guard dog). Perhaps this is a large and dangerous-looking dog? Perhaps you meet this dog in a circumstance where you have previous experience of bad encounters with dogs (say, late at night)? Emotion learning systems can "calculate" (i.e. form a weighted sum) what the likely outcome of such a meeting will be: so that the emotion you experience in a risky context is anxiety. Damasio calls such emotional experiences "somatic markers". They are the psychological representatives of what has happened to your body during previous encounters of this sort.[2] Subjective experience consists, therefore, of a momentary relation between experiencing an object in the outside world, and knowing how we *feel* about that object—a position quite compatible with Freud's. Damasio was unaware of Freud's attitude towards this problem until Mark Solms pointed Freud's position out to him a few years ago. In print Damasio has generously mentioned that, "... we can say that Freud's insights on the nature of consciousness are commensurate with the most advanced contemporary neuroscience views". (Damasio, 1999, p. 38).

Where in the brain?

If we are interested in internally directed perceptual modality, then *where* in the brain should we be looking for this mysterious internal world? Certainly the cerebral hemispheres, sophisticated though they are, are not the right place to look. Doug Watt's chapter outlines the neurobiology of a number of core structures that lie not on the outer surface of the cerebral hemisphere, but deep within the brain. These subcortical structures are vital to the internal world, and are of great complexity. We are particularly concerned here with *core* affect systems: which are found primarily in the upper parts of the brainstem, the hypothalamus, and in a variety of other nuclei (such as the amygdala) that lie in anterior temporal lobes and medial frontal lobes. I recommend Jaak Panksepp's (1998) excellent book for a comprehensive review of this complex topic.

However, in this chapter we will not be concerned with affect *per se*. Affect itself is vital to our discussion, but this piece is more concerned with the relationship between affect and cognition, in particular the potential role that affect has in shaping cognition. What I would particularly like to discuss is a part of the brain called the ventromesial frontal lobes (see *Figure 1*). These lie at the boundary between what was outlined earlier as the perceptual

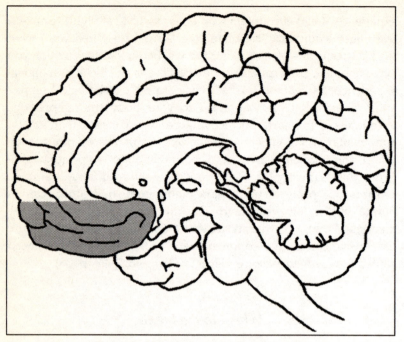

Figure 1. The ventromesial frontal lobes.

organs of the internal and the external worlds. The structures in the upper brainstem, hypothalamus, etc., form the core of our affect system, and hence are the perceptual organ(s) of the internal world. Cognition, crudely speaking, has its substrate in various parts of the cerebral hemispheres, and in some related subcortical structures. In particular, the primary substrate of "high-order" cognition (thinking, problem solving etc) in the human brain appears to be in the prefrontal cortex, especially in the dorso–lateral prefrontal cortex. Key emotion systems appear to achieve access to cognition by virtue of fibre pathways that travel from the core emotion systems forwards *through* the ventromesial frontal lobes, towards the dorso–lateral prefrontal cortex.

An outline of this paper

For these reasons, we should be especially interested in the ventromesial frontal lobes, not because of their role in emotion, but for their role in allowing emotion to make a contribution to cognition. In this paper I will present several lines of evidence in order to support this argument. Firstly, I will discuss a group of neurological patients who have focal lesions in the ventromesial frontal lobes. It is clear, from a variety of lines of work, that a lesion to this brain site has terrible consequences for cognition. "Intelligence" (of the sort measured by standard intelligence tests) remains more or less unchanged in such patients. However, it appears that such intellectual abilities are no longer very "smart" without the input from emotion-learning systems. This paper will briefly discuss the empirical evidence that supports that particular claim.

Having talked about under-activation, and of not having *enough* affect in cognition, I will then present evidence to suggest that *over*-activation of these systems, i.e. an excessive influence of affect over cognition, is also disadvantageous for the mental apparatus. In this case, I will argue, it produces false beliefs, and an inability to properly evaluate the evidence from the external world.

Basic emotion systems

This paper will not discuss affect systems and their architecture in any great detail. Doug Watt's chapter does a good job of that, and I highly recommend Jaak Panksepp's *Affective Neuroscience* (1998) for more information. However, I do want to highlight one emotion system, which we will return to later. This system is one that Panksepp calls the SEEKING system (see *Figure 2*)—though it was originally known (inaccurately) as a "reward" system, and then by the accurate (but long-winded) term "curiosity–interest–expectancy" system. This affective system imbues objects in the outside world with intrinsic interest, and makes us want to go out and explore them. It underlies much of the foundation of play and curiosity in humans.

Its pharmacological basis is mediated by dopamine, in particular the D2 system that psychiatrists are so well aware of in relation to schizophrenia. We will return to the psychiatric issue, and to the treatment of schizophrenia, later in this paper. Also, as perhaps many readers will be aware, the neurobiology of recreational drug abuse is broadly compatible with the neurobiology of emotion, and

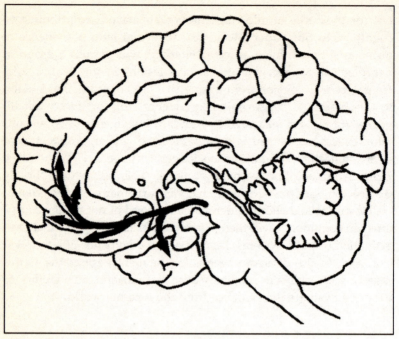

Figure 2. The SEEKING system.

so it is interesting for us to know which recreational drugs seem to modify the operation of this affective "seeking" system. Cocaine and the amphetamines are the principal agents of interest, though there are quite a few others (including nicotine and caffeine) that will modify the system with less spectacular effects. Thus, when you take cocaine it imbues you with an increased sense of interest in the world, and provides objects in the world with additional intrinsic interest—so that you have the energy to pursue whatever interests you. Of course, these days young people go dancing under the influence of such drugs. However, when Freud originally introduced cocaine to the medical community, in the 1880s, he was fond of it because it helped him to work late into the night—which probably suggests more about Sigmund Freud than it does about cocaine. Stimulating this system provides us with increased interest in objects, but it doesn't specify *which* objects, and people are interested in different things. We should also note that this effect only lasts for a while, of course, until the pharmacology of the system has been saturated. When the system has been depleted, the user feels inert and listless. There are also issues of tolerance (discussed below) which mean that such drugs do not, of course, only have the positive-sounding effects already mentioned.

Damage to the ventromesial frontal lobes

To turn from the matter of core emotion systems to the issue of the role of affect upon cognition, we should again focus on the ventromesial frontal lobes—and the ways that they can be damaged. There are a variety of ways in which the ventromesial frontal lobes can become injured. In modern clinical practice, high-speed motor vehicle accidents are undoubtedly the most common cause of such damage. Patients with such lesions represent a great paradox, which neuropsychologists have struggled with for decades. This is because they have substantial lesions to their frontal lobes, an area of enormous growth in recent evolutionary history, and long considered to be the most important, the most "human", part of the mental apparatus. The paradox is why patients with lesions here should look so "normal". Principal amongst the problems to be explained is the fact that they often do very well on intelligence tests, but fail in everyday life. They choose unsuitable friends, enter inadvisable relationships and engage in ill-advised activities (Bechara *et al.*, 1994). This behaviour rapidly leads to financial losses, career termination, and loss of affection of family and friends. Over a number of decades neuropsychologists have attempted to develop tests of these lost abilities: the so called frontal or executive tasks. We hoped that such patients would fail the tasks—so that neuropsychologists could measure the thing that was so obviously wrong with them. Some "frontal" patients *would* do badly, but they never seemed to do badly on the *same* tasks, and some obviously impaired patients would do well on almost *all* the frontal tasks. It is a frustrating circumstance for a clinical neuropsychologist—*knowing* there is something wrong with your patients, but being unable to measure it.

The classical case in this area is Phineas Gage. Many people are now familiar with the case (first reported in 1848 by Harlow). Gage was working in the North Eastern United States, on a railway. An explosive charge went off by mistake, and a tamping rod passed, very rapidly by virtue of the explosion, up through the upper cheek bone and through his ventromesial frontal lobes. The classical description of Phineas Gage uses Harlow's rather archaic language—but the clinical picture remains clear today:

> he is fitful, irreverent, ... impatient of restraint or advice when it conflicts with his desires, at times pertinaciously obstinate, yet capricious and vacillating, devising many plans of future operation which are no sooner arranged than they are abandoned. ... In this regard his mind was radically changed, so decidedly that his friends and acquaintances said that he was no longer Gage. [Harlow, 1868, p. 327]

The implications of findings of this sort are quite frightening. We all consider ourselves to be charming, friendly, socially appropriate individuals. However, if any of us were to have ventromesial frontal lobe lesions (for example in a serious car accident), our friends might judge us no longer to be the person that we previously were, and they might well want to spend less time with us. I must confess that my experience with neurological and neurosurgical patients of this type means that I drive quite cautiously on the roads, and I would advise others to do so too.

The Iowa Gambling Task

As I discussed above, there was a long period in which neuropsychologists had difficulty finding a test on which this class of neurological patient would selectively fail. In the early 1990s, Antonio Damasio's group described the "Iowa Gambling Task" (Bechara et al., 1994)—which has revolutionized the field. In the task the subject is faced with four decks of cards, and asked to choose any deck, in any sequence. They win or lose money with each card turn. Some decks have frequent high gains, but also occasional substantial losses. Sustained playing of these decks leads to overall financial loss. Other decks have more modest payouts, but lead to small infrequent losses, so that sustained playing of the decks leads to small but consistent gains. These are less exciting to play—more akin to "paying your pension" sorts of decks, suitable for those who favour low-risk strategies . The game is complex, and participants do not appear, subjectively, to understand the contingencies of the game (Damasio, 1994). Nevertheless, participants quite rapidly develop a "feeling" about which decks are good or bad, which probably derives from small activations of the autonomic nervous system in the period immediately *preceding* the choice of a high-risk "bad" deck. This autonomic activation, a measurable physiological correlate of emotion, can be tracked using Galvanic Skin Response equipment. This finding is true of more or less *all* neurologically normal individuals—so that everybody starts on the riskier slightly higher payout decks, because they initially seem like a good idea. Gradually, people (even those who regard themselves as "gamblers") move towards decks where, on average, you win rather than lose.

In the classic version you start with a $2000 of monopoly-type money, and you win or lose a few tens or hundreds of dollars. We have tried both that system and much smaller amounts of real money, which appears to make no real difference to the task (Bowman & Turnbull, in press). However, this makes the task a little more ecologically valid, allowing us to work on some patient populations (schizophrenics, for example) in whom small amounts of money seem to be more reinforcing than large amounts of monopoly-type money. Indeed, we have collected some data (Turnbull *et al.*, in press) which suggests that without such explicit reward and punishment relationships, the game is too complex for people to follow, and they cannot learn the task.

I should also stress the point that this learning is happening outside of conscious awareness. We recently tested a patient who was one of the most densely amnesic people that I have ever encountered. He became amnesic following (life-saving) surgery on a brain tumour. Like all densely amnesic subjects, he can remember more or less nothing that happened more than a minute or two ago. In fact, it was very difficult to test him on the Gambling Task for this reason. We explained the rules to him at the beginning. Then he would turn two or three cards over, playing the game normally, then say: "Can you explain the rules to me again?" It took literally hours to test him. When he left the room, and a minute or two had elapsed, he could not report that he had been doing the Gambling Task, or indeed any other psychological test. However, he did seem to retain some *implicit* awareness of our testing. On one occasion he said, conspiratorially, to Mark Solms (who was never involved in testing him) something to the effect that: "I want to tell you something interesting. There seems to some illegal gambling going on around here ...". On another occasion, he walked into the room after a break in testing and said, "I think there's some gambling going on here", and made a "slot machine" arm-pulling movement. Clearly he was (at some level) aware of the gambling *concept*, but only well enough to retrieve the type of gambling that most easily springs to mind (a slot machine), rather than our task (a type of gambling that no one encounters in everyday life). The key point is that, in spite of his dense amnesia, he shows improvement on the Iowa Gambling Task, to a level not much worse than controls. He is consciously unaware of performing the task, but unconscious (implicit) emotion learning systems appear to be functioning at normal, or near normal, levels.

What about patients with ventromesial frontal lesions? Of course, no one can test Phineas Gage, but a number of patients with ventromesial frontal lesions have been described in the more recent literature. Probably the most famous is EVR, who was reported in the middle 1980s, again by Damasio's group. Patients of this sort have now also been tested on the Gambling Task, with the attendant physiological measures (Galvanic Skin Response). It has become clear that *core* affect systems are still intact in such patients. When they turn over a bad deck, they experience a large GSR response, just as anybody else does. Thus, they still experience emotion. The key feature of interest, however, is the ability to have an "advance warning" of a bad deck, which develops in the neurologically normal in the first few dozen trials. This ability to know that you are *going* to choose a bad outcome deck—before you have chosen it—does not develop in these neurological patients. As a result, they begin on the same high-risk decks as everybody else, but they remain there. This failure to predict that particular decisions might result in poor outcomes seems to be the basis for the unfortunate decisions that they make in everyday life—meaning that the Iowa Gambling Task can tap a set of psychological processes (the role of affect in cognition) that other so-called "executive" tasks do not.

In summary, Damasio's Iowa group claims that people use emotion learning systems in performing "cognitive" tasks. This sort of argument will probably come as no surprise to those in the psychotherapeutic community—though no doubt the core finding would be phrased differently. Clinicians are well aware that we experience the affective consequences of our actions, and that well-adjusted individuals learn on the basis of this experience. They also know that some individuals stubbornly fail to learn from negative experiences, and often repeat the same sorts of errors. However, it is clearly of great importance that neuroscience has developed a reliable way of measuring these phenomena, and that it understands something of their neurobiological basis.

A further point is that these sorts of data suggest that we can develop an understanding of that most remarkable of things—a neurobiology of intuition (see Solms & Turnbull, 2002; Turnbull & Solms, in press). What we have here are emotion learning systems, typically operating outside of conscious awareness, which we are capable of drawing upon—if we are prepared to use this class of knowledge. It is, for want of a better phrase, the ability to "listen to your feelings". Further, there seem to be some neurological patients who are not able to do this. Apart from one brief mention of this idea (Damasio, 1994, pp. 187–189) there is otherwise no mention by Damasio's group that their work might represent the investigation of the neurobiological substrate of intuition. However, phrased in this way, some work on "gambling", which would otherwise sound rather uninteresting, is clearly of great interest to the psychotherapeutic community.

Acquired sociopathy

There have also been, in the last few years, some interesting suggestions about the role of the ventromesial frontal lobes in childhood. This work is based on patients injured in serious falls or car accidents—where the injury occurred under two years of age (Anderson *et al.*, 1999). Unsurprisingly, because of lesions to their ventromesial frontal lobes, these individuals behave much like the adult patients described above. Thus, they consistently do badly in relationships, their general social interactions are poor, and their career progression is dreadful. This aspect of their presentation comes as no real surprise to us. However, there is an *additional* factor which appears in these neurological patients, in that they fail to develop some other core psychological abilities. In particular, they seem to lack empathy, and on formal tests of social and moral judgement and reasoning they do very badly. The claim has been made that these represent instances of "acquired sociopathy". A quote from the Anderson paper gives something of a flavour for such patients. Their case was a young woman who would have met many of the criteria for conduct disorder, from their case description. One of the many things that she did, during extraordinarily wild teenage years, was to have unprotected sex. As a result she fell pregnant and had a child. The description of her parenting runs as follows: "There was no evidence that she experienced empathy, and her maternal behaviour was marked by a dangerous insensitivity to the infant's needs" (Anderson *et al.*, 1999).

These are people who become sociopathic not by virtue of poor environmental circumstances—in other words it has nothing to do with non-optimal attachment relationships, as sometimes occurs in dysfunctional families. Here the primary cause is the absence of the neurological structures underpinning the ability to develop empathy. Alan Schore's (1994) book offers a comprehensive review of the importance of the ventromesial frontal lobes for affect regulation, and in these cases of early childhood head injury we see the long-term consequences for development, when affect-regulation is disrupted for neurological reasons.

Of course, no sensible psychologist would imagine that every case of sociopathy is caused by a ventromesial frontal lesion in childhood. In all likelihood, acquired brain injury is a minor cause of sociopathy. Nevertheless, these findings give us some idea of the "scene of action" in this disorder. In addition, we know that, for normal development, one needs *more* than that the basic neurobiology should be present in the developing brain. A central tenet of all psychotherapies is that the developing individual should be surrounded by a stable and reliable socio-emotional environment during the formative years. In this context, there is also some functional imaging work investigating the size of the frontal lobes in the psychopaths, which suggests that they have smaller than average frontal lobe volume (Raine *et al.*, 2000), which probably points as much to "nurture-based" accounts as those relating to acquired brain injury.

Too much intuition?

Thus far, I have argued that affect based knowledge is vitally important for cognition. If it is so very important then perhaps we should get as much of it as we can? In this context, we should ask: "Can you ever have too much intuition?". There is reasonable evidence to support the claim that excessive dominance of affective systems is *not* beneficial for an optimally functioning mental life, which suggests that we need some kind of balance between affect systems and cognition—an argument that seems compatible with classical thinking in psychoanalysis, and throughout the psychotherapies.

There are three classes of knowledge that I would like to bring to bear to support this claim. This chapter will only briefly cover the first two: psychosis and dreaming. The chapter will then spend a little bit more time on confabulation in neurological patients—a topic closer to my scientific home territory.

Schizophrenia, and the neurobiology of affect systems

One of the most important things we know about the neurobiology of schizophrenia is that so called "antipsychotic" medications (also known as neuroleptics, or major tranquillizers) target dopamine systems. I recommend Snyder (1999) for a readable account of this complex field—though information is also available in any basic psychopharmacology text. The finding that dopamine antagonists treat schizophrenia forms the basis of the well-known "dopamine" theory of schizophrenia. Specifically, these agents all target the so-called second, or D2, dopamine system.[3] In fact, we have known since the 1970s that the size of the recommended clinical dose is directly proportional to the extent to which any given neuroleptic agent binds to D2 receptors. Of great interest to us as psychologists, though this fact is typically not mentioned in the pharmacological literature, is that the system known as D2 to psychiatrists is also an *affect* system. Indeed, it is the "curiosity–interest–expectancy", or SEEKING system described by Panksepp. It seems that, in some way which we are not yet able to explain properly, over-activation of this affect system may be responsible for false beliefs (i.e. the positive symptoms of schizophrenia, which are the only aspects of the disorder treated successfully by the neuroleptics).

There is additional evidence in relation to this system, that comes not from people with florid schizophrenia, but from people with stimulant psychoses. If one takes too much cocaine or amphetamines (which promote D2 operation) over a sustained period of time (where one becomes tolerant, and requires larger doses), then one develops a stimulant psychosis. In the earliest stages it presents simply as a mild suspiciousness, but with increasing dosage levels one develops a frankly paranoid set of delusions—apparently indistinguishable from paranoid schizophrenia proper. The treatment, as one might guess, is intravenous injection of the neuroleptics. These lower the operation of this dopamine system, and apparently within minutes the psychotic episode is resolved. On a similar basis one can trigger a florid psychotic episode in a schizophrenic who is otherwise in remission, merely by giving them a small amount of amphetamine. Again, the classic work (done in the 1970s) shows that it takes only minutes to induce the psychotic episode, if the drug is given intravenously (see Snyder, 1999, Chapter 5).

This line of evidence suggests that over-activation of an emotion system seems, in some way, to produce the "false belief" (positive symptom) aspects of schizophrenia. Alas, the literature that shows that this dopamine (affect) system is directly related to schizo-phrenia does not appear to offer any account that clearly explains *why* over-activation of an affect system produces false beliefs. This issue will be addressed later in this chapter.

Dreaming, and the neurobiology of affect systems

The second class of false beliefs to be discussed, albeit very briefly, is related to the neurobiology of dreaming. This field has moved on dramatically in recent years, partly as a result of Mark Solms' work (Solms, 1997b, 2000; see Solms & Turnbull, 2002, Chapter 6 for a review). There appear to be a wide variety of cortical lesion sites that have more or less *no* effect on the dreaming process. However, lesions to the ventromesial frontal lobes have a catastrophic effect on the dream process, and lead to total cessation of dreaming. Thus, people who have previously dreamt every night, say, "you know it's the strangest thing Doctor, but ever since I had my stroke I just don't have any dreams any more". In some cases, particularly the unilateral cases, they recover dreaming. But some people, it seems, never dream again.

The classical orbito–medial leucotomy literature is also of some interest in this regard. We all recall that, before neuroleptics were widely introduced (in the late 1950s and 1960s) one of the treatments for schizophrenia was a *modified* version of prefrontal lobotomy. After the initial introduction of the traditional (large and crude) lobotomies, neurosurgeons started to target, after a trial and error search, precisely the same anatomical sites that have just been described in relation to the pharmacology of schizophrenia and the neurobiology of dreaming. Thus, they began to lesion *only* the ventromesial frontal lobes, in a procedure called an orbito–medial leucotomy. Indeed, it might be argued that neuroleptics are merely targeting this region pharmacologically, where the same effect had previously been produced surgically—so that modern neuroleptic medications are merely "chemical leucotomies" (Panksepp, 1985). As regards dreaming, it turns out that a very successful predicator of whether the surgeons had targeted the correct region to treat the schizophrenia in this surgical procedure was loss of dreams. Thus, in a large proportion of schizophrenic patients who had undergone the modified form of leucotomy, the patients no longer dreamt. More importantly, the non-dreamers were more likely to have been the "good outcome" patients (Solms, 1997b). There is also some pharmacological evidence that over-activation of these systems, which occurs as a side effect of taking L-dopa for the treatment of Parkinson's disease, produces excessively vivid dreams. In summary, functions of the ventromesial frontal lobes seem closely tied to those of dreaming—and dreaming is an exceptional instance of false beliefs experienced by neurologically normal individuals.

Confabulation, and the neurobiology of affect systems

The third class of evidence that this paper will bring to bear is from patients with focal neurological lesions. There are many neurological patients who hold false beliefs—and who are sometimes described as confabulating. They may well hold these beliefs for a range of different reasons, often highly specific in their scope: for example, for parts of the body, time, or place, including famous types such as Capgras' delusion, which occurs both in neurological and psychiatric patients. Patients with Capgras claim that: "this person looks like my husband, sounds like my husband, and dresses like my husband, but actually he's an impostor". These classes of delusional belief are found after a variety of lesion sites, but patients with medial frontal lesions form the clearest examples. The false beliefs are held with great tenacity. These are not instances of delirium, in which patients may believe something strange for a few moments, and then wander off on to a different topic. There is no so-called "clouding of consciousness". Rather, they believe in something that appears very strange to others, and they argue, using the full array of defences, against apparently sensible ideas. Thus, in the Capgras example above, anyone who looks, sounds, and dresses like one's husband is almost certain to *be* one's husband—unless you have some additional evidence to suggest that we might be dealing with an impostor. One of the things that our group have been interested in investigating is a possible role for the way that emotion may influence cognition in these neurological patients.

Mark Solms and Karen Kaplan-Solms had investigated a class of these patients in psychoanalytic psychotherapy, as described in their book (Kaplan-Solms & Solms, 2000, pp. 200–242) and elsewhere (Solms, 1998; see Solms & Turnbull, 2002, Chapter 3 for review). They investigated four patients with confabulation, and made a claim that the false beliefs in these patients were caused by the excess influence of the unconscious over the mental apparatus. I will rephrase that argument in a few moments, using language that is less psychoanalytic. However, the argument is best presented initially using the classical psychoanalytical terminology.

As is well known, Freud outlined four principal properties of the system unconscious in his paper *The Unconscious*. These are: the replacement of external by psychical reality; exemption from mutual contradiction; mobility of cathexis (or primary process thinking); and timelessness (Freud, 1915, p. 187). These are a complex set of principles, which space does not permit me to discuss in detail. The basic arguments are clearly outlined in Freud's original paper. I wish to focus particularly on one aspect of Freud's proposal: that of the replacement of external by psychical reality. This seems reasonably transcribed as arguing that these patients accept views of external reality that are congruent with their internal psychical state. If external reality matches these wishes, they accept it. If not, then they deny, reject, and argue against the evidence of external reality, using the usual array of defences. Given that the internal world is dominated by emotion, it also seems fair to rephrase this argument as saying that they prefer versions of external reality that lead to positive affective consequences.[4] Conversely, when exposed to views of external reality that lead to negative affective consequences they will reject them—again trying to use logical argument to bolster a decision made, at core, for emotional reasons. This, then, would be the reason (or, at least one of the four reasons suggested by Freud) for why people hold false beliefs.

There is a reasonable case to be made that in fact *many* apparently normal individuals have difficulty tolerating views of the world that will lead to negative consequences, and that they (we?) fight against these views of external reality using precisely the same defence mechanisms as neurological patients with false beliefs. Many of us are, for example, biased towards believing that we are more intelligent, charming, and beautiful than we probably are. A key feature of good mental health is the extent to which we are able to *tolerate* the reality of the fact that we are often not all that bright, that we sometimes behave boorishly, and that in the wrong light our cellulite and double chin can seem remarkably unattractive. Thus, false beliefs are the sort of thing that psychotherapists confront in every client. The difference in the neurological patients I wish to discuss is, of course, that the delusions in these patients are so greatly exaggerated, their versions of reality so skewed, that their defences are magnified to the extent of being ridiculous.

It seems appropriate to provide a few examples of the patients described in Kaplan-Solms and Solms (2000).

In one case a patient arrived for his session, and said that earlier that day he had seen an old friend of his, that he had not seen for many years. It turned out that the old friend had lived in a different country, and during the course of the conversation the patient reported that actually, of course, the old friend was dead. In fact, our client remembered his funeral several years earlier. When confronted with the idea that one cannot really be both dead *and* alive, the patient seemed quite accepting of this contradiction. Of course, the patient argued, the man was dead. And, of course, the patient had seen him this morning. What, the patient seemed to be suggesting to the therapist, was the problem here? Indeed, the patient suggested that it must lead to terrible legal complications to be both simultaneously dead in another part of the world and alive here (!).

The patients that I have been more likely to encounter are people who have delusions about place. For example, more than one patient has reported that they are living in a hotel. Discussions with such patients run more or less as follows: the clinician points out that this doesn't *look* like a regular hotel—because, for example, the people are not in separate rooms. Well, says the patient, perhaps it's a rather down-market hotel, and they can't afford to give everyone their own room. But what about the staff, they seem to be in white coats and nurses' uniforms? Well, it's rather a down-market hotel, and perhaps they couldn't afford new uniforms, so they were forced to acquire some second-hand ones from the health service. These sorts of ridiculous arguments, based on flimsy evidence and extremely improbable, are typically used to try to bolster what otherwise would be completely unsustainable claims.

A final example is another from Kaplan-Solms and Solms (2000)—in fact they use it as an example of mobility of cathexis.

A female patient was regularly visited by her husband. When her husband was there (i.e. during visiting time) she was quite happy to treat this person as her husband. However, when he left, she seemed to regard the man in the bed *next* to her as being her husband. It seems that he was far from a carbon-copy of her husband in looks, and she might have gained some further clues about the veracity of her perception from the fact that he wasn't all that delighted with her behaviour. Nevertheless, she was not to be swayed by the evidence of perceptual reality.

Testing false beliefs

The Solms and Kaplan-Solms data are clearly of great interest. They suggest an explanation for why these patients should hold false beliefs—couched in classical psychoanalytic theory, and informed by some important issues relating to the neurobiology of affect. However, there is a central problem with the data presented by Solms and Kaplan-Solms, as viewed when wearing the hat of experimental psychology. Specifically, the approach to data analysis described above suffers from the problem of cherry-picking. Solms and Kaplan-Solms have clearly spent a lot of time with their patients, and have acquired a number of anecdotes and examples which they accurately map onto Freud's account of the properties of the system unconscious. However, it may be that they have included only examples that fit the model, excluding those that run counter to the theory. Such distortions are unlikely to be a *conscious* choice on their part, of course. But we commonly rehearse (and hence recall) material that fits with our preconceptions, putting to one side material that makes less sense.

To verify their claims it is necessary to examine the evidence in a more systematic way—and we have recently made an attempt to do this. How can a more "systematic" investigation be achieved? We have now analysed the data from (in principle) *all* reported cases of confabulation—or at least those accessible from 1980–2000 (Turnbull, Berry & Evans, in press). It seems unlikely that such cases were reported because of a pre-existing bias towards the Solms and Kaplan-Solms theory, and the 1980–2000 data represent a fair starting point from which to select a subset that could test the Solms and Kaplan-Solms model in a reasonable fashion. In particular we wanted to focus on arguments relating to the replacement of external by psychical reality. As suggested above, this seems to suggest that these patients accept views of external reality that are congruent with their internal psychical state. In particular, it might be interpreted as suggesting that these patients far too easily tolerate versions of external reality that lead to positive affective consequences. Hence, their confabulations should lead to a more affectively positive view of reality than truly exists.

To investigate this, the first thing we chose to do was to exclude many types of false beliefs—because they are very hard to measure. We were especially interested in comparing *actual* reality to the *confabulated* version of reality. In some instances, "actual" reality is difficult to establish accurately. For example, in the Capgras delusion, the patient is of the opinion that this person looks and sounds and dresses like her husband, but actually he is an impostor. Here it is hard to know whether there are positive, or negative, affective consequences of this person not being her spouse. For those in love, it would be distressing to believe that their loved one was an impostor. However, for those whose marriage is no longer what it once was, it may *suit* the patient to believe that their spouse is an impostor. Thus, the patient would rather her spouse was not around. Thus, the "impostor" false belief makes her life more pleasant. Because it is difficult to know her *true* feelings on this matter,[5] we have no clear way of measuring whether the affective consequences are negative or positive. However, in some classes of false beliefs we have more certainty—especially in the case of false beliefs about place. Here, we know *where* the patients are, and from their false belief we know where they *claim* they are. From these two known facts we can try to gauge some measure of the "pleasantness" of these two situations.

Considerations of space do not allow a detailed description of the exact method of our study here, but we identified cases of confabulation from the published literature from 1980–2000. We found sixteen cases where the primary error was a false belief related to place. For each case, a set of raters (matched for age, sex, and education with the patients) rated the locations in terms of "pleasantness". The "actual" locations were typically (and un-surprisingly) hospitals. The confabulated locations varied widely. The more poorly rated items on the list were locations such as "my old secondary school", or "my doctor's home". The higher rated items were "staying in a hotel or motel", "on a ferry in the Caribbean", "on a holiday on a barge", "in a bistro" and "at home". In fact, the judges rated being at home as more interesting than being in the Caribbean—which may say something about the stressful nature of foreign holidays.

There was little variance between the raters. Unsurprisingly, being in a hospital was not rated especially high in pleasantness. In *each one* of the other cases the rating for the confabulated location was higher than the actual location. Thus, as the theory predicted, the false beliefs of these patients places them in a more "pleasant" location than they are actually in. In fact, their delusion can be seen as a defence against whatever it is that makes being in a hospital unpleasant (being ill, having had a stroke etc). In sum, the conclusions of Kaplan-Solms and Solms seem to be entirely justified when investigated using a more quantitative approach. However, when wearing an experimental psychology hat yet again, there are some potential attacks on these data—on the grounds that hospitals are not pleasant places *per se*. Thus, one might argue, *any* other location would be more pleasant than a hospital. As a control, we have been investigating two other locations that produce false beliefs—in dreaming and in schizophrenia. In both cases, the false beliefs do *not* follow the pattern seen in the confabulating patients. Thus, you sometimes believe that you are in a *better* place than your bed (e.g. in a sexual dream), and sometimes that you are in a *worse* place (in an anxiety dream). Similarly, the delusions of schizophrenics sometimes make their lives *more* pleasant (e.g. delusions of grandeur), and sometimes *less* pleasant (e.g. delusions of persecution). Thus, we have attempted a degree of experimental control in investigating several classes of false beliefs—and those of confabulators do seem exceptional. Hence, our investigation offers another class of support for the Kaplan-Solms and Solms claim.

Summary and conclusion

In summary, there is clear evidence for the important role that emotion (and emotion-learning systems) play in shaping cognition, especially involving the ventromesial frontal lobes. This class of "perceptual" input represents a vital source of knowledge on which we base our decisions—a class of information which we subjectively experience as "intuition". When such information is *lacking*, individuals appear to retain "intelligence", but behave in a range of ways that are not in their best long-term interests. However, it also appears that *over*-activation of emotional systems has negative consequences for the mental apparatus. In particular, the excessive influence of emotion over cognition seems to lead to false beliefs. This paper reviewed evidence from three classes of false belief: schizophrenia, dreaming, and confabulation. It seems that the ventromesial frontal lobes are centrally involved in *all* of the instances of false belief, and there is reasonable evidence that such disorders result from over-activation of emotion systems, or when such emotion systems are poorly regulated. Emotion is, therefore, an absolutely central feature of the human mental apparatus, and attempts to maintain that "rationality" has little to do with emotion (as experimental psychology and cognitive neuroscience seemed to believe for much of the last century) seem misguided.

Let me finish then, with a brief set of general conclusions. There is clearly enormous common ground between neuroscience and psychotherapy, though the overlap has only become clear recently, as neuroscience has shifted its focus to topics of shared interest, such as motivation, affect, personality, consciousness, dreams etc. It therefore seems clear, as mentioned at the beginning of this piece, that we live in a remarkable period—looking forward to something of a reunification between the two fields. This is, of course, precisely the situation that Freud envisaged when psychoanalysis began. There are numerous occasions in which he argued for the likelihood of future reunification. For example:

> we must recollect that all our provisional ideas in psychology will presumably some day be based on an organic substructure. [Freud, 1914, p. 78]

This also seems like a suitable opportunity to advertise the existence of a science investigating this new field—which seems to have become called "neuropsychoanalysis". There are some twenty special-interest groups internationally with an interest in this topic. We have also had two international conferences: a London meeting in 2000, and a meeting in New York in 2001. Our next meeting is in Stockholm in September 2002. Since 1999 there has also been a journal called *Neuro-Psychoanalysis*, with a remarkable editorial board, including several neuroscientific and psychoanalytic names that psychotherapists in general will recognize, such as Antonio Damasio and Jaak Panksepp (mentioned earlier in this piece), and Eric Kandel (winner of the 2000 Nobel Prize for Medicine and Physiology).

Things, therefore, seem to be going very well. What more does our Society need, and what should its medium-term aspirations be? What we need really is an empirical basis for our discipline, and I am doing everything within my power to promote this, which includes encouraging people to send empirical papers to our journal. This is not all that easy a request to make—for several reasons. What we need, for example, is an empirical basis that does justice to *both* sides of the divide between the two fields. For example, for most of its history psychoanalysis had little to do with controlled empirical investigations of its ideas, and where this has changed recently it has largely been in the direction of outcome studies and treatment efficacy. There has been little work on addressing the core assumptions of psychoanalysis, yet this is precisely where neuroscience can best assist the field.

It is, however, of some interest that there were a few moments in the last century in which there were "experimental" tests of psychoanalytic ideas (for review see Fisher & Greenberg, 1996). Many were carried out by experimental psychologists, using rather sterile experimental paradigms, and many concluded that psycho-analytic ideas were misguided. Psychoanalysts countered, of course, with the quite reasonable point that the studies did not *begin* to approximate the concepts that they were working with. You cannot, to take a trite example, ask people to "repress" the word dog, and then flash words (including dog) on a computer screen, in the hope that this accurately captures the phenomenon of repression. This is a *fair* criticism of the experimental work, which unsurprisingly did not lead to a coherent experimental psychology of psychoanalysis. In the midst of this defence of psychoanalysis, however, one is also entitled to be critical of the field. One cannot choose *not* to do experiments, and yet simultaneously complain when others carry out experiments that you think inappropriate. Yet this is, typically, what psychoanalysts chose to do. If you do not like the nature of the science that others are engaging in, and you feel that they misrepresent your discipline, then you should go out and do experiments of your own.[6] For this reason I have tried to encourage people who are interested in subjective experience, affect, and our general perspective of the world, to engage in empirical work. This is often hard to do, especially for people who do not have an experimental background. However, what any experimentalist would advise is for you to go and get your hands dirty. When you design your first experiment it will seem like a good idea, though the results will (in all probability) turn out inappropriately. You (or others) will be able to see the flaws, and you will be in a position to improve on it in some way. The next experiment will be better. For all of these reasons I would encourage people to engage in the work that deals with the new overlap between these great fields, because we should grasp the opportunity of this incredible period with both hands.

Notes

1. Vestibular sensation, which is central for our ability to balance, might arguably constitute a "sixth" sense that Aristotle omitted. It has an independent class of perceptual organ (the semicircular canals of the inner ear), it "perceives" a property of the world that is different to other organs, and it travels to the brain using a different set of nerve fibres to other sense organs. Similarly, the sense commonly referred to as "touch" would better be viewed as four different types of somato-sensation (best described as the classes of "discriminative" touch, proprioception, pain, and temperature). Each has its own specialized class of receptor (in fact, each class has *more* than one unique receptor type), and again each travels to the brain using an independent set of nerve fibres. Thus, Aristotle's choice of "five" as the key number seems arbitrary in the context of modern neurobiology. However, his *concept* (that a unitary world can be perceived by multiple senses) remains as viable as ever.

2. Damasio points out that such somatic markers need not always be conscious (see Damasio, 1994, pp. 184–187).

3. The newer range of antipsychotic agents are slightly different in their means of operation, in that they target this traditional dopamine system to a lesser extent, but in addition target other dopamine systems, as well as serotonin systems. A detailed discussion of the specifics of each type is beyond the scope of this chapter, but can be found in any psychiatry or neuropharmacology text.

4. This need not be universally true, of course. It is probably more accurate to say that they believe things that are congruent with the emotional consequences of the belief. Perhaps the example of this would be in clinical depression, where the patient strongly denies that *anything* in their life is going well, and that they have *any* degree of competence in more or less *any* domain. Here, the patient accepts only versions of reality that are untrue, but they are the versions that appear (at least to the neutral observer) to lead to *negative* affective consequences.

5. It is of some interest, of course, that psychotherapists represent one group who *would* claim that we can establish the patient's underlying opinion about their spouse. However, this can only be done with a

substantial investment of time, and in the context of a sound therapeutic relationship. This sort of information is certainly not available in the published literature on patients with Capgras' delusion.
6. There have been few examples of empirical work of this sort in psychoanalysis—though the work of some, such as Howard Shevrin, stand in stark contrast to this position (see Shevrin *et al*, 1996, for a review). However, work of this sort has received nothing like the recognition that it deserves—both outside, and even *within*, psychoanalysis.

References

Anderson, S. W., Bechara, A., Damasio, H., Tranel, D., & Damasio, A. (1999). Impairment of social and moral behaviour related to early damage in human prefrontal cortex. *Nature Neuroscience, 2*: 1032–1037

Bargh, J. A., & Chartrand, T. L. (1999). The unbearable automaticity of being. *American Psychologist, 54*: 462–479.

Bechara, A., Damasio, A. R., Damasio, H., & Anderson, S. W. (1994). Insensitivity to future consequences following damage to human prefrontal cortex. *Cognition, 50*: 7–15.

Bowman, C. H., & Turnbull, O. H. (in press). Real versus facsimile reinforcers on the Iowa Gambling Task. *Brain & Cognition.*

Damasio, A. (1994). *Descartes' Error*. New York: Grosset/Putnam.

Damasio, A. R. (1999). Commentary on Panksepp. *Neuro-Psychoanalysis, 1*: 38–39.

Damasio, A. (2000). *The Feeling of What Happens*. London: William Heinemann.

Fisher, S., & Greenberg, R. P. (1996). *Freud Scientifically Reappraised: Testing the Theories and Therapy*. Wiley-Interscience: New York.

Freud, S. (1914). *On Narcissism. S.E., 14*: 73–102.

Freud, S. (1915). *The Unconscious. S.E., 14*: 166–215.

Harlow, J. (1868). Recovery from passage of an iron bar through the head. *Massachusetts Medical Society Publication, 2*: 327–347.

Kaplan-Solms, K., & Solms, M. (2000). *Clinical Studies in Neuro-Psychoanalysis*. London: Karnac Books.

Panksepp, J. (1985). Mood changes. In: P. Vinken, G. Bruyn & H. Klawans (Eds.), *Handbook of Clinical Neurology, Volume 45* (pp. 271–285). Elsevier, Amsterdam.

Panksepp, J. (1998). *Affective Neuroscience: The Foundations of Human and Animal Emotions*. New York: Oxford University Press.

Panksepp, J. (2000). On preventing another century of misunderstanding: towards a psychoethology of human experience and a psychoneurology of affect. *Neuro-Psychoanalysis*, 2: 240–255.

Raine, A., Lencz, T., Bihrle, S., LaCasse, L., & Colletti, P. (2000). Reduced prefrontal grey matter volume and reduced autonomic activity in antisocial personality disorder. *Archives of General Psychiatry*, 57: 119–127.

Schore, A. (1994). *Affect Regulation and the Origin of the Self*. Mahwah, NJ: Lawrence Erlbaum Associates.

Shevrin, H., Bond, J. A., Brakel, L. A., Hertel, R. K., & Williams, W. J. (1996). *Conscious and Unconscious Processes: Psychodynamic, Cognitive, and Neurophysiological Convergences*. New York: Guilford Press.

Snyder, S. H. (1999). *Drugs and the Brain*. New York: Scientific American Library.

Solms, M. (1997a). What is consciousness? *Journal American Psychoanalytic Association*, 45: 681–703.

Solms, M. (1997b). *The Neuropsychology of Dreams*. Mahwah: Lawrence Erlbaum Associates.

Solms, M. (1998). Psychoanalytic observations on four cases on ventromesial frontal lobe damage [German]. *Psyche-Zeitschrift Fur Psychoanalyse Und Ihre Anwendungen*, 52: 919–962.

Solms, M. (2000). Dreaming and REM sleep are controlled by different brain mechanisms. *Behavioural and Brain Sciences*, 23: 843–850.

Solms, M., & Turnbull, O. H. (2002). *The Brain and The Inner World: An Introduction to the Neuroscience of Subjective Experience*. London: Karnac Books.

Turnbull, O. H., Berry, H., & Bowman, C. H. (in press). Direct versus indirect emotional consequences on the Iowa Gambling Task: "Frontal" performance in the neurologically normal? *Brain & Cognition*.

Turnbull, O. H., Berry, H., & Evans, C. E. Y. (in press). A positive emotional bias in confabulatory false beliefs about place. *Brain & Cognition*.

Turnbull, O. H., & Solms, M. (2003). Memory, amnesia and intuition. In: V. Green (Ed.), *Emotional Development in Psychoanalysis, Attachment Theory and Neuroscience: Creating Connections*. London: Taylor & Francis.

CHAPTER SIX

Psychotherapy and neuroscience: how close can they get?

Chris Mace

W hile the potential contribution of neuroscience to psychotherapy can seem huge, this chapter is a plea for caution. It examines the gap between what may seem possible and where we actually are. An understanding of current theories and models of how the brain works can be heuristically extremely useful to all of us. It helps us to think in new ways that are clinically helpful, and can extend lines of reasoning along paths we may not otherwise follow. Biological models of the mind have a long and honourable tradition in this respect, and reflect the personal involvement of several psychotherapeutic pioneers in neurology. Freud had a very detailed understanding of contemporary neuropathology—I have traced elsewhere how contemporary understanding of causation in neurological disease underpinned Freud's thinking about psychopathology for the remainder of his career (Mace, 1992). This eventually led Freud to renounce his attempts to seek a single psychological cause for a given kind of symptom formation. However, this mission is one which others (e.g. Gabbard, 2000) have not abandoned a century later. By yielding a unique importance to Freud's early "Project for a scientific psychology" (Freud, 1895), some modern commentators

have made claims—for his attempts to apply neurological understandings to all mental functions—that exceed his actual ambitions.

Some of Freud's immediate successors used biology to derive new
analytic understandings that were not directly linked to therapeutic
innovation. Paul Schilder's concept of "organic repression"
(Schilder, 1935) represented the most significant conceptual link
since George Groddeck in explaining how emotional events might
be associated with lasting illness.

In developing a quite different conception of the role of
psychotherapy in health, the founder of group analysis, S. H.
Foulkes, turned to an alternative tradition of neurological thinking
in preference to the localizationalist schools that had inspired Freud.
The organismic emphasis of Kurt Goldstein (1939) extended the
holistic tradition in biology advocated by Claude Bernard. It
highlighted emergent properties of higher levels of organization
that could never be reduced to the contributions of their
constituents. Goldstein therefore emphasized the primacy of the
neural network and was highly sceptical of the philosophy of
functional localization that was central to lesionist thinking. For
Foulkes, Goldstein's organismic view did more than provide a
metaphor for the primacy of the collective to the individual. It was
key to understanding how individuals might influence one another
immediately and unconsciously through a process akin to musical
resonance, and to Foulkes' perception of the interdependence of
figure and ground in human groups (Foulkes, 1964).

It is important to recognize that such references to neurology
have been heuristic. They have served to enrich the models
psychotherapists use, but not to validate them. By having a parallel
system of explanation, to which repeated reference can be made and
comparisons sought, a process of triangulation allows new ideas to
emerge that would have been highly unlikely without the anchor
that the foreign explanatory system provides. Naturally, the new
understandings that result from triangulation will be heavily
coloured by thinking in the other domain. The extent to which the
new concepts are actually justified must be tested in the original
domain, in this case psychotherapy. If these concepts implicate the
brain, then testing will require examination of brain events in the
course of psychotherapy.

An heuristic appreciation of new views on the sequencing of

developmental processes, on the expression of emotion, or on which human motives may correspond to a subset of primary drives associated with those older, more primitive areas of the brain known as the basal ganglia, can each shape our views of how to proceed when doing therapy and the kinds of association to expect. But this is not the same as direct observation of the brain at work. A parallel can be found in the uses Renaissance artists made of the developing science of optics. Many artists were content to apply understandings of perspective derived from visual experiment to their own work so their depictions acquired a greater degree of realism. Others, through devices like the camera obscura, used optic technology to enhance the precision of their vision as they drew (Hockney, 2001). Their work acquired a far sharper realism as their art was transformed by other science rather than borrowing from its theory.

As I write, minimally invasive techniques of examining brain function while subjects are alert and awake are available that would have been unimaginable even 15 years ago. Despite this, and despite a growing interest in the brain by psychotherapists, little work continues to be done to observe what actually transpires in the brains of those providing and receiving psychotherapy as it happens. In terms of the analogy with drawing, the camera obscura has yet to be brought into the studio. There has been much resistance, historically, to any project threatening to align the objective and subjective aspects of psychotherapy more closely than before—witness the hysteria that could surround the use of audio-visual recordings within therapy sessions. Claims that these may seriously pollute the patients' reactions, or discourage therapists from accessing their own subjectivity in their recollections, will be familiar to most people who have had a traditional training in psychotherapy within the last 30 years.

Here, uncritical faith in a subjectivity that could be threatened by external observation, risks becoming an unfalsifiable dogma if examination of how far it is justified is prevented. It can also prevent study of the subjective via a potentially crucial, if external, vantage point that could ultimately strengthen its claims. Fortunately, through initiatives in training and research, many therapists have come to appreciate the potential of auditory and visual records to enhance understanding of the therapeutic process in ways that do not supplant the personal. This may be an important lesson to remember at a time when the potential for neuroscientific understanding of psychotherapy, based on actual observation, has barely begun life.

Having illustrated the contrasts between the use of biological metaphors in psychotherapy and the biology of psychotherapy, I shall illustrate the potential of a more thorough integration of neurobiology by reference to three questions. All are key to psychotherapeutic practice: namely the selection of patients for treatment; what the results of the treatment are understood to be; and the process the treatment follows.

Selection of patients for psychotherapy

On the face of things, assessment of whether someone is likely to benefit from psychotherapy, or be put at risk by it, would appear to be one facet of a rich and many layered enterprise that is relatively open to objective empirical investigation. Paradoxically, while psychotherapy research has become a significant industry over the last 30 years, and started to contribute a good deal of understanding concerning the kinds of therapeutic events that make for better outcomes, it has had little to contribute to the prediction of outcomes before therapy begins or how clinical assessments should be conducted (Mace, 1995). This state of affairs is reflected in the absence of any independent treatment of assessment in successive editions of the *Handbook of Psychotherapy and Behaviour Change*, a compendium that is effectively the psychotherapy researcher's bible (Bergin & Lambert, 1994).

Although therapists make all kinds of predictions in the course of preliminary assessments, these are notoriously unreliable and are not nearly as dependable as judgments made once therapy has begun. In addition, although clinical assessment would seem to invite the use of auxiliary aids to detect factors not immediately available on interview (the original rationale of projective tests such as the Rorschach inkblots), formal tests seem only to have found widespread acceptance among cognitive and behavioural therapists. Any test that improved the accuracy of assessments of prospective patients' capacity to benefit from therapy should deserve serious consideration in the present context. There are now signs that readily measured neurobiological characteristics could increase the accuracy of pre-therapy assessments.

An example follows. For two decades, US sleep researchers have investigated associations between the physiological profile of patients' sleep at night (sleep "architecture") and depressed mood. A number of sleep changes have been significantly associated with specific depressive symptoms, if not all cases of depression. A recent comparative investigation tried to determine whether differences in sleep architecture were predictive of response to psychotherapeutic and pharmacological treatments (Thase *et al.*, 1997). Three changes commonly occur together, namely decrease in the latency period before rapid eye movement (REM) sleep appears after commencement of sleep; decrease in overall sleep efficiency; and density of the REM periods during the sleep cycle. These had already been shown to be associated with a poorer response to cognitive–behavioural psychotherapy in an earlier study. In this study, all participants had had at least one previous episode of depression and were clinically depressed at the time of entry. This was further classified as "mild" or "severe" using a standard rating scale. All subjects had their sleep architecture recorded over two nights in a sleep laboratory before receiving interpersonal therapy for up to 16 sessions. Anyone who failed to respond to psychotherapy received antidepressant medication for a further period, during which further psychotherapy was also provided. The sleep recordings identified two groups at the outset, 41 subjects whose sleep pattern was abnormal in the respects listed above, and 50 without significant change from normal. Although there was a tendency for more people having milder depression to have normal sleep, this was non-significant, and the sample can be analysed as four subgroups according to severity of depression and normality of sleep.

Figure 1 shows the clinical progress of each of these four groups through the 16 weeks. The vertical axis represents the percentage who achieve clinical remission. It is clear from this that, after the 10th week, people who entered the study with a normal sleep pattern are significantly more likely to enjoy a clinical remission after psychotherapy than those whose sleep architecture was rated "abnormal". At the same time, the severity of the initial depression had no bearing on the likelihood of success. Although surprising,

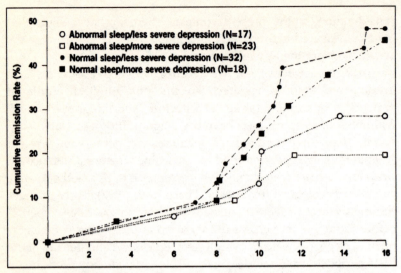

Figure 1. Cumulative remission rates of patients with major depression, stratified by sleep profile and severity of illness, treated with interpersonal psychotherapy.

this finding was consistent with other studies of interpersonal therapy that had shown it could be effective across a wide spectrum of severity, possibly more so than other treatments.

The implication for psychotherapy assessors is striking. On the one hand, clinical indicators that are relatively simple to ascertain, such as the severity of a patient's mood disturbance, are unhelpful in predicting response to the therapy. On the other, neurobiological changes that are evident only from physiological investigation appear to be reliable predictors. As these do not correlate with any other kind of observation that could be made during an assessment interview (and there is no reason to suppose that they do), it would appear that direct assessment of brain functioning can usefully be incorporated into assessment procedures predicting likely response to treatment.

The study illustrates an important theoretical possibility. Like most isolated studies, it should be taken to be neither authoritative nor flawless. The authors chose to emphasize other aspects of their findings, particularly the observation that most of the patients who did not respond to psychotherapy did go on to respond to medication, irrespective of both severity and sleep pattern. They tended to see psychotherapy as little better than a placebo of limited range, ignoring the fact that therapy continued during the medication phase. *Figure 1* also presents the study's results in a way that is likely to misrepresent the actual differences between these groups. Fewer and fewer patients were staying in the study as time passed, but more were leaving from the abnormal sleep groups. This made it progressively harder for those groups ever to achieve a comparable cumulative remission rate, even if therapy was effective in those who remained. While these caveats do mean the results of the study need replication before they should be accepted, the principle remains that biological markers may assume more importance in assessment for psychotherapy in the future.

Outcome in psychotherapy

The question of clinical effectiveness has been a prominent theme of psychotherapy research since its inception. As techniques of evaluating the overall efficacy of a treatment have developed, researchers have moved away from simple evaluation of outcome towards studies that combine this with attempts to identify processes by which the outcomes might have been achieved. These may account for relative differences in the outcomes obtained within a sample of patients. Thus, it is increasingly common for studies to combine assessment of outcomes in terms of symptoms or personal functioning with study of favoured intervening variables, such as the quality of the working relationship between therapist and patient. These are usually measured either by repeated questionnaires or by audio or video recording of a treatment in progress. In principle, these might be complemented by some direct measurement of the patient's physiological state.

Intrusive as these may be, they are trivial in comparison to the disruption that, until very recently, most methods of assessing changes in brain functioning (e.g. wearing a cap containing 20 or more interconnected electrodes) would involve. However, functional imaging studies, sensitive to transient changes in blood flow, are able to pinpoint differential changes in energy use in the cortex and mesial brain structures by techniques that are little more intrusive physically than an X-ray. Their virtue is not only relative ease, but a far more direct correspondence between test output and the maps of localized brain function already familiar to neuro-physiologists, potentially simplifying interpretation of the images they provide. This simplicity is, however, deceptive. There are a variety of protocols for constructing functional images from raw emissions, but they can lead to important discrepancies between observations of the same phenomena depending upon which methodology is used. Methodological variation may be one significant reason why, in an area of great interest to psychothera-pists, the range of findings associated with mood change remains very varied. Nevertheless, images are available whose resolution was unattainable a decade ago, while the sensitivity of newer techniques to change makes possible inspection of brain events accompanying participation in psychotherapy.

A recent example of this approach comes from a UK study of the treatment of depression by interpersonal therapy and antidepressant medication (Martin *et al.*, 2001). Despite significant methodological weaknesses, this work's findings have potentially important implications for the mode of action of psychotherapeutic treatments. Martin's team studied 28 middle-aged volunteers with high scores on a depression inventory who underwent functional brain imaging. All had been free of treatment for at least six months. Fifteen were treated with the antidepressant venlafaxine, and 13 received interpersonal therapy. Both the scans and the clinical ratings were repeated after six weeks. Symptomatically, members of both groups had improved significantly, those having medication slightly more so. Functional imaging six weeks into treatment showed three sets of changes. These are illustrated in *Figure 2*, which is a summation across the sample of significant differences between finishing activity and starting activity.

The top row of three diagrams in *Figure 2* depict the blood flow activation seen across the interpersonal therapy (IPT) patients; those on the second row are from the venlafaxine patients. There are two principal areas of activation in each group, but only one of these is common to both. This is the spot just to the right of the midline, towards the front of the brain where, on side view, the brainstem becomes surrounded by the frontal lobes. It corresponds to activation of the right basal ganglia. Two other "hotspots" are apparently unique to either of the other groups: the midline area

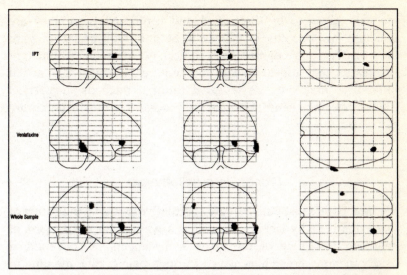

Figure 2. Regional cerebral blood flow activation with interpersonal psychotherapy (IPT) (*n* = 13), venlafaxine (*n* = 15), and whole sample (*n* = 28) on statistical parametric mapping 96 analysis of variance "Z maps" (*P* = 0.01), for scan 2. For scan 1, the columns, left to right, show sagittal, coronal, and transaxial grids.

found in the IPT group corresponds to activation in the right posterior cingulate gyrus; the activation on the surface of the cortex in the venlafaxine patients corresponds to the right posterior temporal lobe.

One interpretation of these results is that, while activation of the basal ganglia accompanies a non-specific elevation of mood, the changes specific to each kind of treatment reflect differences in their mechanism of action. As in the previous discussion, there are significant factors that mean the details of this study should be interpreted with caution. Other findings, that are very common among untreated patients with depression (such as deactivation of dorsolateral prefrontal areas), were not found with this sample, compromising their representativeness. A lack of qualitative data makes it hard to link the possible difference in mode of action with any specific clinical effects. In addition, a contemporary comparative study of similar treatment regimes, using different imaging methods, failed to show changes in activation specific to one treatment (Brody *et al.*, 2001). However, treatment specific changes are only likely to be discovered and confirmed when they are searched for. This study is likely to be important in encouraging investigators to recognize that clinical outcomes from different treatments, that appear similar, may not be equivalent. The actual differences may only be revealed through methods that reflect differences in the neurophysiological processes with which they are associated.

Process in psychotherapy

My final point must remain more speculative, but is an indication of work that is badly lacking, as well as a warning of the dangers of neurocentrism. One of the great achievements of conventional psychotherapy research, achieved through painstaking attention to in-session events, is its support for the importance of the relationship between therapist and patient in influencing the outcome. Much of this work, encapsulated in efforts to operationalize the concept of "therapeutic alliance", is relatively independent of therapists' chosen therapeutic models. It has been one way of highlighting how it is events between therapist and patient, rather than "in" one of them alone, that are crucial if therapy is to work well. There are increasing grounds too for thinking that non-verbal processes based on very rapid, mutual tuning of behavioural interaction, are important to therapeutic success (Stern *et al.*, 1998). Indeed, there are parallels between the importance of vocal synchrony in the mother/infant interactions Professor Trevarthen discusses elsewhere in this volume, and this aspect of therapist/patient relationships.

The idea that events between therapist and patient are key is overtly opposed to what may be termed the instrumental view of therapy. According to the instrumental view, therapy is fundamentally about fixing something within the cranium of the person named the patient: the professional participant's task is simply to find the best means of doing this. Neuroscience, with its capacity to image and analyse activity within the patient's brain as a window on a disordered mind, is in danger of reinforcing this instrumental view. Indeed, the two previous discussions provide good-enough examples of it at work. In them, psychotherapy is one treatment among others. It may be synergic with treatments that work directly on the biological level (e.g. psychotropic drugs). The problem is that a unidirectional view of the therapeutic process is reinforced. The fact that therapists are not only deeply affected by the process, but that this might be critical to its success, is discounted when the therapist is only a supplier of interventions in the same way that a pharmacist dispenses a drug "treatment".

The evidence from work by Stern, Trevarthen, and others implies that the parts of the therapist's behaviour we take to be the effective ingredient—the words—may not be as crucial as many believe. This is an important point in itself, with its corollary that developmental understanding of interaction can prompt a recon-ceptualization of therapeutic communication. However, evidence that mutual responsiveness is key to effective work is also a vital corrective to the instrumental fallacy. In order to understand what is going on in biological terms in such a highly synchronized and interdependent situation, it would be necessary to examine events associated with the therapist as much as any identified with the nervous system of their patient. Nearly a century after physics has accommodated itself to the impossibility of isolating observers from the systems in which they participate, the entrance of psychotherapy research to the arena of mind mapping may prompt reconsideration of the influence of investigators' own brains across many studies of psychological processes. In investigations of psychotherapeutic treatments, it would seem unwise not to monitor the events in a therapist's brain accompanying those studied in his or her patient if the biology of what is going on is ever to be adequately described.

Conclusions

In moving from speculation to science, it is evident very little has been established so far about brain processes during psychotherapy. The few studies that have been performed *in situ* are imperfect, but tantalizingly so. They do indicate areas in which further work could revolutionize practice and theory. It is also apparent that some of the basic assumptions of neuroscientific investigation need revising if this work's full potential for influencing the practice of psychotherapy is to be realized.

References

Bergin, A. E., & Garfield, S. L. (1994). *Handbook of Psychotherapy and Behaviour Change* (4th edn). New York: Wiley.

Brody, A. I., Saxena, S., Stoessel, P., Gillies, L. A., Fairbanks, L. A., Alborzian, S., Phelps, M. E., Huang, S-C., Wu, H-M., Ho, M. L., Ho, M. K., Au, S. C., Maidment, K., & Baxter, L. R. (2001). Regional brain metabolic changes in patients with major depression treated with either paroxetine or interpersonal therapy: preliminary findings. *Archives of General Psychiatry, 58*: 631–640.

Freud, S. (1895). Project for a scientific psychology. In: *S.E., 1*: 283–397.

Foulkes, S. H. (1964). *Therapeutic Group Analysis*. London: George, Allen & Unwin.

Gabbard, G. (2000). *Psychodynamic Psychiatry in Clinical Practice* (3rd edn). Washington: American Psychiatric Press.

Goldstein, K. (1939). *The Organism: A Holistic approach to Biology derived from Pathological Data in Man*. New York: American Book Company.

Hockney, D. (2001). *Secret Knowledge*. London: Thames and Hudson.

Klerman, G., Weissman, M. M. *et al.* (1984). *Interpersonal Psychotherapy for Depression*. New York: Academic Books.

Mace, C. J. (1992). Hysterical conversion I: a history. *British Journal of Psychiatry, 161*: 369–377.

Mace, C. J. (1995). Introduction. In: C. Mace (Ed.), *The Art and Science of Assessment in Psychotherapy* (pp. 1–7). London: Routledge.

Martin, S. D., Martin, E., Rai, S. S., Richardson, M. A., & Royall, R. (2001). Brain blood flow changes in depressed patients treated with interpersonal psychotherapy or Venlafaxine hydrochloride. *Archives of General Psychiatry, 58*: 641–648.

Schilder, P. (1935). *The Image and Appearance of the Human Body*. New York: International Universities Press.

Stern, D. with "the process of change study group". (1998). Non-interpretive mechanisms in psychoanalytic therapy: the "something more" than interpretation. *International Journal of Psychoanalysis, 79*: 903–921.

Thase, M. E., Buysse, D. J., Frank, E., Cherry, C. R., Cornes, C. I., Mallinger, A. G., & Kupfer, D. J. (1997). Which depressed patients will respond to interpersonal psychotherapy? The role of abnormal EEG sleep profiles. *American Journal of Psychiatry, 154*: 502–509.

CHAPTER SEVEN

Constructing a psychobiological context—science, neuroscience, and therapeutic collaboration

Cairns Clery

Introduction

This paper begins with some brief general remarks on the consistent societal resonance, or pulling power over time, of scientific method, linking it with some systemic implications for psychotherapeutic practice during periods of multi-modal/interdisciplinary collaboration or cross-fertilization. It then presents a pragmatic discussion about some of the experiential consequences of taking a neuroscientific perspective in psychotherapy by way of a specific focus on events in a therapeutic alliance with a traumatized, severely self-harming, adolescent girl. As is clear from other presentations herein, psychobiological knowledge is increasing at a rapid pace. This paper suggests that psychotherapists should "make haste slowly" in incorporating it into their practice. The paper eschews analysis and openly cherry-picks certain neuroaffective findings to propose that their subjective deployment can be of assistance in understanding complex and disturbing material. This in turn may help patients.

Psychotherapy and scientific developments

By turning its attention to human affect, neuroscience is now offering a psychobiological approach to the understanding of feelings using the properly scientific language of neurophysiology, for example by way of computerized tomographic and magnetic resonance imaging hardware. It is providing a language for describing how both feelings and awareness of them arises, based on phenomenological observations. For psychotherapists, this effectively means that neuroscience must now be taken into the mainstream of therapeutic theory and practice in terms of our thinking about what it is to be a human being.

The clinical question is how, and how can doing so help us to help our patients?

Psychotherapists of all schools have a practice interest in successfully deploying theoretical ideas to help patients feel that the quality of their lives has been improved. Patients may not be told explicitly about the therapeutic beliefs or the particular approach being deployed by their therapist, but theories—which, however dazzlingly formulated and widely tested, can still accurately be described as ideas or fantasies—are taken by psychotherapists like potions or psychological medicine to help them in their work with patients. A social constructionist might say it is as if in our therapeutic work we were behaving like experimental scientists whose relationships with our patients (if not the patients themselves) were the experiments.

But a successfully tested hypothesis in the true, i.e. scientific, sense of the term is like a potion of potions, as rare in the laboratory of individually troubled lives which is the psychotherapist's professional consulting room, as the philosopher's stone. In fact, like the philosopher's stone it is mythologized. In reality science is not about using ideas or theories to describe or dictate what we already know. Science is about clarifying what we don't know (Kuhn, 1962). So it is important to remember that just because there is an observable fit between a patient's pathology and a particular theory, it does not mean that this latter is necessarily "true" of the former. Although it may be.

The very existence of the philosophy of science as a field of enquiry attests to the reality of the socially and historically constructed belief that science (capital S) has a glamour or mystique which we must admire, i.e. make projections upon and idealize, because its methods are quintessentially empirical, tried, and tested. In the meantime, we work with our own affect to attune ourselves to our patients and their predicaments using empathy, intuition, imagination, experience etc, trying and testing our own personal and professional skills and trainings against the problems they want help with. In the process, we are aware that the therapeutically effective minutiae of what we do, and how we are, in our relationships with them are not often readily available to the scrutiny of an exact science. Videoed sessions and/or live supervision, where practicable, can be helpful, but in the end what works is what the therapist and her/his patients *together actually feel is working*.

So, we have to be very cautious about embracing any scientific developments, however attractive they may be, without at the same time keeping the notion of objectivity in very clear inverted commas (Maturana & Varela, 1987), recognizing that even if we do utilize scientific advances to help us with own thinking—and there is every reason why we should—ours is an intersubjective (Watzlawick, 1984; Kaplan-Solms & Solms, 1999) recursive field, within which we are always at risk of unconsciously making linear unsystemic idealizations of what science can "objectively" offer us.

Little more than a decade ago Goldberg and David (1991) could justifiably write that traditional science was widely perceived by therapists as mundanely technological, linked with those in political power, and therefore reactionary. But the wheel has since turned and the opposite is now the case in our postmodern world. Scientific perspectives are now seen as revolutionary because they allow new stories to be told. The reattachment of neuroscience to psychotherapy is, therefore, having a profound paradigmatic effect on the practices and beliefs of psychotherapists. So of course it is important to keep abreast of the details involved in this process. But it is also vital to remain conscious of the degree to which, as a profession, we are suffused with and contained by a scientistic world view. This causes us to make a potential (and perhaps not dissimilar to what Greenough and Black (1992) referred to, in infant brains, as experience-expectant) attachment to any genuine scientific developments, such as those currently emanating from affective neuroscience, which lend more credibility to what we do, and/or to reject those which undermine it.

Actively recognizing that the idealization of scientific method is a dynamic embedded in our broadest socially constructed inter-subjective therapeutic assumptions helps prevent the reification of one particular set of theories or piece of research. It also helps neutralize the attendant risk that psychotherapy might thereby and subsequently start to lose its identity as a discipline in its own right. At the other extreme, however, a resistance to change by way of rigid and blinkered attachment to therapeutic dogma, in the face of findings from other disciplines, will render us redundant, depending upon otiose therapeutic reframing rituals as a substitute for discourse and development. Indeed, history shows that major paradigmatic shifts have precisely such an effect on the beliefs and behaviours of adherents of belief systems of all kinds, religious, political, and so on (Ponting, 2000). The existence of so many different schools and umbrella organizations (UKCP, BCP, and BACP etc.,) evidences that, as psychotherapists, we are no different. Not to put too fine a point on it, ours is a discipline notoriously prone to polarization and splitting.

Between embracing neuroscience as explanatorily all powerful, on the one hand, and complete denial of its usefulness, on the other, therapists should continue to take a pragmatic approach in their work with patients. Doing so nevertheless involves the revolutionary recognition that some knowledge and understanding of neuroscientific developments is now *just as* relevant to, and containing of, what we do with our patients as any of the major theories already informing our practice.

Neuroaffective research and the pragmatics of psychotherapy

There is neuroscientific evidence (Schore, 2000) suggesting that, rather than focusing exclusively as therapists on the theoretical constructions we put on the material our patients bring us, it is more helpful to become keyed in or attuned (Stern, 1995) to our patients' affective preoccupations by way of our emotional imagination or empathy. Doing so will better assist them to cope with their problems than wordily interpretative rationalizations.

Schore describes this process as affect regulating. A patient's agitated feelings, which prior to therapy have been mainly personal, subjective, and intrapsychic, in therapy become interpersonal, intersubjective, and mutualized, processing between patient and therapist and linking them together in an attachment system, analogous to that between an infant and her/his mother, until the therapist has sufficiently enabled the patient to cope with more equanimity with both their arousal and/or the stress factors which trigger them. But, of course, patients are often extremely disturbed and their preoccupations can be seriously and continuingly traumatic and/or retraumatizing (van der Kolk, 1991; Kalsched, 1996). It is, therefore, inevitable that as therapists we are going to have to deal with how we ourselves are affected by such material (de Zulueta, 2000). This will be part and parcel of the intersubjective reality of the relationship and absolutely requisite if the patient is to be provided with a proper service.

Particular psychotherapeutic approaches help identify and inform the treatment of these subjective and intersubjective events, and supervision assists in understanding them better. But the therapeutic task is usually, and in large part, about helping a patient to *know* what s/he is feeling, which requires the therapist to have some sense of her/his own feelings in order to differentiate what belongs with whom. Now, awareness of feelings, as distinct from feelings themselves, is one of the defining characteristics of what it is to be a human being. It follows that neuroaffective evidence, which demonstrates how awareness of feelings develops in the primary attachment relationship between infant and adult (usually the mother), must therefore be relevant to the therapeutic alliance between patient and therapist; both in terms of content, that is, what is known of the patient's developmental and attachment history, and in terms of the systemic and dynamic analogues and re-enactments currently occurring in the intersubjective relational process going on between them.

But what constitutes the healing element in this process, and can it actually prompt permanent synaptic change in the brain function of the patient? Or is increased cognitive awareness the most a patient can expect? A systemic approach, for example, might help a patient make contextual or environmental changes, and/or a psychodynamic one might help the patient to gain insight into why s/he cannot make deep and permanent personal or biological changes; but realistically can the aim of therapy be no more than an enabling of a more adaptive position on the part of the patient rather than the facilitation of real neurophysiological change? The work of Gould at Princeton, and of Gage at the Salk Institute for Biological Studies in La Jolla, California (both cited in Holloway, 2001), would seem to support the view that genuine synaptogenesis, similar to that occurring during the period of neural plasticity in early childhood, can also occur later on in life, at least during critical or sensitive periods.

Schore himself refers to the work of Barbas (1995), arguing that because the orbito–frontal cortex retains some capacity for plasticity in adulthood, an affect-regulating relationship with a therapist should now be viewed as capable of prompting actual psychobiological change. He discusses the MRI evidence for dyadically created therapeutic engagement or attunement with patients in terms of its analogical equivalence with the right brain to right brain states of emotionally connected mothers and their infants and small children. Although more independent corroborations, which take account of all the complexities, may be necessary before there can be neuroaffective certainty about the therapeutic relationship, talking in terms of neural equivalences or similarities can helpfully reflect the actuality of the process until then. Ultimately, of course, the patient/therapist relationship cannot actually be describable as neurologically identical with what happens in the mother/infant dyad, because of the enormous structural differences in terms of age, development, frequency of contact, familial ties etc.

In the meantime, psychotherapists can nevertheless take heart from the fact that the key centrality of the therapeutic relationship itself is now beginning to be grounded in empirical neuroscientific evidence. And we need to remind ourselves that, irrespective of the therapeutic method or ideology our particular training has provided us with, be it contextual revisioning, insight-oriented interpretation, cognitive hierarchializing, etc., and irrespective of how helpful and necessary such approaches may be for us as therapists, *in themselves* they are incapable of bringing about any actual structural changes in the brains of our patients whatsoever. To believe otherwise is to have fallen into a state of what Kant called categorical confusion.

Schore's original contribution to the practice of psychotherapy lies specifically in the attention he has drawn to the neuroaffective finding that it is the therapist's "emotionally responsive interventions [which] are transformative for the patient" (Schore, 2000). In other words, in the intersubjective setting of a therapeutic session, it is our humanity, our feelings, and our awareness of feeling which is the main agent of psychobiological change in our patients, rather than expertly worded formulations or ideologically correct hypothetical constructions.

Case study

Kathryn is an intelligent creative 17-year-old girl currently studying for A levels at a college. She was admitted to a regional inpatient psychiatric unit for adolescents when she was 15 years old following two serious overdoses. Five months previously she had been diagnosed with symptoms of depression and an eating disorder by her (boarding) school doctor who treated her pharmacotherapeutically, with an SSRI, without informing her mother. The overdoses came as a complete surprise to her mother as Kathryn had given her absolutely no reason to suspect that anything was amiss when she saw her at the weekends and during school holidays.

Kathryn is the second of two children. Her brother is 10 years older than her and had been living overseas for some years at the time of her admission. The first three years of her life were characterized by marital discord between her parents, who separated when she was three. It can, therefore, be hypothesized that there were at least some maternal and neonatal stress factors during her earliest years. Kathryn moved with her mother to London when she was six and her parents tried to revive their marriage by living together again. Divorce proceedings began shortly after. Three years later her mother took her to live with her new partner and his son in the west country. She continued to have intermittent contact with her father.

Between the ages of 10 and 13, Kathryn was raped at home in the evenings after returning from school before her mother or her violent angry partner got back from work. They both worked until late in the evening. The perpetrator was the apparently innocuous 22-year-old son of her mother's partner, who in fact threatened to kill both her mother and herself if she told anyone about what he was doing to her.

Early on during those three years she inadvertently discovered that scratching herself on the top of her leg in the toilets at school provided her with a diversion from all the terror and anxiety she was experiencing at home, and was an activity she could feel in control of. Over time this scratching developed into frequent and deliberate self-harm involving extensive and deep cutting to various parts of her body. When she was 14 her mother ended the relationship with her partner and moved back to London with Kathryn, who then went to boarding school.

On admission to hospital, she was in a dissociated state and in the weeks immediately following struggled to talk about her feelings, except reluctantly to own to her dangerousness in terms of self-harm and suicidality. She was placed on continuous observations by nursing and medical staff, because of the high risk she posed. As soon as these were lifted she immediately lacerated herself with glass she found in the hospital grounds and the observations policy had to be reinstated. A pattern of lifted and reinstated continuous observations developed as Kathryn kept on attacking herself whenever the opportunity presented, i.e. after each attempt to trust her to try and take more responsibility for her own safety. After four months she disclosed what had happened to her to a member of the staff team, who by unfortunate coincidence then left the unit. Kathryn asked if she could see me for individual therapy instead. She was offered therapy, but insisted she did not want to meet with a female therapist. We agreed to meet three times weekly and continuously review whether to increase or decrease the frequency of sessions.

Trauma re-enactment in therapy

Male nurturance in therapy with women, as Doherty (1991) shows, is qualitatively different from that provided by females. It is further complicated when the problems the patient is bringing to therapy are directly related to adult male violence and she herself is still not yet fully mature. Notwithstanding that Kathryn had got to know me a little whilst a patient on my unit and so was able to make a more informed/empowered decision about who she wanted as a therapist, how was her insistence on seeing a male therapist to be understood? Kathryn told me that, although she loved her mother, she repeatedly and confusingly found herself behaving hatefully towards her, as if it had been her mother's fault that her own position as someone in need of protection (by virtue of being a 10-year-old child) had been inverted so that it was she who was looking after her mother (by complying with the rapist and thus keeping them both alive). But she also hated herself for having complied with his demands, as if she had not in fact been helpless and a child and as if there had been some choice about the matter. Consequently, her view of herself and her mother as females, and by extension of women in general, was negative. She told me she understood this, but it did not affect the way she felt; she might be prepared to accept a female therapist in the future but it was absolutely out of the question at this time.

De Zulueta's (1993) psychobiologically based concept of violence as "attachment gone wrong" describes the kind of self-directed violence Kathryn continued to perpetrate long after the direct threat to her own and her mother's life had become historical. Throughout the years of her abuse Kathryn had been able to preserve a minute but intact sense of herself as still "good" because she had protected and prevented her mother from being killed. This had been achieved by successfully keeping secret, but from her point of view effectively lying to her mother about, what was being done to her. Despite, and because she suffered from painful eczema at the time of her abuse, Kathryn had been able to disguise her own attacks on her body as a scratched response to her inflamed skin condition. But they were actually an adaptive coping response (Crowe, 1996) to the appalling circumstances she was in. A lie had had to be placed between herself and her mother in order to keep them both alive, but it severed the quality of the bond between them, separating them emotionally and depriving Kathryn of the close attachment relationship she actually needed more than at any time since she was an infant in arms. And the price she paid for this "lie" was self-harm. Van der Kolk *et al.* (1991) conducted a four-year empirical study into the childhood origins of self-destructive behaviour and observed that it is mainly associated with a combination of childhood trauma, together with a lack of secure attachments. Kathryn's situation fulfilled both these criteria.

Kathryn's "lie"—which was actually of course not a lie but a withholding of the truth—continued to organize her relationship with her mother and to a lesser extent her more distant father, for more than two years after the abuse was over; two years during which her self-harm escalated from scratches to cuts with razor blades, which she used to retraumatize herself with. The lie, or withheld truth, she was trying to maintain had evolved during that time and become maladaptive. It was now her sense of herself as someone who was bad and who, therefore, deserved to have pain inflicted upon her, that she had to keep from her mother. If she could believe this construction, then it would mean that her self-harm could be given some justification. As an intelligent 15-year-old she knew the girl she had been between the ages of 10 and 13 had not actually been bad, although the rapist had told her she was. She had felt bad. But she had since learned to put all her bad feelings into her cuts. The logic was straightforward: cutting was bad. She was a cutter. Therefore, she was bad. And as her self-harm was abusive she felt she had to punish herself more severely for punishing herself (Clery, 1998). But, however badly she wounded herself, she did not actually feel much if any pain at all. She told me she would love it if she did. It was an appalling spiral which left her severely depressed.

To add insult to injury, as a sleepless psychiatric patient, she was also suffering flashbacks and auditory hallucinations, particularly at night, hearing the voices of her abuser and his frighteningly aggressive father—classical symptoms of post-traumatic stress disorder (PTSD). Cutting herself provided her with temporary, but by now alarmingly pleasurable, relief from these symptoms. But the pleasure she took in cutting was not simply a matter of diversion from the psychotic intensity of her PTSD symptoms, or of masochistic eroticization, there was actually an addictive quality to it. She admitted that cutting got her "high". Van der Kolk's (1989) neuroaffective observation that repeated self injury at times of stress triggers endogenous opioid systems into releasing endorphins which can have an anaesthetizing effect on unbearable feelings, is relevant here. But, for Kathryn, it was simply another source of shame which was only slightly alleviated by being informed about its psychobiological basis.

Bentovim (1995) writes about some families whose functioning can be understood as organized around some unspoken traumatic experience, such as sexual abuse; that there can be a tacit or secret agreement between otherwise innocent parties, a conspiracy of silence, in order to preserve the trauma-organized system. Kathryn also sought to replicate this pattern of secrecy in her relationships with members of the wider system, for example enjoining the school doctor into treating her, aged barely 15, with serious anti-depressant medication without her mother knowing anything about it. Or again, and more obviously, the repeated demand in therapy that her mother be kept in ignorance about what had actually happened to her or else she would kill herself. Her suicidal fantasies—jumping off a high building or a bridge or hanging herself; methods she rightly felt were more likely to achieve the desired outcome than the taking of overdoses—had to be viewed very seriously, and a careful risk management approach adopted. She told me there was no question she would kill herself if her mother ever found out what had happened to her in the past, effectively threatening me with what her abuser had threatened her with in the past (her own death), if I tried to work with her towards a healthier relationship with her mother. In this way she continued to hold onto the emotional core of the now pathological belief that her mother needed protecting or she (Kathryn) would cause her to die. But in the intervening years, and without realizing it, she had modified it, adjusted it, and adapted it so that it had become her own feelings and coping strategy (i.e. self-harm and silence) that she was now protecting her mother from, for fear of killing her emotionally with the truth, not only of what had happened in the past, but also of what she was continuing to do to herself in the present.

But maybe the truth will out as part of the therapeutic process. Kathryn did know her mother knew things were seriously wrong. After all she was in hospital, and as part of the contract between the responsible adults in her life, nursing staff informed her mother every time Kathryn was known to have harmed herself. Indeed, on one occasion when she had gone home overnight her mother had had to apply a tourniquet and ring for an ambulance after Kathryn opened an artery. So her cutting was not really a secret at all any more. After her mother finally worked out what had happened in the past and told Kathryn she now "knew" why she behaved as she did, Kathryn was angry but relieved and she did not in fact try to kill herself.

Alexithymia

Years of silence had taken their toll. Of the 150 minutes a week in which we met for sessions, approximately 120 were spent in silence. But many of those were anguished as Kathryn tried to find words for her feelings and experiences as an alternative to cutting or suicidal ideation. She would toss and turn in her chair, literally rolling her eyes and moaning, as if the struggle to either speak or harm herself was physically hurting her. Tears would stream down her face. She knew she wanted to stop harming herself and she knew she did not want to stop at all. She knew she was ambivalent. But insight was no cure. It did not change what she felt. And she experienced this conflict in such stark concretized—or more accurately, corporealized—terms that when she did successfully resist cutting herself she would instead find herself hallucinating blood running down her arms or legs, a sensation which she found more horrible than the real thing. Such symptoms were so overwhelming that she would often leave a session prematurely, telling me she hated me for trying to help her find a different way of coping and that I was her enemy. At other times she would leave a session early because the aforementioned pattern of trauma-organized secrecy would interpose itself into our therapeutic relationship and she would find herself wanting to look after me by protecting me from the full horror of what she was feeling. Then, despite all attempts to dissuade her, she would go off with the express intention of deliberately harming herself again.

The primacy of relationship

This would prompt terrible feelings of guilt on my part. I would feel completely inadequate to the task of meeting her therapeutic needs, part of the problem, ashamed of how frightened that made me feel, and castigating myself for it. In other words, consequent upon extremely upsetting right brain to right brain interactions with Kathryn, by just staying with what she was feeling, I would find that I had attuned myself to the affective reality of her PTSD to such an extent that I myself felt extremely stressed. And like Kathryn I would then effectively retraumatize, if not actually hurt myself. Not with razor blades or broken glass but by being hypercritical of my therapeutic competence and deriding my professional skills as negligible or non existent and because of that, no better than her abuser.

At the same time, quality supervision together with the support of a skilled multidisciplinary team, enabled me to struggle into a cognitive understanding that this sense of my own hopelessness was a cybernetic or countertransferential affective process and I was not as professionally ineffectual as I felt I was. My collegiate relationships thus contained and enabled me to realize that I did in fact have some choice about how I viewed myself after a session with Kathryn, which, in turn, reflected the fact that she had some choices too.

So it was therapeutically important to help Kathryn give herself permission not to feel she had to talk in therapy; to rediscover her autonomy, her right to choose how she wanted to use the sessions, and to disabuse her of the notion that she would have to force herself to speak the unspeakable if she was to recover. It helped to know something about the psychobiological basis for her anxiety, to understand about the raised cortisol levels in cases of dissociation and PTSD (Graham *et al.*, 1999). I would reassure her that she did not have to talk, that there was categorically no therapeutic requirement that she coerce herself into talking if she was to get better. The neuroimaging work of Rauch *et al.* (1998), showing the switch-off effect on left brain languaging and verbalization processes of emotional (right brain) states in cases of PTSD, provided hard evidence for this approach, so that I could let her know that for people with her kind of problems, talking about feelings was actually (neuro)physiologically difficult, that making herself do so when she didn't yet feel able to simply reprised the helplessness she had felt during the traumatic years of her abuse and actually made talking more difficult. Adopting a developmental model, we discovered that, for Kathryn, therapy was almost like starting life again, as if she were a small baby who did not yet have words, but could nevertheless affectively communicate perfectly well without them until such time as she did. Then it became easier for her and in time she was able to talk about what she wanted to talk about and to not talk about what she did not want to.

In the end, a neuroscientific developmental perspective helped me carry hope for Kathryn that, although she had a deep desire to be dead, mitigated only by her love and hate for her mother, as a young adolescent the process of neural plasticity had not yet completely stabilized and her therapeutic relationship with me could, therefore, just make a difference to her affective experience of herself. If, at the end of a session I was left with some of her despair, then it was just possible that she could be left with some of this hope. And after some months the frequency of her self-harm did in fact reduce.

Conclusion

In our clinical work with patients we have to be prepared to expose ourselves to their feelings if we are to be of any real help. This means we too will be affected by who they are and what they bring us. Psychotherapeutic theories and neuroscientific developments are both crucial in helping us to work more effectively, but in the end it is our actual relationships with our patients and with our colleagues which enables and contains real change. This is the revolutionary point at which the views of both psychotherapists and affective neuroscientists now converge.

References

Barbas, H. (1995). Anatomic basis of cognitive–emotional interactions in the primate prefrontal cortex. *Neuroscience and Biobehavioural Reviews, 19*: 499–510.

Bentovim, A. (1995). *Trauma Organized Systems*. London: Karnac.

Clery, C. (1998). Deliberate self-harm and sexual abuse in adolescence: some treatment issues in individual therapy. *European Journal of Psychotherapy, Counselling and Health, 1*(3): 353–364.

Crowe, M. (1996). Cutting up: signifying the unspeakable. *Australian and New Zealand Journal of Mental Health Nursing, 5*: 103–111.

van der Kolk, B. A. (1989). The compulsion to repeat the trauma: re-enactment, revictimisation, and masochism. *Psychiatric Clinics of North America, 12*(2): 389–410.

van der Kolk, B. A., Perry, J. C., & Herman, J. L. (1991). Childhood origins of self-destructive behaviour. *American Journal of Psychiatry, 148*: 1665–1671.

De Zulueta, F. (1993). *From Pain to Violence: the Traumatic Roots of Destructiveness*. London: Whurr.

De Zulueta, F. (2000). Speaking at the Bowlby Memorial Lecture in London. March.

Doherty, W. (1991). Can male therapists empower women in therapy?

In: T. J. Goodrich (Ed.), *Women and Power: Perspectives for Family Therapy*. New York: W. W. Norton & Co.

Goldberg, D., & David, A. S. (1991). Family therapy and the glamour of science. *Journal of Family Therapy, 13*: 17–30.

Graham, Y. P., Heim, C., Goodman, S. H., Miller, A. H., & Nemeroff, C. B. (1999). The effects of neonatal stress on brain development: implications for psychopathology. *Development and Psychopathology, 11*: 545–565.

Greenough, W., & Black, J. (1992). Induction of brain structure by experience: substrate for cognitive development. In: M. R. Gunnar & C. A. Nelson (Eds.), *Minnesota Symposia on Child Psychology 24: Developmental Behavioural Neuroscience* (pp. 155–200). Hillsdale NJ: Lawrence Erlbaum.

Holloway, M. (2001). *Young Cells in Old Brains*. Scientific American, September.

Kalsched, D. (1996). *The Inner World of Trauma: Archetypal Defences of the Personal Spirit*. London: Routledge.

Kaplan-Solms, K., & Solms, M. (1999). *Clinical Studies in Neuropsychoanalysis—Introduction to a Depth Neuropsychology*. London: Karnac.

Kuhn, T. S. (1962). *The Structure of Scientific Revolutions*. Chicago: University of Chicago Press.

Maturana, H., & Varela, F. (1987). *The Tree of Knowledge: The Biological Roots of Human Understanding*. London: Shambhala.

Ponting, C. (2000). *World History: A New Perspective*. London: Chatto & Windus.

Rauch, S. L., Shin, L., Whalen, P., & Pitman, R. (1998). Neuroimaging and the neuroanatomy of post-traumatic stress disorder. *CNS Spectrums, 3*(7): July/August.

Schore, A. N. (2001). Minds in the making: attachment, the self-organizing brain, and developmentally oriented psychoanalytic psychotherapy. *The British Journal of Psychotherapy, 17*(3).

Stern, D. N. (1995). *The Interpersonal World of the Infant*. New York: Basic Books.

Watzlawick, P. (Ed.) (1984). *The Invented Reality: How do we know what we believe we know? Contributions to Constructivism*. New York: W. W. Norton & Co.

CHAPTER EIGHT

"At the border between chaos and order": what psychotherapy and neuroscience have in common

Roz Carroll

"Understandings that are derived at the border between chaos and order where, according to some, many of the problems of nature lie, may not provide exact solutions but rather those which can allow application and understanding to emerge"

Coveney & Highfield, 1995, p. xiii

"Psychotherapy and psychoanalysis appear to be far closer to forms of intermittent turbulence and uncertainty than to ordered systems ... one of the goals of [...] modelling is to discover the underlying order beneath the surface chaos of the psychotherapeutic interaction"

Langs, 1988, p. 206

We are at a point in history where re-convergence between psychotherapy and the rapidly developing field of neuroscience has immense significance and potential—a potential which is revolutionary in its implications. The neuroscience represented in this book really does reflect a cutting edge distinct from mainstream science. It offers psychotherapy a great deal more than just fragments of interesting information and alternative models of the mind. It highlights a new way of thinking in science which—I am going to argue—is not just a familiar way of thinking for psychotherapy but actually is fundamental to its inception.

Freud's neurological studies, from 1880 onwards, preceded and informed his development of psychoanalysis. In his day, neurology consisted in the attempt to correlate clinical problems with specific locations in the brain. But he became dissatisfied with the limitations of this "localization" approach, because it did not address the *dynamic* nature of neurosis (i.e. its clinical difference from the specific effects of brain damage). Freud had both the desire and the imagination to sense a potential integration of neurological, behavioural, mental, and somatic functions, but the scientific tools and conceptual models of his era were not adequate to the task. He never up gave the idea entirely, but turned his attention to the development of psychoanalysis.[1]

In the twentieth century, the two burgeoning fields of psychoanalysis and neuroscience continued to develop in different directions. Dialogue between the two disciplines was hampered by differences in discourse, aims, and modes of research. There was a largely unbridgeable gap between the scientific language of neurons, neurotransmitters, and sensory–motor functions and the psychotherapeutic models of intrapsychic and interpersonal processes. Paul Whittle has called it, "the faultline running down the middle of psychology" with experimental psychology (which has been incorporated into neuroscience) on one side, and psychoanalysis and other forms of psychotherapy, on the other (Whittle, 2000).

But there has been a gradual turning of the tide. Until fairly recently, "the self has been viewed as a metapsychological phenomenon that was not accessible to scientific investigation" (Schore, 1994: p. 490). Now a small but significant group of radical thinkers in neuroscience and related fields have made significant strides towards integrating into its conceptual models aspects of human functioning which are very much closer to psychotherapy's concern with the self: feelings, the dyadic nature of consciousness (and the unconscious), the construction of meaning (internal working models), and the critical significance of early developmental experience. Psychotherapy, under pressure to produce "scientific" evidence, has much to gain from the impetus and dynamism of contemporary neuroscience. What is most heartening is that affective neuroscience is providing increasing evidence that underlines the need for a relational approach to human suffering, and points away from reductive thinking that has tended to characterize many medical model solutions. (Panksepp, 1998; Schore, 1994; Solms & Kaplan-Solms, 2000; Trevarthen, 2001; Watt, 2001).

Neuroscience's spectacular development, over the last decade in particular, is a result of three main factors:

— A surge in interdisciplinary thinking, including the emergence of many new fields, such as developmental neurochemistry, infant psychiatry, and neuropsychoanalysis, has resulted in the processing, cross-referencing and integration of vast amounts of data. A proliferation of connections between previously separate fields is a result of the crystallization of a few core concepts, such as self-regulation, attachment, and parallel process, which are recognized and studied by many disciplines from different perspectives. Integration is occurring in the context of a clearer recognition of the hierarchy of logical types, in other words different levels of organization, from the micro (atoms, molecules, organisms upward) to the macro (social, cultural, cosmic). Whilst appreciating the distinctions between different "levels of description", integrational theorists are overcoming the obstacles created by perceived hierarchies of discourse, which are about politics and power (Carroll, 2002a).
— Advanced technology, such as MR (magnetic resonance scanning) and PET (positron emission topography), for monitoring activity in various regions of the brain, techniques for tracking biochemical changes in the body, use of video to study the choreography of mother–infant interactions, and computers which can handle complex data, all contribute to a dynamic microscopic and more complete picture of human internal life. The micro level is absolutely critical in distinguishing subtle processes which have hitherto been disregarded or denied as scientifically unproveable.
— A shift has taken place in the overarching models of science, as far reaching as the changes following Einstein's theory of

relativity. Field, chaos and complexity theories have superseded mechanistic models which compared the brain to a computer. The implications for psychotherapy of this paradigm shift will be the main theme of the chapter.

A scientific revolution

To understand what it is that has enabled neuroscience to begin to get to grips with the subtle, multilayered, and often convoluted process of human relating, it is necessary to appreciate the revolution that has taken place in science over the last century. This new scientific paradigm, stemming from general systems theory, has arisen from the attempt to describe the behaviour of non-linear dynamic systems. These systems manifest characteristics such as chaos, complexity (or in some cases catastrophe), and self-organization by which names the theory is also known.[2]

In *Table 1*, I have contrasted the basic terms, principles, and characteristics of classical and new science (non-linear dynamic

Table 1. Classical versus new science.

Classical Science	New Science
Causality	Emergent properties
Linear	Non-linear
Objective	Includes subjectivity
Isolates events	Emphasizes context
Matter	Process
Focuses on stability	Focuses on sensitivity
Logic	Deeper pattern
Closed system	Open system
Reductive	Complex
Predictability	Chaos
Explicit/observable	Implicit/hidden
Time is uniform	Sensitive critical periods
Cause–effect	Feedback loops
Sequential	Experience-dependent
Mechanistic	Self-regulating
Fixed relations	Self-organizing
Objects (physical)	Fields
Particulate	Parallel

systems theory). This over-simplifies a historical process which is itself complex and chaotic, but gives an overview of the critical change in framework for thinking about non-linear processes.

Classical science explains closed systems which behave in ways that are predictable, stable, and knowable, for example, the physical behaviour of mechanical objects, such as clocks. New science was born from the attempt to understand dynamic, complex, open systems, such as the ecosystem, the weather system, and the behaviour of living creatures. In these systems, change is a matter of complex interconnected events, where there can be an extraordinary sensitivity to timing and minute changes in the environment, mediated through ubiquitous networks of feedback loops.

Psychotherapy has long wrestled with the implications of biology and its associations with determinism. The new biology— within the framework of self-organization theory—emphasizes interaction and contingency as major principles of formation, and therefore is more aligned with the emphasis on historical and relational principles of psychotherapy. In addition, new developments in science have enabled a more profound recognition of the structure–function relationship: structure is the record of previous history and determines *capacities*, but not content. The characteristics of the human mind arise from and are grounded in the structure of the brain and the body in interaction with the environment (Damasio, 1994, 1999; Johnson, 1987; Panksepp, 1998; Schore, 1994; Totton, 1998).

The formulation of principles which describe dynamic non-linear processes has led to tremendous advances in fields such as neuroscience. The brain itself is now conceived of as dynamic and non-linear, a complex hierarchy of systems and sub-systems. Interest is increasingly focused on neurochemistry in the dynamic equation of psychological functions. This implicates the totality of bodily processes interacting with brain structures to produce a radical "new anatomy", where all psychological functions, even specific ego functions, are conceived of as emergent properties of a complex "brain–mind–body" (Carroll, 2001; Schore, 2000: p. 40).

The prototype and initial bridging concept between biology and psychology was self-regulation, modelled on physiological homeostasis and incorporating the behavioural concept of adaptation. Feedback is the essential mechanism of self-regulation that allows living organisms to maintain themselves in a state of dynamic balance. Mother and baby can be conceived of as homeostatic regulators of each others' emotional states. The baby's behaviour is feedback—a communication to the mother. Her attuned response acts as benign feedback, helping to maintain equilibrium in the infant. The theory of self-regulation has been taken up by infant research and recent psychoanalytic theorists, where it has been strongly identified with the concept of affect regulation (Fonagy, 2001). Integrating across a variety of disciplines, Allan Schore demonstrates how the infant acquires regulatory capacities as a set of representations of interactions between itself and the caregivers. These representations correlate with structural changes in the brain enabling increasing self-regulation (Schore, 1994).

Whilst self-regulation remains a core model of developmental process, it has been extended by the evolution of self-organization theory which adds to it the elements of form and complexity. Prigogine, a pioneer of chaos theory, differentiated between systems that were "in equilibrium", "near equilibrium" and "far from equilibrium". Self-regulation theory emphasizes how the organism maintains equilibrium. Prigogine (1984) showed that systems far from equilibrium give birth to new structures—they can develop in a non-linear way. Chaos emerges when the trajectory of a system reaches a threshold of change (bifurcation point) far from equilibrium. At this moment of instability, the system may break down and follow an earlier pattern imprinted in its structure (repetition). Or as a result of its exquisite sensitivity to any fluctuation in the environment, it may break through to a new pattern of higher order and complexity.

The trajectory of self-organization is influenced by attractors, which, in terms of a human process, can mean a memory, a thought, or feeling—an attractor is like a groove which gets carved as experience gets repeated. Periodic attractors are those which recur and are characteristic of a stable system. Strange attractors emerge when a system is far from equilibrium and they can lead to dramatic shifts and reorganizations of structure. The difference between self-regulation and self-organization is that in the former the process is one of adaptation, translation, and change in surface structure. In contrast, self-organization manifests deep structural changes, where new forms emerge spontaneously. Self-organizing systems evolve hierarchically, they move from one level of development to another. Each new level builds on the previous one and is increasingly complex and differentiated. This helps elaborate a model of human development which includes both gradual progress and quantum change. Allan Schore, for example, has convincingly shown how the infant's experience in the attachment relationship is internalized as structural changes in the brain, in the form of increasing complexity, connectivity, and differentiation between parts. This directly correlates with the precise character of each individual infant's psychological story, with huge implications for their future emotional and physical well-being (Schore, 1994).

Self-organizing systems develop by coupling with other systems through ongoing feedback. Recurrent interactions trigger mutual structural changes. Neuroscientists Maturana and Varela coined the term "structural coupling" to describe the general principle of living systems interacting with their environment (Maturana & Varela, 1980). Structural coupling graphically describes human relationships, where people have ongoing reciprocal impact on each other. What is more, they insist, a structural couple is a *learning system*. Through experience we generate internal working models which we then enact, though with varying degrees of awareness. As Capra explains in *The Web of Life*:

> At a certain level of complexity a living organism couples structurally not only to its environment but also to itself, and thus brings forth not only an external but also an inner world. In human beings the bringing forth of an inner world is linked intimately to language, thought and consciousness. [1996, p. 270]

Self-organization is the critical property of living systems because it makes them both flexible and responsive to change, including sudden change, and robust and stable, able to maintain self-referral and coherence. The brain is self-organizing, with the evolutionary older parts tending to have more "fixed programmes", and the later-developing mammalian system being associated with the capacity for a wide range of feelings linked to survival and social functioning. It is now suggested that the plasticity of the neocortex, especially the orbito-frontal area, is influenced by the quality of structural coupling in the attachment relationship. Self-and-other representations become increasingly differentiated and integrated over specific developmental stages. In this way a hierarchical organization of sub-systems allows for emergent complex emotions, thoughts and actions (Schore, 1994, p. 491). Whilst such concentrated change cannot occur in the adult brain— because the sensitive "windows" of development have passed and with it the young brain's neural plasticity—the adult brain continues to evolve according to the principles of self-organization (Schore, 1994, p. 468).

Allan Schore points out that the term self-organization is a misnomer in two ways (Schore, 1997, p. 607). Self-organization describes a fundamentally *dyadic* process, not a self-centred one; and it refers to a continual flux of *dis*-organization and *re*-organization. With this minor caveat, self-organization theory provides a framework for thinking about multiple levels, the effect of relationships, non-linear change, the role of history, repetition, communication, sensitivity, and subtlety: in other words, the very phenomena that interest psychotherapists.

Psychotherapy—at home with chaos and complexity

Psychotherapy has always sought to work with the non-linear, apparently irrational, uniqueness of each individual or group. Its key thinkers have been gifted in seeing through the veil of madness to a deeper pattern, which takes account of the context and dynamic from which it emerged. Freud said of the unconscious: "we call it a chaos ..." (1933), and he described it as a dynamic system. Many of the regulatory principles outlined in Freud's "Project" (1950 [1895]) have been found to be quite compatible with modern systems theory (Pribam & Gill, 1976). However, Freud lacked the conceptual models of our contemporary scientific paradigm, and so was forced to develop psychoanalysis as a separate discipline.

Freud struggled to integrate functional, topographical, systemic, dynamic, and economic points of view.[3] Arguably, self-organization theory could provide the framework for such an integration. Certainly Freud was struck by the principle of the reciprocal bodily and psychological process of trying to maintain equilibrium, and the paradoxical behaviours and spontaneous (unconscious) forms— symptoms, dreams, jokes—that resulted from juggling internal conflicts. He identified the shifts between "bound" and "mobile" states on many levels (word presentation, ego organization, affect, energy). He used terms such as "fixation", "excitation", and "lability" to describe what Allan Schore, using the language of non-linear dynamic systems theory, is correlating in neurological detail with attractors and state transitions (Schore, 1997). Today Christopher Bollas is further developing this idea of constant flux or disorganization—reorganization (what he calls condensation and dissemination) as *the* work of the unconscious and psychotherapy (Bollas, 1997).

Interestingly Reich and Jung *were* able to find an explicit place for self-regulation, both in their distinctive metapsychological positions and, more significantly, in the actual process of the therapeutic work. Reich anticipated contemporary neuroscience in his emphasis on the autonomic nervous system, now recognized as a core structure involved in emotional self-regulation: "the development of character is a progressive unfolding, splitting and antithesis of vegetative (i.e. autonomic) functions" (Reich, 1973, p. 302). He maintained that physiological systems, such as the muscular system, had a correlating psychological function, based on their structural—or as he put it functional—identity. In his development of vegetotherapy (i.e. a therapy which directly addresses the autonomic nervous system), Reich worked with the breathing pattern to release chronic contraction in the tissue, which arrests pulsation, the fundamental rhythm of self-regulation (Reich, 1972, 1973). Meanwhile, Jung had a powerful perception of the patient's spontaneous productions—symptoms, imagery, dreams—not simply as diagnostic, but as potentially healing in and of themselves. The Self is seen as having deeply rooted, innate self-regulating capacities which can be effectively utilized in psychotherapy (Conger, 1988; Jung, 1921; Samuels, 1989).

Self-regulation, as a broad term, remains a key concept in subsequent therapeutic traditions—particularly the humanistic—where it includes a variety of therapeutic activities. The elaboration of an impulse indirectly through a specific medium, such as art, or directly with the therapist allows for its recognition and assimilation. In other therapies (NLP, family therapy, Gestalt, T.A) systems and field theory have been used explicitly to model dynamic processes.

Meanwhile, the thinking of Klein, Winnicott, and Bion was characterized by the attempt to find a language to describe *intensity*.

Working typically with a more disturbed client group, they anticipated the relevance of catastrophe, chaos, and paradox in non-linear dynamic systems theory by perceiving such change processes of human experience in these very terms! In psychoanalysis, the therapist is conceived as having a more active role in the regulation (containment) of the patient through holding and interpretation (Grinberg, 1977).

Despite the wide variations in theory and technique which characterize the field of psychotherapy today, *therapy in general seems to offer a particular opportunity for intensifying the ordinary self-organizing process of life*. Its formal structure sets limits of one kind, in order that other limits—such as the constraints of "normal" social discourse—can be suspended. Secondly, it radically increases feedback to the system (the client) in a multiplicity of ways. Self-regulation is supported through the provision of a stable, empathic, boundaried space. This acts as a container for meaningful crises and transitions to more complex and differentiated states.

Psychotherapy pays close attention to the trajectory of the client's thinking and feeling. As the therapist perceives a crisis or fluctuation in the trajectory (both backward and forward), he/she makes a therapeutic decision—perhaps to actively support the emergence of a new state, or perhaps just to continue to wait and see what unfolds. Or the therapist may perturb a familiar trajectory either inadvertently or deliberately through an intervention. Psychotherapy inevitably evokes pain and fear in the client because it amplifies the conflict between established structures which are breaking down and an emergent process which is unfamiliar.

The aspects of the feedback process in psychotherapy could be broken down in various ways and into various categories. In the next section I am going to focus on three fundamentally interrelated facets of this process, which I am calling "representing", "feeling", and "relating". In terms of self-organization theory, representing refers to the pattern of organization, feeling is the state, and relating the structural couple.

Psychotherapy as a self-organizing process [4]

Since its inception, psychotherapy has used the telling of a story as a means for the client to present and represent him/herself. The modes of this representation in psychotherapy have proliferated, as have controversies about the nature of representation itself. Whilst neuroscientists would agree that representation is intrinsically overdetermined and complex, they are as much in dispute over the scope of the term representation as psychotherapists. In general though, representation is recognized as an activation or reactivation of a neural pattern. Neuroscientists commonly use the metaphor of an on-line function (reminding us of Freud's meaning "*re*-presentation"). Damasio and Schore, both from quite different perspectives, are arguing that representations are based on patterns of relationships, the object plus its effect on the subject (Damasio, 1994; Schore, 1994). Of equal significance is the substitution of the idea of "mental" content for a more holistic embodied concept for all representation. Damasio suggests that the neural patterns from which representations derive are essentially *images in multiple sensory modalities of texture, movement and intensity* (1999, p. 318). His work supports the emphasis on innate imagery, increasingly recognized in psychotherapy as underpinned by bodily processes (Samuels, 1989; Landale, 2002). All the major theoreticians in neuroscience are moving—in their different ways—towards recognizing psychological process as fundamentally embodied (Carroll, 2002a). This is part of the cultural and scientific paradigm shift and is reflected in the growing interest in the role of the body in psychotherapy. Body psychotherapy, for example, includes the explicit use of the feedback from the body to the brain to enhance and clarify object relations (Carroll, 2002b).

Naturally, representation of the client to him or herself happens in numerous ways. Psychotherapies vary most obviously in the way in which they implicitly and explicitly manage this feedback process: verbal interpretations, questions, and reflections; eye contact, non-verbal attunement, movement, and qualities of presence; techniques such as visualization, bodywork, hypnosis, and other structured interventions, such as maintaining boundaries. All these interventions are, to one degree or another, interpretative within a framework. Every therapist imparts a set of principles and concepts which, whatever their intrinsic value, reframes the client's experience, and therefore re-presents it.

Representation is complex, conflicted, and multi-levelled: conscious and unconscious, triggered self-reflexively and directly and indirectly in relation to the therapist. And it is holistic: affecting many systems of the brain and the body, producing images, sensations, fantasies, feelings, and thoughts. The nature of the brain makes this inevitable—for representation of the self is distributed through many systems of the brain, from the brainstem to the cortex. Rather than a central coordinating area for processing in the brain, neuroscientists suggest that massive parallel neural connections between brain regions (known as "re-entry") happens via reciprocal electrical signalling, such that different regions mutually influence each other. In *The Mind-Brain Relationship*, Pally explains that:

> Synchronisation of activity made possible by re-entry enables rapid shifts in activity in large populations of neuronal groups. Re-entry functions to select the particular neural pathway that underlies the perceptual behaviour and experience [...] by linking widely distributed areas into complicated patterns [...] This is why consciousness takes time. Stimuli, memory or emotion must persist for sufficient duration to enable re-entry to produce the synchronisation of firing necessary to integrate widely distributed neural networks. [2000, pp. 163–164]

The nature of the process which precipitates integration between parts of the brain is very complex and still relatively uncharted. Still, a few basic integrative patterns have been of particular interest: left-brain to right-brain connections; vertical integration of brain systems, from cortex to brainstem; and functional circuits governing specific emotions, behaviours, and psychological functions. Insights into brain functioning confirm how psychotherapy can have a beneficial effect just from the cumulative consequence of making connections, representing and re-associating significant information. The use of metaphor, for example, is a highly integrative form of representation because it activates many brain regions simultaneously.

The complementary styles of the right and left cortex, popularized in the 1960s by Gazzaniga and Sperry, have been increasingly differentiated with significant resulting implications for psychotherapy (Pally, 2000, pp. 105–136). The left and right brains are lateralized for special functions, although in the healthy brain the two work synergistically. The right brain is associated with emotional processing and attachment; contextual, spatial, and global thinking; socio-emotional and non-verbal information; and integration of information from the body. The left brain identifies detail, sequential information, causal relationships, logic, and language. The left brain plays an important role in verbalizing and therefore optimally interpreting and articulating feelings. When it is not integrated with right-brain functions, it operates more like a confabulator, generating plausible explanations that are not based on deeper emotional connections (see Turnbull in this volume). Therapeutic work can support increasing representation across the two cortices through the use of arts, music, movement and bodywork (which nourish the right brain), and by attention to the client–therapist relationship (Robbins et al., 1986).

Equally, however, increased understanding of the complexity of brain organization confronts us with the stubborn hard-wiredness of deep psychological–neurological structures. Despite the relative plasticity of the cortex, which allows for the tremendous intellectual and creative scope of the human mind, its deeper interconnections with older parts of the brain limits its ultimate range of function. Neurodevelopment follows the principles of self-organization in that higher structures mirror and recapitulate the organization of lower systems. In other words, a "basic fault" will manifest higher up the system. In addition, whilst the cortex is designed to process novelty, it is in the lower brain structures that behaviours not subject to conscious control are maintained and consolidated. In studies, it has been shown that as long as the individual tries to control his behaviour or makes a conscious mental exertion, the alpha wave, which reflects spontaneous reorganization of brain activity, is not achieved (Robbins et al., 1986, p. 117).

The challenge of facilitating structural change is compounded by the sheer multiplicity of neurological systems organizing behaviour. This means that attention and energy are easily displaced into the circuits with which therapist and client are most comfortable. Freud identified this process of displacement of instinctual energy over a century ago. In a landmark work, *Affective Neuroscience*, Jaak Panksepp (1998) has delineated seven emotional operating systems, distinguished by specific neural circuits and integrated cognition/ affect /behaviour patterns, that come close to what we might call "instincts". Panksepp regards these not as drives but as regulatory mechanisms emerging from the intrinsic potentials of the nervous system. Neurobiologically, the systems identified are: the seeking system (governing curiosity, searching and meaning-making); the rage system (aroused by frustration); the fear system (fight/flight/freeze); the panic system (separation distress); the lust system (sexual behaviour); the care system (maternal behaviour); and the play system.

Whilst some of these categories are predictable, others radically reformulate our established categories of affect with surprising implications. Panksepp suggests that the function of the play system—which he links with play in the sense of "rough and tumble" activity—is to integrate a wide variety of somatic and other information, in a complementary role with dreaming (1998, pp. 280–299). Meanwhile, the seeking system is linked with the pleasure of discovery, and is implicated in the neurochemistry of dreaming. Investigation of this neurobiological system, connected with foraging behaviour, can help us understand why we are driven to search for meaning in psychotherapy (and elsewhere) and why its elaboration is so intrinsically satisfying, quite apart from the benefits to be gained from insight. Dysregulation of this system leads to an excess of meaning-making—manic activity which is ungrounded and unstable (1998, pp. 144–163).

Yet what strikes me about these neurologically identifiable systems is that they correlate quite highly with the orientation and emphases of various therapeutic traditions: those which have given pre-eminent place to attachment, such as attachment-based psychoanalytic psychotherapy (separation distress system); the Freudians with their emphasis on sexuality (lust system); the Kleinians who work particularly around themes of frustration and envy (rage system); the Jungian emphasis on active imagination and dream analysis (the seeking system); body psychotherapy which is premised on somatic integration (the play system); and finally therapies which specialize in working with trauma (fear system). Obviously no psychotherapy is limited to one system and these links between neurological system and school are somewhat stereotypical. But I hope the point is still valid: that the development of psychotherapies may be influenced by the particular system that their founders tended to self-organize around. The positive side of this is that self-organization in one system does affect neighbouring systems, so that there will be a knock-on effect from work done on any aspect.

Naturally it is also the case that these distinct circuits are complexly interrelated and reciprocally linked. Nor should these neurological structures be mistaken for the manifest themes in psychotherapy. They constitute deep organizational patterns which have ramifications on many structural levels of the brain. The best hypothesis about the key to structural reorganization fits with current psychotherapy thinking: that it is not in identifying the content, but in creating the therapeutic context for activating cortical, limbic, and brainstem simultaneously—a neurological firing on all cylinders. Douglas Watt, commenting on the phenomenon of repetition compulsion, suggests that both "cortical and subcortical systems need to be 'on-line' and (re-)activated in order for them to be modified by new contingencies" (Watt, 2001, p. 8).

How—as it were—can the therapist maximize this "on-lineness" so that critical reorganization can take place? Recall that what nourishes self-organization is *feedback* which, I suggest, in a cultivated and often highly sophisticated way is the essence of psychotherapy. Indeed, psychotherapy is a specialized form of mutual feedback, a double loop which focuses around the client's self-organization, whilst nested within the organization of the psychotherapy relationship (and beyond that the supervision). It depends on the reflective use of relating, paying particular attention to subtle changes and nuances that hint at hidden dynamics. When a behaviour, phrase or gesture—or all three together—are noted, even if not verbalized, awareness is amplified. Empathy in the therapist, and the client's attachment to the therapist, and curiosity in them both, will increase the potential for resonance. The structure of therapy itself reinforces the propensity to heightened engagement stimulated by high levels of attunement. In contemporary psychotherapy, there is now a marked emphasis on the psychotherapeutic relationship itself as the critical factor organizing change. The therapist–client couple has been variously theorized and utilized, including via the attachment model and the erotic couple of the Jungian *coniunctio* (Samuels, 1989). This correlates with the concept of structural coupling, a phrase which evokes the prototypical human pairings of mother–infant and adult lovers.

The Process Oriented Psychologist, Mindell, suggests that the varieties of psychotherapy are "spontaneous creations which arise by amplifying events in given channels of the client therapist interaction" (Mindell, 1989, p. 8). The implication is that not only are different schools of psychotherapy self-organizing, but so is each therapist in his or her experience of the countertransference. With each new client the therapist allows the emergence of a self-organizing structure between themselves and the client (Ogden's "analytic third"). The recognition of countertransference as an ordering principle is thoroughly congruent with chaos theory (Field, 1996). Countertransference is characterized by an extreme sensitivity to relational cues; its meaning has to be derived from the context. Its manifestations are inherently non-linear and unpredictable and we tend to notice them first either in a very subtle and novel detail of our own process or through finding our own internal trajectory knocked dramatically askew.

Transference reflects a relatively closed feedback loop, because it constitutes the repetition of a past pattern, rather than an open loop in the present. The therapist aims to feedback the information in this unconscious behaviour in the face of the tricky fact that transference is precisely what blocks the client from receiving feedback. It is interesting to note that in dynamic systems theory *two* contrasting kinds of feedback are recognized: amplifying or (+ve) feedback which expands and intensifies patterns; and dampening or (–ve) feedback, which has the opposite effect. In the psychotherapy relationship, both participants are subject to their own self-regulating defences (internal feedback). When a certain threshold of arousal occurs, he/she will unconsciously inhibit further arousal (–ve feedback). This is in tension with the curiosity to explore and amplify feelings which may lead to a pleasurable, or uncomfortable, increase in self-awareness (+ve feedback).

This has numerous ramifications, which may be perceived by the therapist in terms of the client's language (narrative content, imagery), behaviour (looking away, making faces), and other body phenomena (breathing, tone of voice), and in the countertransference. The therapist's intervention may help amplify subtle transactions which are then experienced in their intensity as pain, excitement, fear etc. (increasing positive feedback). Or they may provoke further defensive contractions in the client, who is attempting to limit the catastrophe and chaos of experiencing intensity. The tension between these forms of feedback are at the crux of psychotherapy. With an imbalance of negative feedback, the individual/system becomes static and closed. Too much positive feedback dysregulates in the other direction—there is chronic instability.

At the risk of over-generalizing, we could say that the humanistic tradition has been characterized by its emphasis on positive feedback, "letting it happen", expression etc. Its *raison d'etre* was the encouraging of growth. By contrast, some psychoanalytic psychotherapies have focused on naming and interpreting defences, in order to modify the effect of negative feedback. In practice, all therapies probably use a mixture of both. We work with the dynamic tension between safety and not being too safe, between conscious insight and disinhibition, between structuring and disrupting.

The paradox of therapy is that when the client can bear what is unbearable to think and feel, their experience changes—the self reorganizes. The critical factor here is spontaneity which is equivalent to chaos, in the sense that scientists are using the term. Chaos, in this context, represents "a lifting of constraints on information processing" (Schore, 1997, p. 614). The client—and sometimes the therapist—inevitably fear chaos in the worst sense of the word, as a meaningless loss of control. Yet an outburst of feeling may prove an important turning point allowing for a deeper holding or tolerance of destructiveness, or an insight into the creative force of what has been repressed.

Spontaneity is the hallmark of reorganization. It is a term more frequently used in humanistic practice and conveys its fundamental optimism about human nature and the trajectory towards self-actualization. It has also been associated with the emphasis on discovering internal *freedom to act*. In psychoanalysis, free association is the focal vehicle for a spontaneous process. The emphasis here is on *freedom to think* through getting at the roots of unconscious restraints on thought.

It is widely agreed now that the client needs to *experience* feelings in the relationship with the therapist. This makes sense because, as Doug Watt has argued, "emotion binds together virtually every type of information that the brain can encode [...] running from top to bottom of the neuro-axis" (1998, p. 19). Intensity of feeling, transitions between feelings, and the identifying of unfamiliar feelings, all feed self-organization. The therapist plays a critical role in influencing—via subtle cues and interpretations which reflect both strategic focusing and unconscious avoidance in the therapist —both the specific feeling and the intensity that the client is encouraged to experience.

These are bodily relational processes. The ability of the client to occupy and differentiate a multiplicity of psychological "positions" (in the broadest sense) depends on their capacity to shift between different psychobiological states associated with different affects. Schore argues that pathology is directly equivalent to inefficient state regulation originating in early failures of the attachment relationship. He notes that chaos arises at the point of phase transition, in other words at the critical point when new feelings are emerging (1997). At this point, the client is extremely sensitive to "perturbation", a disturbance in the form of interruption or non-attunement. As therapists know, timing is crucial and "minute perturbations can change the whole trajectory" (Schore, 1997, p. 602).

At the current moment both neuroscience and psychotherapy would probably agree that change is not linear but rather a continual process of organization, disorganization, and reorganization. Despite the need of the therapist to maintain the therapeutic position, many argue now that at critical moments neither therapist nor client may be "in control" and that the therapist's access to a meta-level—a containing overview—will be disrupted before it is recovered (Soth, 2000, no. 18, p. 10). Psychotherapy, in other words, joins neuroscience in researching "at the border between chaos and order" (Coveney & Highfield, 1995, p. xiii).

Notes

1. The importance of Freud's 1895 essay *Project for a Scientific Psychology* (1950) was noted by neuropsychologist Pribam and Gill (1976), and has been commented on by Wilden (1972), Solms and Kaplan-Solms (2000), and Totton (1998).

2. Non-linear dynamic systems theory is the over-arching term, whilst chaos, complexity and self-organization form overlapping branches of theory. Field and information theory are also part of the new scientific paradigm. I have tried to minimize use of technical terms and lengthy

explanations of concepts in order not to obscure the emphasis on basic principles. As a non-scientist, I followed the descriptions outlined in Coveney and Highfield (1995), Capra (1996), Sardar and Abrams (1998), and for the broadest overview Wilber (1995).

3. For a spectrum of analyses of Freud's overlapping models of metapsychology, see Wilden (1972), Ricoeur (1970), Solms & Kaplan-Solms (2000). I am particularly indebted to Nick Totton's (1998) discussion of Freud in relation to various neuroscientific and psycho-analytic perspectives, including Damasio, Kristeva, Stern, and Winnicott.

4. Various writers have made links between chaos theory and psycho-therapy, including Field (1996), Scharff and Scharff (1998), and Robbins *et al.* (1986). Allan Schore's paper on non-linear processes in early development (1997), as well as his discussion of research in psychotherapy using a chaos model (1994, pp. 469–472), was an important influence. I am also grateful to Michael Soth, Nick Totton, and Kathrin Stauffer for their inspiration and help in developing this chapter.

References

Bollas, C. (1997). *Cracking Up: The Work of Unconscious Experience.* London: Routledge.

Capra, F. (1996). *The Web of Life: A New Understanding of Living Systems.* New York: Anchor Books.

Carroll, R. (2001). The new anatomy; an exploration of the body systems integrating neuroscience, psychotherapy and psychoanalysis. http://www.thinkbody.co.uk.

Carroll, R. (2002a). Interdisciplinary thinking at its best: an introduction to some neuroscientists. *The Psychotherapist, 18,* Spring.

Carroll, R. (2002b). Biodynamic massage in psychotherapy: re-integrating, re-owning and re-associating through the body. In: T. Staunton (Ed.), *Advances in Body Psychotherapy.* London: Routledge.

Conger, J. P. (1988). *Jung and Reich: The Body as Shadow.* Berkley: North Atlantic Books.

Coveney, P., & Highfield, R. (1995). *Frontiers of Complexity.* London: Faber.

Damasio, A. (1994). *Descartes' Error: Emotion, Reason, and the Human Brain.* London: Putnam.

Damasio, A. (1999). *The Feeling of What Happens: Body, Emotion and the Making of Consciousness.* London: Heinemann.

Field, N. (1996). *Breakdown and Breakthrough: Psychotherapy in a New Dimension*. London: Routledge.

Fonagy, P. (2001). *Attachment Theory and Psychoanalysis*. New York: Other Press.

Freud, S. (1932). *New Introductory Lectures on Psycho-analysis*. S.E., 22.

Freud, S. (1950 [1895]). *A Project for a Scientific Psychology*. S.E., 1.

Grinberg, L. (1977). *New Introduction to the Work of Bion*. New Jersey: Aronson.

Johnson, M. (1987). *The Body in the Mind: The Bodily Basis of Meaning, Imagination and Reason*. Chicago Press.

Jung, C. G. (1921). Psychological types and the self-regulating psyche. In: S. Storr (Ed.), *The Essential Jung*. Princeton University Press, 1983.

Landale, M. (2002). The use of imagery in body psychotherapy. In: T. Staunton (Ed.), *Advances in Body Psychotherapy*. London: Routledge.

Langs, R. (1988). Mathematics for psychoanalysis. *British Journal of Psychotherapy*, 5: 2.

Maturana, H., & Varela, F. (1980). *Autopoiesis and Cognition*. Dordrecht, Holland: D. Reidel.

Mindell, A. (1989). *Rivers Way: The Process Science of the Dreambody*. London: Arkana.

Pally, R. (2000). *The Mind-Brain Relationship*. London: Karnac.

Panksepp, J. (1998). *Affective Neuroscience: The Foundations of Human and Animal Emotions*. Oxford University Press.

Pribam, K. H., & Gill, M. M. (1976). *Freud's "Project" Re-assessed*. New York: Basic Books.

Prigogine, I., & Stengers, I. (1984). *Order Out of Chaos*. New York: Bantam.

Reich, W. (1972). *Character Analysis*. New York: Farrar, Strauss and Giroux, 1990.

Reich, W. (1973). *The Function of the Orgasm*. Reprinted Souvenir Press, 1983.

Ricoeur, P. (1970). *Freud and Philosophy: An Essay on Interpretation*, D. Savage (Trans.). New Haven: Yale University Press.

Robbins, A. *et al.* (1986). *Expressive Therapy: a Creative Arts Approach to Depth-Oriented Treatment*. New York: Human Sciences.

Samuels, S. (1989). *The Plural Psyche*. London: Routledge.

Sardar, S., & Abrams, I. (1998). *Introducing Chaos*. Duxford: Icon.

Scharff, J. S., & Scharff, D. E. (1998). *Object Relations Individual Therapy*. London: Karnac.

Schore, A. (1994). *Affect Regulation and the Origin of the Self*. Hove: Lawrence Erlbaum.

Schore, A. (1997). Early organization of the non-linear right brain and development of a predisposition to psychiatric disorders. *Development and Psychopathology*, 9: 595–631.

Schore, A. (2000). Attachment and the regulation of the right brain. *Attachment and Human Development*, 2(2).

Schore, A. (2001). The American Bowlby: an interview with Allan Schore, www.psychotherapy.org.uk.

Solms, M., & Kaplan-Solms, K. (2000). *Clinical Studies in Neuro-Psychoanalysis*. London: Karnac.

Soth, M. (2000). Body/mind integration. *AChP Newsletter*, no. 17–19.

Totton, N. (1998). *The Water in the Glass: Body and Mind in Psychoanalysis*. London: Rebus Press.

Trevarthen, C., & Aitken, K. J. (2001). Infant intersubjectivity: research, theory and clinical application. *Journal of Child Psychology and Psychiatry*, 42(1): 3–48.

Watt, D. (1998). Affective neuroscience and extended reticular thalamic activating system (ERTAS) theories of consciousness. Association for the Scientific Study of Consciousness Electronic Seminar: http://server.phil.vt.edu/Assc/esem4html.

Watt, D. (2001). Psychoanalysis and neuroscience: alienation and reparation. *Neuro-Psychoanalysis*, 2(4).

Whittle, P. (2000). Experimental psychology and psychoanalysis: what we can learn from a Century of Misunderstanding. *Neuro-Psychoanalysis*, 1: 233–245.

Wilber, K. (1995). *Sex, Ecology and Spirituality*. London: Shambala.

Wilden, A. (1972). *System and Structure: Essays in Communication and Exchange*. London: Tavistock.

INDEX

Abrams, I., 209–210
abuse
    alcohol/drug/substance 117, 141
    child, 4, 82, 125, 127–128 183–184,
        187
Adolphs, 23, 30, 39
affect regulation, 16, 24–26, 31, 35,
    67–69, 124, 157
affective neuroscience, 1–2, 4–5, 79,
    84, 86, 112, 141, 177, 193
Ainsworth, M. D. S., 7, 16–17, 39,
    128, 130
Aitken, K. J., 20, 78, 211
akinetic mutism (AKM), 93, 95
    102–107
Alborzian, S., 171, 174
Amini, F., 28, 34, 39
amygdala, 20–21, 24, 96–97, 99,
    101–103, 106, 108, 124, 139
Anders, T. F., 21, 39
Andersen, S. M., 31, 39
Anderson, S. W., 25, 39, 147–148,
    161

Aristotle, 160
Arnsten, A., 126, 130
Atchley, P., 29, 39
Atchley, R. A., 29, 39
attachment(s), 7, 11–13, 16, 18–19,
    28, 81, 85, 88–89, 99–100, 109,
    122, 127, 130, 193, 203–204
    and affects, 12
    and the brain, 117
    behaviour(s), 19, 21, 106, 121, 127
    bond, 16
    communications, 38
    control system/system, 19, 128,
        179
    development of, 123
    disorganized, 128
    disorder(s)s, 26, 129
    dyadic, 38
    dynamics, 36
    emotions of, 66
    experience(s), 19, 35, 109–110
    figure(s), 128–129
    -focused psychotherapy, 27, 204

formation of, 129
functions, 28, 34
"gone wrong", 183
histories, 26
history, 179
interactions, 26
interactive, 15
mechanism of, 23
mechanisms, 82
model, 38, 205
needs, 111–112, 128
neurobiological correlates of, 129
organization, 128
pathologies, 26–27
patterns, 34
process(es), 12, 82, 86
-related information, 33
relationship(s), 9, 12, 23, 27–28,
    129, 148, 179, 183, 197, 208
research, 8
right brain, 23, 35
secure/security/insecurity of, 24,
    26, 38, 128–129, 183
studies, 28
theory, 8, 12–13, 26, 66
to the therapist, 205
transactions, 11
Attention Deficit Hyperactivity
    Disorder (ADHD), 126
attunement/misattunement/
    reattunement, 15–16, 28–29,
    32–33, 37, 124, 180, 201, 205,
    208
Atwood, G. E., 36, 49
Au, S. C., 171, 174
autonomic nervous system (ANS),
    22, 35, 61, 85, 93, 145, 199
autoregulate/autoregulation, 25,
    33, 35
Axis I/II disorders, 83–84

Baars, B. J., 111, 113–114
baby/babies, 3, 16–17, 54–58,
    60–72, 75–76, 119, 121, 187, 196
Bagby, R. M., 27, 50
Bandler, R., 102, 113

Barbas, H., 24, 38–39, 180, 188
Bargh, J. A., 136, 161
Barnett, L., 28, 42
Baron-Cohen, S., 24, 50
Barr, R., 127, 131
Bateson, G., 55
Bateson, M. C., 55–56
Bauer, R. M., 22, 40
Baxter, L. R., 171, 174
Bechara, A., 24, 39, 143–144, 161
bed nucleus of stria terminalis
    (BNST), 101, 103
Beebe, B., 35, 39
Beeman, M., 30, 39
Belsky, J., 38, 46
Bentovim, A., 184, 188
Bergin, A. E., 166, 174
Bernard, C., 164
Berry, H., 145, 155, 162
Bihrle, S., 148, 162
Bion, W. R., 29, 39, 199
Black, J., 121–122, 131, 177, 189
Blanck, G. 113
Blanck, R., 113
Blehar, M., 128, 130
Blonder, 29–30, 40
Bloom, E., 119, 132
Bollas, C., 199, 209
Bond, J. A., 161–162
Bookheimer, S. Y., 36, 43
Boring, A., 127, 131
Boris, N. W., 117, 133
Bosquet, M., 123, 132
Bowers, D., 22, 30, 40
Bowlby Memorial
    Lecture/Conference, 2, 7, 12
Bowlby, J., 7–9, 11–12, 19–24, 26, 30,
    38, 40, 82, 113, 127–128, 130
Bowman, C. H., 145, 161–162
Bownds, M. D., 121, 131
Boyer, L. B., 35, 40
Bradley, S., 12, 27, 40
brainstem, 20, 73, 91, 92–93, 95–97,
    99, 106, 110–111, 119, 137,
    139–140, 170, 202, 205
Brakel, L. A., 162–163

Brammer, M. J., 37, 50
Brammer, M., 21, 41
Bråten, S., 76
Brazelton, B., 55
Brazelton, T. B., 14, 45
Brenner, C., 9, 40
Brody, A. I., 171, 174
Brothers, L., 24, 40
Brown, 37
Bruckbauer, T., 24, 42
Brumaghim, T., 125, 132
Bruner, J., 55
Bruschweiler-Stern, N., 19, 30,
    49–50
Bucci, W., 30, 40
Buck, R., 29, 41
Bullmore, E., 21, 41
Bullowa, M., 56
Burns, A. F., 29, 40
Buysse, D. J., 167, 174

Cameron, A. A., 102, 113
Capgras' delusion, 152, 155, 161
Capitanio, J. P., 16, 46
Capra, F., 197, 209
Carmichael, S. T., 21, 41, 46
Carroll, R., 1, 5, 191, 193, 195, 201,
    209
Carroll, R., 1, 5, 191, 193, 195, 201,
    209
Casey, B., 127, 131
Cassidy, J., 24, 45
Cavada, C., 21, 41
Chalmers, D., 113
Chartland, T. L., 136, 161
Checkley, S. A., 37, 50
Cherry, C. R., 167, 174
Cheverud, J., 21, 42
Chiron, C., 10, 41
Chisum, H., 121, 131
Chua, P. M.-L., 31, 45
Cicchetti, D., 125, 132
Clarke, D., 127, 131
Clery, C., 5, 175, 184, 188
Cliffer, K. D., 102, 113
cognitive, 3, 24

abilities, 125
aspects, 86
awareness, 179
drives, 85
experience, 72
extensions, 92, 110
functions/activity, 85, 92,
    105–107, 111
impressions, 37
information, 13
learning, 66
operations, 92, 95
psychology/psychologists,
    73–74, 136
science/neuroscience, 3, 38, 74,
    135–136, 158
therapists, 166
trends/processes, 4, 11, 92, 100,
    110
understanding, 187
Colletti, P., 148, 162
Company, T., 21, 41
computerized tomography (CT),
    105, 118
confabulation/confabulator,
    151–152, 155–157, 203
Conger, J. P., 199, 209
Cooper, G., 23, 30, 39
Cornes, C. I., 167, 174
Costall, A., 76
Courchesne, E., 121, 131
Coveney, 191, 208–209
Cox, S. G., 37, 50
Craik, F. I. M., 25, 41
Critchley, H. D., 20–21, 41
Crnic, K., 38, 46
Crowe, M., 183, 188
Cruz-Rizzolo, R. J., 21, 41
Cue, K. L., 28, 42

Daly, E., 21, 41
Damasio, A. R., 3, 22, 25, 39, 41, 84,
    79, 94, 96, 100, 110–111,
    144–147, 158, 160–161, 195, 201,
    209
Damasio, H., 39, 161

dance, 53–54, 60, 72, 75
David, A. S., 177, 189
David, A., 21, 41
Davidson, R. J., 37, 41
Davidson, R., 124, 131
Dawson, G., 124–125, 131
De Bellis, M., 127, 131
de Leeuw, R., 78
de Zulueta, F., 179, 183, 188
Deci, E. L., 18, 15, 46
Depaulis, 102, 113
depression, 62, –63, 84, 86, 87–91,
        160, 167–168, 170–171, 181
Derryberry, D., 30, 41
development, 25–26, 66, 94, 148
    abnormal/failure of/
        maladaptive, 25, 122–123,
        127, 129–130
    adult affective, 37
    early, 8, 11, 31, 137, 193, 209
    emotional, 4, 27, 33, 37, 67
    human, 7, 11, 197
    interpersonal, 123
    neurobiological, 38
    of speech and language, 55, 123
    of the brain/mind, 3, 8–9, 54, 73,
        92, 117, 119, 121–123, 125,
        129, 198, 203
    of the infant/of infant
        intelligence, 3, 13, 15, 18–19,
        55, 67, 124
    scientific/neuroscientific,
        176–178, 188, 193
developmental
    disorder(s), 35 landscape, 82
    history, 179
    model, 187, 196
    neurological damage/"arrests",
        25, 27, 82
    neuroscience/
        neuropsychoanalysis/
        psychoanalysis, 11, 25, 29,
        38, 74, 86, 187
    pathway, 109
    psychology/psychologists,
        11–12, 67–69

research/hypotheses/concepts,
        8, 11, 82–83,
    studies, 28, 34 needs, 32
    understanding, 173
disinhibited attachment disorder,
        129
Dobbing, J., 11, 41
Doherty, W., 182, 188
Dolan, R. J., 10, 21, 31, 41, 45
dopamine, 87–89, 101, 103,
        105–106, 118–119. 126, 141,
        149–150, 160
Dosamantes, I., 35, 42
Dozier, M., 28, 42
Draghi-Lorenz, R., 69, 76
dreaming, 149–151, 157, 204
Drevets, W. C., 21, 41, 46
Dulac, O., 10, 41

Earls, F., 127, 132
Edelman, G., 19, 42
ego function(s)/organization, 2,
        195, 199
Eisenberg, L., 11, 42
electroencephalograms (EEGs), 18,
        118, 125
Elliott, R., 20, 41
Emde, R. N., 17, 27, 42
emotional
    arousal, 31
    availability, 17
    brain, 21, 37, 195
    capacities, 13
    conditioning, 97
    connections, 203
    difficulties, 129
    disorders, 36
    dynamics, 68
    evaluations, 68
    events, 164
    experience(s)/information,
        18–19, 24, 33–34, 139
    experiences, 28, 35–36
    face of the object, 20
    facial expressions, 21, 30
    history, 27

imagination, 178
involvement, 56
learning, 99
neglect/abuse, 4, 128
primitives, 85, 100
processing, 203
reactivity, 124
response(s), 25–26, 35–36, 138
self-regulation, 199
self/state(s), 20, 23, 25, 27–28,
    31, 36–37, 83, 125, 196
significance, 37
stimuli, 10, 26, 92
syntax, 76
system(s), 73, 203
systems, 107, 157
transaction(s)/communication(s),
    3, 11, 16–18, 26, 28–29,
    121
trauma, 81
well-being, 197
English and Romanian Adoptees
    Study Team, 123, 129,
    132
event-related potentials (ERPs),
    118, 125

Fairbanks, L. A., 171, 174
Falk, D., 21, 42
Feldman, R., 13, 19, 42
Field, N., 206, 209
Field, T., 15, 42, 132
Fink, G. R., 24, 42
Fisher, S., 159, 161
Fitzgerald, H. E., 117, 130
Fogel, A., 15, 42
Fonagy, P., 24, 27, 42, 196, 210
Fosshage, J. L., 32, 42
Foulkes, S. H., 164, 174
Fox, 125, 131
Frank, E., 167, 174
Freeman, W. J., 111, 113
Freud, S., 2, 8–12, 18, 21–23, 2
    8–31, 33, 42–43, 79, 81, 94,
    112–113, 136, 138–139, 142,
    152–153, 155, 158, 161,

163–164, 174, 192, 198, 201,
    203, 208–210
Freudian(s), 1, 204
Freund, S., 22, 44
Frey, K., 125, 131
Fridlund, A., 31, 43
Friedman, N., 35, 43
Frustaci, K., 127, 131
functional magnetic resonance
    imaging (fMRI), 19, 36, 118

Gabbard, G. O., 31, 43, 163, 174
Gage, P., 143–144, 146, 180
Galin, D., 10, 43
Gallup, G. C. Jr, 22, 44
Galvanic Skin Response, 145–146
Gans, J. S., 34, 43
Garavan, H., 19, 43
Garfield, S. L., 174
Gazzaniga, 202
Gedo, J., 27, 43
George, C., 128, 133
Gewirtz, H. L., 18, 46
Giedd, J., 127, 131
Gill, M. M., 198, 208, 210
Gillies, L. A., 171, 174
Glaser, D., 4, 117, 127, 131
global state functions (GSF), 94–95,
    102, 110
Goldberg, D., 177, 189
Goldstein, K., 164, 174
Goleman, D., 37, 43
Goodman, S. H., 189
Gow, S. A., 37, 50
Go–No-Go paradigm, 93
Graham, Y. P., 187, 189
Gratton, A., 23, 50
Greenbaum, C. W., 13, 19, 42
Greenberg, L. S., 12, 44
Greenberg, R. P., 159, 161
Greenough, W., 121, 177, 189
Grinberg, L., 200, 210
Groddeck, G., 23, 43, 164
Gunnar, M., 127, 129, 131
Gur, R. C., 26, 45
Gur, R. E., 26, 45

Ha, Y., 37, 50
Hariri, A. R., 36, 43
Harlow, J., 143–144, 161
Harrison, A. M., 19, 34, 49–50
Heilman, K. M., 22, 40
Heim, C., 189
Heiss, W.-D., 24, 42
Helmkamp, R. C., 21, 42
Henry, J. P., 9, 43
Herman, J. L., 183, 188
Hertel, R. K., 162–163
Hess, E. H., 13, 43
Hessl, D., 125, 131
Hetherington, C. R., 37, 50
Highfield, 191, 208–209
Hildebolt, C., 21, 42
HIV/AIDS, 105
Ho, M. K., 171, 174
Ho, M. L., 171, 174
Hockney, D., 165, 174
Hodges, J., 129, 132
Hofer, M. A., 24, 46
Hoffman, J., 14, 45
Hollinger, P. C., 34, 43
Holloway, M., 180, 189
Holmes, J., 28, 36–37, 44
Hoppe, K. D., 10, 44
Hornak, J., 34, 46
Horvath, A. O., 12, 44
Howard, R. J., 37, 50
Huang, S.-C., 171, 174
Hugdahl, K., 24, 30, 34, 44
Hynd, G. W., 18, 49
hypothalamic–pituitary–adrenal
    axis (HPA), 23, 126
hypothalamus, 20, 22–23, 73, 9
    2–93, 95–97, 99–103, 106,
    110, 126, 139–140

infant–mother/caregiver
    bonding/relationship/dyad,
    11, 15–16, 18–19, 23–24,
    28–29, 32, 53–55, 60, 124, 127,
    172, 179–180, 193, 196, 205
intrinsic motive pulse (IMP), 70
Iowa Gambling Task, 144, 146

Ishii, Y., 13, 51
Itoh, H., 13, 51

Jackson, J. H., 22, 44, 94
Jacobs, T. J., 34, 44
Jambaque, I., 10, 41
Janer, L. D., 10. 51
Jansen, 104
Javors, M., 118, 132
Jessel, T. M., 98, 114
Johnson, M., 195, 210
Joliot, M., 111, 114
Jones, N., 125, 132
Joseph, R., 37, 44
Jung, C. G., 199, 210
Kalsched, D., 179, 189
Kandel, E. R., 98, 114, 158
Kant, E. 180
Kantrowitz, J. L., 32, 44
Kaplan, N., 24, 45
Kaplan-Solms, K., 37, 44, 136,
    152–155, 157, 161, 177, 189, 193,
    208–209, 211
Kapur, S., 25, 41
Kawashima, R., 37
Keenan, 22, 25, 44
Keshavan, M., 127, 131
Kessler, J., 24, 42
Khan, I. A., 102, 113
Kim, S. W., 24, 51
Kimura, K., 13, 51
Kindlon, D., 127, 132
Klein, M., 31, 199
Klerman, G., 174
Klorman, R., 125, 132
Knight, R. T., 24, 50
Kohut, H., 33, 44
Konigsberg, L., 21, 42
Konishi, Y., 13, 51
Kraus, R., 31, 44
Kuhl, J., 18, 25, 46,
Kuhn, T. S., 176, 189
Kupfer, D. J., 167, 174

LaCasse, L., 148, 162
Lachmann, F. M., 35, 39

Lambert, 166
Landale, M., 201, 210
Lane, R. D., 31, 45, 114
Langs, R., 191, 210
Lannon, R., 28, 34, 39
Larrieu, J. A., 117, 133
Larson, C. L., 367, 41
LeDoux, J., 79, 84, 103, 108, 114
Lee, D., 74
left brain/hemisphere, 10, 18,
    21–22, 24, 29–30, 35–36, 58,
    110, 124–125, 187, 202–203
Lehmann, D., 21, 30, 46
Lencz, T., 148, 162
Lester, B. M., 14, 45
Levin, F., 10, 45
Lewis, J. M., 35, 45
Lewis, M., 69
Lewis, T., 28, 34, 39
Lieberman, M. D., 38, 45
Llinas, R., 111, 114
Loewald, H., 32, 34, 45
Lounes, R., 10, 41
Luria, 94
Lutolf, P., 31, 44
Lyons-Ruth, K., 19, 30, 49–50

Mace, C. J., 5, 163, 166, 174
MacLean, P. D., 114
magnetic resonance imaging
    (MRI), 105, 118, 176, 180, 193
Maidment, K., 171, 174
Main, M., 24, 45, 128, 132
Mallinger, A. G., 167, 174
Malloch, S., 53, 58–59, 62, 76
Manzella, L. M., 31, 39
Marcus, D. M., 29, 45
Markowitsch, H. J., 24, 42
Martin, E., 170, 174
Martin, S. D., 170, 174
Mathias, C. J., 20, 41
Matsui, M., 26, 45
Maturana, H., 177, 189, 197, 210
Mazakopaki, K., 70
Mazziotta, J. C., 36, 43
McCutcheon, B., 22, 44

McGrath, J., 34, 46
McLaughlin, J. T., 10, 33, 45
Mead, M., 55
Mesulam, M.-M., 19, 21, 45, 93,
    96–97, 114
Mezzacappa, E., 127, 132
Miller, A. H., 189
Miller, L., 10, 45
mind, 4, 7–12, 22–24, 31, 34, 38, 54,
    56, 68, 74, 135, 137–138, 163,
    195, 203
  disordered, 172
  mapping, 173
  mind–brain, 117–118
    language/disciplines, 87, 91
  models of, 192
Mindell, A., 205–206, 210
missing link, 23
Mlot, C., 10, 45
monoamines, 80, 84, 87–88, 90, 100
Moore, R. W., 29, 40
Morgan, A. C., 19, 30, 49–50
Moroz, T. M., 25, 41
Morris, J. S., 10, 45
Moscovitch, M., 25, 41
Moskowitz, M., 35, 43
mother and baby interaction, 55–66,
    70–72, 75–76, 124–125, 127–128,
    172, 179–180, 193, 196, 205
Mun, E. U., 117, 130
Munder-Ross, J., 31, 46
Muramoto, S., 13, 51
Murphy, D., 21, 41
Murray, L., 62–63, 125, 132
music/musical analysis/music
    therapy, 53, 56, 58, 60–61, 62,
    64, 70, 72, 74–76, 203
musical intelligence, 3
Nabbout, R., 10, 41
Nahum, J. P., 19, 30, 49–50
narrative, 61, 76, 206
  awareness, 3
  cycle, 61
  "dynamic envelopes" of, 61
  melody/melodies, 53, 62, 65, 72,
    75

patient's, 35
therapeutic organization of, 36
Nelson, C., 117, 119, 122, 123, 132
Nemeroff, C. B., 189
neurodevelopment/neurodevelop-
mental theory/research, 4,
109–112
neuropsychology, 2–3, 73
neurotic
patients, 8
processes, 3
Newman, J., 111, 113–114
nonverbal communication/
behaviour, 13, 18, 21, 28–31,
33–36
tranference–countertransference,
31, 37
norepinephrine (NE), 87, 89, 101,
103

O'Connor, T., 123, 129, 132
O'Sullivan, B. T., 37, 44
obsessive compulsive disorder
(OCD), 86–87
Ogden's analytic third, 206
Ohman, A., 10, 45
orbitofrontal cortex, 19–22, 24,
38
Ornstein, R., 10, 23, 46
Osborne, N., 72
Osofsky, J. D., 130, 132
Osterling, J., 125, 131

Pally, R., 202, 210
Panagiotides, H., 125, 131
Panksepp, J., 77, 79, 88, 92, 100, 103,
106, 109, 114, 135, 137, 139, 141,
149, 151, 158, 161–162, 193, 195,
203–204, 210
Papez, J., 114
Papoudi, D., 20, 78
Papousek, H., 13, 46, 77
Papousek, M., 13, 46, 77
Parker, J. D. A., 27, 50
Parkinson's disease, 151
Pascual-Leone, A., 22, 44

patient(s), 5, 8, 12–13, 27–38, 82, 87,
93, 105–107, 141, 143–149,
151–157, 160–161, 165–173,
175–181, 184, 188, 199–200
periaqueductal grey (PAG), 95–96,
99–110
Perry, J. C., 183, 188
persistent vegetative state (PVS),
95, 107
Petrovich, S. B., 18, 36
Phelps, J. L., 38, 46
Phelps, M. E., 171, 174
Philips, M., 21, 41
Phillips, D., 117, 133
Pibram, K., 2
Pinker, S., 76
Pitman, R., 187, 189
Pizzagalli, D., 21, 30, 46
Pliszka, S., 118, 132
Plum, F., 103, 105
Polan, H. J., 24, 46
Pollak, S., 125, 132
Ponting, C., 178, 189
Pöppel, E., 74
positron emission tomography
(PET), 118, 193
Povinelli, D., 37, 46
Preuss, T. M., 37, 46
Pribam, K. H., 2, 198, 208, 210
Price, J. L., 19, 21, 41, 46
Prigogine, I., 196, 210
primary narcissism, 3
projective identification, 2, 31
proto-conversation(s), 2, 17, 55, 58,
61, 63, 67, 83
proto-conversation(s)/-conversa-
tional, 2, 17, 55, 58–59, 61, 63,
67
prototype(s), 87, 103, 106, 111, 195
emotion(s), 80, 83, 88, 96,
99–100–101
mammalian, 85
states/affective states,/behav-
iour 83, 85–86, 88, 94, 99,
103–104, 106, 108–111
work, 83

psychotherapy
    activity, 94
    appraisal, 94
    brain systems, 93
    cognitive–behavioural, 12
    deficits, 93
Putnam, K. M., 37, 41
Puttler, L. I., 117, 130

Quay, H., 118, 132

Rai, S. S., 170, 174
Raine, A., 148, 162
rational empiricism, 73
Rauch, S. L., 187, 189
Reddy, V., 68, 76–77
Regard, M., 21, 30, 46
Reich, W., 199, 210
Reinkemeier, M., 24, 42
Reinoso-Suarez, F., 21, 41
Reite, M., 16, 46
resonance, 16–17, 28, 32, 164, 175,
    205
reticular activating system (RAS),
    103
Reznik, I., 31, 39
Ribary, U., 111,114
Richards, M., 55
Richardson, M. A., 170, 174
Ricoeur, P., 209–210
right hemisphere/brain/cortex,
    9–12, 18–21, 38, 110–111,
    115, 124–125, 171, 180–187,
    202–203
Robbins, A., 203, 209–210
Roberts, J. Z., 20, 78
Robertson, D., 21, 41
Rogeness, G., 118, 132
Roland, P. E., 37, 44
Rolls, E. T., 24, 34, 46
Rorschach test, 166
Roschmann, R., 28, 51
Rosetta Stone, 2
Ross, T. J., 19, 43
Royall, R., 170, 174
Rutter, M., 123, 129, 132

Ryan, N., 127, 131
Ryan, R. M., 18, 25, 46

Sable, P., 28, 47
Sadato, N., 13, 51
Samuels, S., 199, 201, 205, 210
Sander, L. W,, 19, 30, 32–33, 47
    49–50
Sanders, G., 22, 44
Sands, J., 11, 41
Sardar, S.,209–210
Saxena, S., 171, 174
Scarr, S., 123, 133
Scharff, D. E., 209–210
Scharff, J. S., 209–210
Schiff, N.,103, 105
Schilder, P., 164, 174
schizophrenia/schizophrenic(s),
    141, 145, 149–151, 157
Schore, A., 2, 5, 7, 9, 11–12, 16, 19,
    23–26, 28, 31–32, 34–35, 37–38,
    47–49, 69, 77, 114, 124, 133, 148,
    162, 178–181, 189, 192–193,
    195–199, 201, 207–211
Schultz, W., 21, 41
Schwaber, E. A., 33–34, 49
Schwartz, G. E., 10, 51
Schwartz, J. H., 98, 114
SEEKING system, 141–142, 149
selective serotonin reuptake
    inhibitors (SSRIs) 86–87, 181
self, a/the, 9, 16, 25, 37, 54, 67, 75,
    82, 110, 128, 192, 197, 199, 202
    proto-self, 100
    self-image, 10, 86. 90
self-organizing brain/system, 7, 9,
    19, 194–198, 200, 203–206, 208
Semrud-Clikeman, M, 18, 49
separation distress, 83, 85–86,
    88–89, 100–101, 107, 204
serotonin, 86–87, 89, 103, 118–119,
    160
Shevrin, H., 161–162
Shin, L, 187, 189
Shonkoff, J. 117, 133
Siegel, D. J., 9, 49

Sinclair, 63, 125, 133
sleep research/sleep abnormality,
    167–169, 184
Smith, H. F., 22, 32, 49
Snow, D., 22, 49
Snyder, S. H., 149–150, 162
sociopathy/sociopathic, 147–148
Solms, M., 27, 37, 44, 49, 136–137,
    139, 145, 147, 150–155, 157,
    161–162, 177, 189, 193.
    208–209, 211
Solomon, J., 128, 132–133
Soth, M., 208–209, 211
Sperry, 202
Sroufe, L. A., 16, 49
Stauffer, K., 209
Stein, E. A., 19, 43
Stengers, I., 196, 210
Stern, D. N., 11, 30, 34, 49–50, 61,
    68, 77, 124, 133, 172–174, 178,
    189, 209
Stoessel, P., 171, 174
Stolorow, R. D., 36, 49
Stone, M. H., 10, 49
Stone, V. E., 24, 50
Strange Situation Test, 128
stress/stressful/stressors, 23, 25,
    27, 33, 35, 82, 90–91, 104,
    117, 119, 123, 126–130, 179, 181
    post-traumatic stress disorder
        (PTSD), 83, 127, 184,
        186–187
Stuss, D. T., 25, 37, 41, 50
Sullivan, R. M., 23, 50
synchrony/asynchrony, 16, 18–19,
    28, 60, 125, 172
Syrota, A., 10, 41

Tanaka, M., 13, 51
Target, M., 24, 27, 42
Taylor, D., 123, 133
Taylor, G. J., 27, 50
Taylor, J. G., 111, 113
Taylor, V., 123, 133
Teasdale, J. D., 37, 50
Tejedor, J., 21, 41

Thase, M. E., 167, 174
Thatcher, R. W., 38, 50
Theory of Companionship, 66
therapist/psychotherapist, 1, 3–5,
    12–13, 27–38, 81, 85, 135,
    153–154, 158, 160, 164–166, 169,
    172–173, 175–183, 188, 198–203,
    205–208
time in the mind, 61, 74
Totton, N., 195, 208–209, 211
Townsend, J., 121, 131
Tranel, D., 23, 30, 39, 161
transference–countertransference,
    31–32, 34, 35, 37, 81, 206
Trehub, S. E., 77
Trevarthen, C., 17, 20, 53, 57, 77–78,
    172–173, 193, 211
Tronick, E. Z., 18–19, 50, 78
Tucker, D. M., 30, 41
Tulving, E., 25, 41
Turetsky, B. I., 26. 45
Turnbull, O., 4, 135–137, 147, 150,
    152, 161–162, 203

UK Council for Psychotherapy
    (UKCP), 1–2, 178
unconscious, the, 12, 22–23, 29–31,
    38, 136, 152, 155, 192, 198–199,
    201
    activities, 29
    avoidance, 208
    behaviour, 206
    communication(s), 14, 26, 34
    excess influence of, 152
    influence, 164
    limbic/emotional learning, 34,
        146
    processes, 12, 21, 24–25, 33, 95,
        136
    relational, 31
    restraints, 207
    states, 29, 32
Van Amelsvoort, K. M., 21, 41
van der Kolk, B. A., 179, 183–184,
    188
van Rees, S., 63, 70–71, 78

Vannier, M., 21, 42
Varela, F., 177, 189, 197, 210
ventral tegmental area (VTA), 99,
    101, 105, 107
ventromesial frontal lobes, 139–141,
    143–144, 146–148, 150–151, 157

Wade, D., 34, 46
Wall, S., 128, 130
Wallerstein, R. S., 31, 50
Wang, G., 111, 114
Warrenburg, S., 10, 51
Waters, E., 128, 130
Watt, D. F., 3, 10, 50, 79, 81, 100,
    103, 108, 115, 137, 139, 141,
    193, 205, 207, 211
Watzlawick, P., 177, 189
Weinberg, M. K., 19, 49, 50
Weissman, M. M., 174
Westen, D., 26, 50
Westlund, K. N., 102, 113
Wexler, B. E., 10, 51
Whalen, P., 187, 189
Wheeler, M. A., 25, 44

Whittle, P., 192, 211
Wilber, K., 209, 211
Wilden, A., 208–209, 211
Wilden, A., 209, 211
Williams, S. C. R., 37, 50
Williams, S., 21, 41
Williams, W. J., 162–163
Willis, W. D., 113
Winnicott, D. W., 27, 51, 62, 199,
    209
Winocur, G., 25, 41
Winson, J., 10, 51
Wittling, W., 23, 28, 61
Wu, H.-M., 171, 174

Yamada, H., 13, 51
Yan, M. X.-H., 26, 45
Yirmiya, N., 13, 19, 42
Yonekura, Y, 13, 51

Zald, D. H., 24, 51
Zeanah, C. H., 21, 39, 117, 130, 133
Zeddies, T. J., 31, 51
Zucker, R. A., 117, 130

CL

616.
891
4
UNI

6000466257